WEEKEND

BRAG ABOUT

100 ADVENTURES IN BRITAIN'S GREAT OUTDOORS

Christopher Nye

Survival Books · Bath · England

First Edition 2011

Copyright © Survival Books 2011
Photo editor: Peter Farmer
Cover design: Kate Buckle
Maps © Jim Watson

Survival Books Limited, Office 169, 3 Edgar Buildings
George Street, Bath BA1 2FJ, United Kingdom
☎ +44 (0) 1935 700060, ▤ +44 (0)1935 700060
✉ info@survivalbooks.net
▢ www.survivalbooks.net

British Library Cataloguing in Publication Data
A CIP record for this book is available
from the British Library.
ISBN: 978-1-907339-39-4

Printed and bound in Singapore by Stamford Press

Acknowledgements

The author wishes to thank all the people who helped produce this book, particularly the many adventure companies who gave so generously of their time and advice. Thanks are also due to my partner Denise for her patience while I disappeared to do those activities that I missed in my bachelor days, and her ideas for all manner of new and dangerous sports she suggested I try. Thanks also to our son Dylan, who inspired me to find adventures for younger folk. I also wish to thank my sister Louise for the loan of her horses and my brothers Jeremy (for ideas and encouragement) and Simon (for the use of his country home).

Thanks are also due to Peter Read for the commission in the first place and for editing, Lilac Johnston for proof-reading, Di Bruce-Kidman for DTP, Peter Farmer (the photo editor) for the wonderful photographs (not forgetting the contributing photographers listed on pages 365-367), Lara Dunn for her expert advice on technical matters, Kate Buckle for the superb cover design and Jim Watson for the maps. Finally, a huge thank you to Land Rover for sponsoring this book.

Survivalphotos

Natural History & Travel Photography

I have a comprehensive library of images, covering Flora and Fauna, cultural photographs of countries from around the world, plus one of my favourite subjects, macro photography of the smaller end of life. If you are interested in any of these subjects, please see my website or contact me directly.

Contact: Peter Farmer

www.survivalphotos@aol.com

survivalphotos@aol.com

Contents

Introduction

"What did you do at the weekend?" Do you hate that question? If the truth is something like got up late, re-organised sock drawer, wandered downtown, watched *The X Factor*, opened (second) bottle of wine, passed out on the sofa – then maybe you ought to get out more and live a little closer to the edge.

There's a wild world of adventures on your doorstep, from exploring vast subterranean caverns lit only by the lamp on your helmet to rediscovering the hunter inside as you pull the bow back and let loose an arrow at a (model) deer. This afternoon you could be climbing without ropes at a bouldering site, foraging for food and cooking it on a wild camping expedition, or on horseback cantering along a sandy beach. Tomorrow, why not try snorkelling down to barnacle-encrusted shipwrecks, clambering up a waterfall in a Welsh valley or testing your off-road driving skills in deepest Devon…

We've rounded up 100 plus activities from every corner of Britain to suit all fitness levels, from iron man to obese, every pocket from loaded to empty and every age from 8 to 88. It's for whatever you call a 'weekend', not just Saturday and Sunday but a day off mid-week, a week's holiday or even just an afternoon. There are ideas to fill any gap in your schedule up to and including taking the rest of your life off and paddling the world in a canoe, camping on the riverbank and eating what you can pick or catch. Some activities you do alone, most with friends old or new, and there are also options for team-building sessions.

Many won't cost much, if anything, to try, and most have the option of equipment hire and gentle instruction (if necessary). We've listed a few specific locations, so that you can easily find the closest venue, and added an 'Accessibility Index' that grades each activity on how easy it is to arrange. There are easier options for most of them, so you can start gently, maybe even take the kids, and gradually work your way up to weekend marathons and death-defying feats.

There's really no excuse for being bored these days. *Weekends to Brag About* provides you with the inspiration for countless unique experiences, a sack full of dirty clothing on Monday morning and an exciting tale to tell the folks at work.

"What did you do at the weekend? Well I was sailing at 3,000ft over this mountain…"

Have a GREAT weekend!

Christopher Nye

March 2011

Ullswater, Lake District National Park

1

BANISH BORING WEEKENDS

- ❖ **Wake Up Your Weekend**
- ❖ **The Best of British**
- ❖ **Activities Without Barriers**
- ❖ **Join Up, Join In**
- ❖ **Safety First!**
- ❖ **At a Glance**

WAKE UP YOUR WEEKENDS

It's Friday morning, and you're at the office, factory or school, getting ready for the weekend but not expecting it to be anything special. If your weekends add up to a predictable routine of shopping, television and a trip to the pub, it's time to shake them up a bit and give yourself something to **really** look forward to. This book is full of ideas for activities to transform your time off into an exhilarating and extraordinary adventure. Some can be arranged in an afternoon, while others take a bit more planning, but all are achievable, enjoyable and anything but dull. So what have you got to lose?

Modern life, while free from the dangers and stresses faced by previous generations, promises so much yet often delivers so little. You're in no danger of being stamped on by a woolly mammoth or asked to storm a foreign beach under enemy fire, but where are the thrills? You won't find them on Facebook, in the Sunday newspapers or on reality TV.

Psychologists agree that it's generally by **doing** things that we make ourselves happy. The technical term for this is 'flow': the positive feelings that envelop you when you're absorbed in an activity. If you can get your brain engaged in something that's challenging but not beyond you, such as hill walking, pony trekking or tobogganing, then feelings of anxiety and boredom are replaced by profound excitement and happiness.

In this state, time flies by without you noticing discomfort, politics, debts, petty squabbles, even hunger or thirst – all you care about is the task in hand. It's called flow because people have likened the feeling to being carried down a river. Sportsmen and women experience it while playing; artists, musicians and writers also experience flow, which is why some don't eat properly, wash or talk to anyone for days during a creative period. Flow is what therapists try to induce in celebrity drug addicts at rehab centres when they attempt to get them to reconnect with the world by doing menial tasks. Indeed, there's a whole branch of medical treatment called occupational therapy which is based on the idea that if you can get people to forget about their illness or problem by doing something, they'll get better without even realising it.

If you want to experience your own flow, read on. This book is packed with ideas to revitalise your weekends, whether you want

The worse the weather,
the better it gets.

You can rely on British weather to be unreliable. But unruly weather only makes the Land Rover Experience even more fun. You'll be warm and dry inside our latest model Land Rover and Range Rover vehicles as you tackle the exhilarating slopes, obstacles and challenges of our off-road course.

For a great day out, rain or shine, call us on 0800 110 110
or visit www.landrover.co.uk/experience

experience

Isle of Skye, Scotland

to suck a little more of the marrow out of life by scaring yourself silly, get fitter without boring yourself at the gym, find something fun to do with your partner or children, or simply need a break from your job, home or family for a day or two. Whatever your motives, we promise that you'll get a great feeling from climbing a cliff or a waterfall (frozen or not) or cycling along a woodland track at night, dodging badgers. We guarantee that if you have a go at orienteering this weekend, or learn to sail a dinghy, or run a fast cross-country course while harnessed to your dog, you'll be proud of yourself come Monday morning.

It could be that you've heard of some of these activities but you don't know if they're expensive or how fit you need to be to do them, or whether you're too old and overweight (you probably aren't). Maybe it all looks a bit too difficult or scary? You'll never know unless you take the first step...

THE BEST OF BRITISH

Until a few years ago, if you asked a friend where they were going on holiday and they mentioned somewhere in the UK, you probably felt a bit sorry for them. Not any more. These days, saying "Oh, we're off to the Serengeti" is more likely to earn you a lecture on global warming. After 40 years of flying out of it at the first opportunity, the British are rediscovering their own island paradise.

From Vacation to Staycation

In 2007, a new word entered the holiday lexicon as people opted for a 'staycation': a holiday spent at home rather than in an exotic overseas destination. This option has become increasingly popular among the British, partly as a response to the credit crunch, poor exchange rates and disruptive events such as the Icelandic volcano eruption in April 2010, but also because they're discovering just how much the UK has to offer.

There are benefits to spending your leisure time in Britain, starting with the water. British rivers are reputed to be the cleanest since before the Industrial Revolution. We have a coastline of some 11,000 miles (17,000km) – more than double that of Spain – so you may even have your bit of coast to yourself. The Gulf Stream flows up from Florida and across the Atlantic, bringing warm water to our beaches, thus ensuring that the UK is a gentle, verdant oasis in comparison with say Siberia or Canada's Labrador Coast, both of which are on a similar latitude. Unless you go ice climbing in the Cairngorms, you rarely have to cope with -15ºC (5ºF) days. Nor are you likely to die of heatstroke as there's always somewhere to shelter from the sun. What's more, according to a United Nations report, Britain has more woodland than at any time since 1750.

And it's all on your doorstep. Even in central London you're never more than half an hour's drive from a grassy hill and the furthest point inland from the sea is just 70 miles (113km). The UK has a network of trains and buses that make travelling to beauty spots almost a joy compared with the agony of shuffling through airport departure lounges. Plus, we are waking up to the realisation that cheap flights aren't so cheap after all when you consider the greenhouse gases pumped into the atmosphere. A return flight from London to Barcelona pumps 277kg (611lb) of polluting CO_2 into the air per passenger – that's the weight of an average family – while going on a UK camping expedition adds little or nothing. Even a return train journey from London to Edinburgh produces ten times less pollution than the Barcelona flight.

Staying on home turf gives you the opportunity to do new and exciting things, instead of aimlessly wandering around foreign cities as a tourist. You can take your ropes and crampons on the bus or train, pop your kayak on top of your car, fill the caravan with the kids' bikes and head for the hills, lakes and beaches.

The UK's service economy is making a huge effort to tempt us to spend our leisure time in Britain. New National Parks have been created – the most recent being the South Downs in 2010 – while there are dozens of Areas of Outstanding Natural Beauty (AONBs) and thousands of Sites of Special Scientific Interest (SSSIs). Pro-active organisations such as the Forestry Commission, Natural England, National Waterways, Scottish Natural Heritage and National Trails all promote Britain's great outdoors and help you to enjoy it. The main British 'countryside' organisations are described below.

Peak District National Park

National Parks

Britain has 15 National Parks (🖥 www.nationalparks.gov.uk) which recently enjoyed their 60th birthday, having been created after the Second World War to ensure that people could visit the beautiful coasts, mountains, moors, woods and wetlands they had recently so stoutly defended. Each has a National Park Authority whose job it is to protect and promote the parks, which are great places for walking, mountain biking, camping, climbing and many other

activities. They are easily accessible with good transport links and also provide accommodation for visitors.

Areas of Outstanding Natural Beauty

A rung below National Parks, are the 38 Areas of Outstanding Natural Beauty/AONB (💻 www.aonb.org.uk) in England and Wales and eight in Northern Ireland, covering some 20 per cent of the countryside and including areas as large as the Cotswolds. As well as being beautiful places to visit, they're the habitats of special plants and wildlife, and many have interesting historic and cultural connections, yet people often don't even know they're in an AONB or that they have one on their doorstep. The Scottish equivalent is the National Scenic Area (NSA) of which there are 40, run by Scottish Natural Heritage (💻 www.snh.gov.uk).

Natural England

The independent public body, Natural England, provides advice to the UK government on safeguarding England's natural environment. It regulates Sites of Special Scientific Interest, posting signs telling visitors that they're somewhere special and mustn't do anything to damage the environment or disturb the wildlife, such as wild camping. For more information, visit the Natural England website (💻 www.naturalengland.org.uk).

Sites of Special Scientific Interest

England's 4,000 Sites of Special Scientific Interest/SSSIs (💻 www.sssi.naturalengland.org.uk) cover around 7 per cent of the country, so there's likely to be one near you – check out the maps on the 💻 www.natureonthemap.org.uk website. They're notable for rare flora and fauna, and include rivers teeming with trout, wetlands popular with wading birds, and meadows filled with wild flowers or endangered creatures. Although usually owned by farmers, they're regulated and overseen by Natural England (see box).

National Trails

There are 15 National Trails (💻 www.nationaltrail.co.uk) covering every corner of England and Wales and stretching for over 2,500miles (4,000km), plus four in Scotland where they're known as 'long distance routes'. They're way-marked with an acorn logo, normally on an oak post, so they're easy to follow, and they link up ancient lanes, footpaths and bridle paths to offer the best routes through Britain's beauty spots. The longest is the South West Coast Path at 630 miles (1,014km); other popular trails including the North Downs Way (153mi/246km) and the Pennine Way (268mi/167km) down the central spine of northern England. There are stretches for bicycles and horses,

Lake District National Park

often with hire companies along the way, and also access for wheelchair users. For walks in Wales, visit the Countryside Council for Wales website (💻 www.ccw.gov.uk).

Forestry Commission

The Forestry Commission (💻 www.forestry.gov.uk) is the guardian of over one million hectares of woodland in England, Scotland and Wales. As well as safeguarding and enlarging the forests, it also makes them more accessible and fun for visitors. As the largest provider of outdoor recreation in the country, the Forestry Commission organises pop concerts in the woods, cani-cross events (cross-country running with your dog), and maintains trails for mountain biking, horse riding and carriage driving. Nature lovers can learn how to recognise trees, the best ways to climb them, and which mammals, insects and birds they might encounter. For outdoor adventurers of any age, the Forestry Commission is a great place to start.

British Waterways

Half the UK population lives within five miles of one of the 2,200 miles (3,541km) of canals and rivers maintained by British Waterways (💻 www.britishwaterways.co.uk/home), and we should be enjoying them more. Through Waterscape (💻 www. waterscape.com), British Waterways encourages people to use their local waterways for boating, barging, fishing, swimming, rafting, cycling and hiking along towpaths, and almost anything else that's legal, as well as recruiting volunteers to help clear canals. As a testament to its success, there are more boats on British canals today than there were in their industrial heyday. Waterscape is also a great resource for boating holidays, accommodation and weekend volunteering projects.

ACTIVITIES WITHOUT BARRIERS

You may be young, elderly, penniless or disabled, but you've never had a better chance of doing an adventure activity. There's a wealth of information available and fewer barriers to accessing adventure, with charities, clubs, individual sports' governing bodies and private companies reaching out to all sectors of the community.

There are programmes to enable young people to enjoy adventure activities, with the aim of reversing the trend towards childhood obesity and giving underprivileged kids access to adventure. Projects include Tall Ships Races, where children from all backgrounds get the chance to sail a three-masted barque, the scholarship scheme run by the British Gliding Association, and the excellent Pony Club, which has over 500 centres around the country for kids who don't own a pony. For children of all ages and abilities, groups such as the Scouts and Girl Guides are still a great way to get a taste of adventure.

You're never too old to try something new and there are many options for older people to take up a new challenge, with retirees' clubs promoting the 'bucket list' approach: ticking off the things you want to experience or achieve before you 'kick the bucket'. You can organise a club yourself or there are plenty of companies happy to grab the 'grey pound'.

New technology gives people with disabilities access to many more sports and activities. Specially adapted ski-bikes allow amputees to ski and water-ski, and aids for wheelchair users are so advanced that they enabled quadriplegic yachtswoman Hilary Lister to sail round Britain controlling the sails and rudder by blowing into a tube. Technology has also made previously dangerous activities safer. You don't need to be a strong swimmer to tackle river rapids anymore; almost anyone can do it with a wetsuit, life jacket and helmet. The development of sturdier yet lighter hang gliders means that you can now soar up to thousands of feet, and if anything goes wrong, you have your own neat little parachute on your back. There are even riding jackets with airbags fitted to take some of the danger (but not the thrill) out of cross-country horse riding and drag hunting, and avalanche airbags for off-piste skiers.

If you have a disability, check out tourism and governing body websites to find out whether you can do an activity and find a suitable place to stay while you're doing it. For example, Enjoy England (💻 www.enjoyengland.com), the official website for English tourism, uses symbols to denote whether accommodation is suitable for mobility-impaired, visually-impaired or hearing-impaired people, while the UK government's information website (💻 www.direct.gov.uk) has information about charities, companies and organisations which help disadvantaged and disabled people to have as much fun doing adventure activities as everyone else.

JOIN UP, JOIN IN

What did people do with their weekends before the arrival of Saturday television and Sunday shopping? You may have a rosy image of people in the '50s spending their weekends cycling into the countryside for a picnic with the church youth club, going pigeon racing, doing flower arranging or choir singing, playing cricket on the village green, staying up late with a flask of cocoa at the astronomy club or dressing up for a historical re-enactment. And you'd be right; half a century ago, clubs were the social hub and people preferred doing things together.

These days, we do things together far less. In his book *Bowling Alone*, Harvard professor Robert Putnam explains how the club habit has been lost in American society over the past generation. In some cases, people still do the activity but on their own. Take ten-pin bowling as an example; in the US, people formed bowling teams, clubs and leagues, but now they go bowling alone. Putnam found that the number of Americans attending club meetings had dropped by almost 60 per cent over the last 25 years, due to the competing attractions of TV and the internet, the pressure on families with both parents working and other reasons. The situation is at least as bad in the UK, where many of us commute long distances to work and don't have the time or energy to be the treasurer of the local archery club in the evening. Putnam

calculates that for every extra ten minutes of commuting we lose 10 per cent of our 'social capital', i.e. our connections with friends.

Yet there are many advantages in getting together to do adventurous things, rather than doing them alone or paying a commercial operator. Clubs are cheaper. Members can pool their resources to buy expensive equipment such as a glider, dive boat or vehicle. At the very least, they offer a chance to swap opinions and ideas. In a club, the donkey work and administration is done for free by volunteers and becomes part of the fun. Most of all, it's a chance to meet like-minded people, exchange information and improve your proficiency without needing to pay an instructor. Going coasteering with a commercial operator costs at least £40, which is fine for a one-off experience, but if you enjoy it you can join a club and do it every weekend for little or nothing, even sharing the cost of transport. Other club members can also be a motivating force to tempt us out at the weekend when our own inertia is holding us back, and leaping into the foaming sea or off a mountain feels a little unattractive.

Be Prepared... for Fun

One of the easiest and most worthwhile ways for young people to get involved in adventure activities is with the Scouts, Girl Guides, Boys' Brigade or Woodcraft Folk. Whether you're young enough to be a member or old enough to be a volunteer leader, it's a great way to spend your weekends doing anything from abseiling to zorbing. In some areas young people are on waiting lists due to a lack of volunteers, so you'll also be helping the 'Big Society' along – and you don't even need to have any kids of your own.

SAFETY FIRST!

One of the blessings of living in the UK is that you're on pretty safe ground. In some countries, even to go for a 'walk in the woods', you may need to take a compass, bear-scarer, emergency rations, first-aid kit and fire starter. In the UK you're rarely far from civilisation and unlikely to be attacked by wolves or enveloped in a mudslide or forest fire. The notion that we're probably going to die if we do anything out of the ordinary has come from insurance companies and well-meaning people misunderstanding the principles of health and safety, and from a media which focuses on reporting tragic accidents rather than pointing out the millions of people who have accomplished the same activity safely. This reaction doesn't treat all sports or their participants in the same way: if you're privileged or wealthy enough to climb to the 'death zone' of Mount Everest or sail around the world single-handedly, you're an inspiration, but if you're a kid having fun leaping from a breakwater into the sea, you're an irresponsible menace.

You should never disregard safety, but for the more gentle DIY activities such as trail running or wild swimming, you should be trusted to look after yourself. If you're going cave diving or base jumping, then take all the precautions in the world and be guided by the experts, but you don't necessarily need walking boots to go walking, a helmet to go tobogganing or a self-inflating mattress to enjoy wild camping – it's just more 'comfortable' if you do. The golden rule of any adventure activity is to know your own capabilities and never let yourself be pressured into doing something that you feel is beyond you.

Whatever you do – even a bit of DIY at home – it's important not to be reckless and to take sensible precautions, which can be done without diminishing the fun factor. Don't underestimate the dangers of some activities and sports, particularly when combined with inclement weather. For example, winter hill walking can seem a fairly benign activity, yet every year there are fatalities; and still every time you go out in winter you'll see people who are unprepared for the weather conditions, not only putting their own lives at risk but those of the mountain rescue teams who may have to rescue them. Even experienced mountaineers can have unfortunate accidents in winter while 'just walking'.

Ironically, often the safest activities are the most extreme. When the point of the exercise is to try something that carries the risk of almost certain death if anything goes wrong, such as bungee jumping, skydiving or snowholing, companies organising these activities are obsessed with safety as their licence to operate depends on avoiding accidents. Operators of bungee jumping, for example, have systems that include three safety back-ups, known as 'triple redundancy'. Most water sports have strict safety regulations – not imposed by Health & Safety but formulated by experts and organisers who are intimately aware of the dangers. In some activities, e.g. paragliding and scuba diving, you must undergo training and/ or be qualified before you can go solo. Whatever the activity, it pays to heed the advice of experts, take all necessary safety precautions, and (hopefully) give the A&E department a wide berth. The advantage of safety features (and training) is that they provide extra confidence, thus allowing you to go higher, faster and further.

Many of the most dangerous activities are governed by the Adventure Activities Licensing Authority (AALA, 🖳 www.hse.gov.uk/aala), part of the Health and Safety Executive (HSE), or by a voluntary system called Adventuremark (🖳 www.adventuremark.co.uk) from the Adventure Activities Industry Advisory Committee (AAIAC, 🖳 www.skillsactive.com). If you're unsure about an operator, check their licensing status with the national association. Most sports' governing body websites (listed by activity in this book) provide a cool and rational assessment of the safety of their sport, while also offering advice on how to avoid accidents. There are also some excellent independent websites, such as Safesport (🖳 www.safesport.co.uk), which provides comprehensive safety advice and information.

If the foregoing catalogue of disaster and impending doom hasn't terrified you into staying in bed, then all that remains is to wish you the best of luck… **Hals und bein bruch!** ('neck and leg break') – as the Germans so charmingly put it when wishing someone good luck.

Warning!

If you're tempted to participate in extreme sports while abroad, you should be aware that in some countries the training, regulations and equipment aren't always up to British standards, and some operators have a cavalier attitude towards safety.

AT A GLANCE

All major activities described in this book have an 'At a Glance' information box, which provides an overview. This includes an accessibility rating, fitness level indicator, degree of difficulty, equipment hire or cost, white knuckle (how scary) rating, season and other considerations, which are explained in detail below.

Accessibility Rating

How spontaneous can you be about starting an adventure activity or sport? The accessibility rating indicates how easy it is to find a location, centre or organiser for an activity at short notice, ranging from least (1/5) to most (5/5) accessible; for example, base jumping, isn't very accessible (1/5), while hill walking (5/5) is. Some activities, such as whale watching, are only possible in a few remote areas at certain times of the year, but they offer the advantage of not requiring special equipment or training, while surfing may be inaccessible in many parts of the UK, but you can bodyboard on most beaches. Activities which you can do as a 'passenger', e.g. a tandem parachute jump or gliding/ microlighting, count as accessible, as do certain activities

that are easy to do but can only be done at certain times, e.g. storm watching.

Activities are graded by imagining the typical reader on a Friday afternoon contemplating a weekend accompanying their spouse around the shopping mall or taking the kids to their granny's for tea. How easy would it be to organise something more exciting? For most people, a quick 'Google' for an adventure activity organiser is enough to book yourself in for the next day (or check 🖳 www.toad.uk.com). By this time tomorrow you could have a beatific smile on your face having just done your first tandem skydive!

As a rough guide, the accessibility rating (out of five) is as follows:

Accessibility Rating

1 impossible as it requires extensive training and/or money and there are only a few providers

2 almost impossible, but more accessible than 1. above

3 can just about be done at short notice, but possibly only at a simplified or beginner's level

4 easy to organise, but you may need to buy or hire specialist equipment

5 no barriers – events are organised most weekends where you can hire equipment or just go it alone, e.g. hill walking

---

Fitness Level

Few activities require participants to be super-fit, while most will help you get fit, usually while taking your mind off all the energy you're expending and the muscles you're working. This book offers only a guide and different operators and locations will vary, while some activities (such as mountain biking and hill walking) depend on the terrain – start gently and work up to those weekend marathons. Also bear in mind that although you may be very fit for one sport, this may not help much when you take up a completely different sport, with different fitness and physical demands.

Some activities don't need much fitness in themselves, such as tobogganing or hang gliding, but may require a fair bit of puff to get up the hill in the first place. However, given that some of the most testing adventure sports have programmes for wheelchair users, they could also have options for the chronically unfit, so it's always worth asking.

Some activities such as aerial sports and horse riding have a weight limit, therefore if you're particularly heavy you should inquire in advance.

As a rough guide, the fitness rating (out of five) is as follows:

Fitness Rating

1 unfit (inactive)

2 moderately fit (regular walker)

3 quite fit (regular jogger or sports participant)

4 very fit (serious fitness addict, e.g. distance runner)

5 super fit (marathon man/woman)

Degree of Difficulty

Is an activity technically demanding, requiring long training or experience even to have a go, or can a beginner have a stab at it? Surfing has a high degree of difficulty, for example, while mountain biking has very little or none (provided you can ride a bike). Even with the most difficult activities, you have to start somewhere, but there may be easier ways into a sport, such as stand-up paddleboarding as a warm up for surfing, or bouldering before tackling ice climbing. Activities are rated from 1 to 5, where 1 is no skill required and 5 is extremely technically or physically demanding, requiring extensive training and/or experience.

As a rough guide, the difficulty rating (out of five) is as follows:

Degree of Difficulty

1 no skill required, e.g. bungee jumping, zorbing

2 some skill necessary but it can be quickly learned

3 the basics can be picked up in a few hours

4 requires several days training and possibly a written examination

5 requires extensive experience and/or study, e.g. base jumping

---

Equipment

Getting out and having fun is more important that spending lots of money and many activities can be enjoyed for free or for very little cost. For some sports the cost of equipment is prohibitively expensive and only for the privileged few, while for others all you need is a suitable jacket and footwear and you're in business. Even 'expensive' sports can usually be enjoyed relatively inexpensively until you become serious

and need to buy your own equipment. It's better to try out an activity at a club or centre where equipment hire (which will also include special clothing if necessary) is included, rather than splashing out.

The rating system indicates whether you can hire equipment (sometimes the only option) and/ or what a beginner can get away with paying. Low cost generally means less than £50, medium cost from £50 to £500, and high cost over £500 (and possibly many thousands of pounds).

White Knuckle Rating

How scary or dangerous is it? It depends on the individual and how brave or daring he or she is – many activities are daunting at first. So was starting school, but it gets easier the more you do it – even skydiving. We have rated activities from one to five, where one is relaxed and five is terrifying! Often the rating for a specific activity depends on a range of factors such as the speed, terrain, weather conditions, etc. – some activities can be enjoyed at fairly low pulse ratings, right up to off the scale.

As a rough guide, the white knuckle rating (out of five) is as follows:

White Knuckle Rating

1 not frightening at all, e.g. crop circle hunting
2 there may be small heights, speed or animals involved
3 it takes a bit of nerve
4 potentially very scary, but the pleasure makes up for it, e.g. rock climbing or cave diving.
5 the point is to scare you to death, e.g. bungee jumping, cliff jumping or rap running

---

Ben Nevis, Scotland

Look Before You Leap

The most dangerous extreme sport is base jumping or BASE jumping, which involves jumping with a parachute from a fixed point such as a building, antennae, span (bridge) or earth (cliff) – hence the acronym. Between 1981 and 2010, there were a reported 157 fatalities, while other research suggests that one in 2,300 jumps ends in a death.

Season

Most activities are available for most of the year, by wearing a wetsuit or just wrapping up warm, although many are dependent on good weather (or 'bad' weather in the case of winter sports) and are therefore not practised in winter. Some are available only at certain times of the year, such as drag hunting, which takes place during the autumn and winter. Others are positively dangerous out of season or not really worth the effort (good luck finding a snake in winter – they're all hibernating). It's always best to ask a local organiser for guidance or to check that they're still operating outside the normal season. For example, you could go zorbing at any time of year, but most operators shut down in winter.

Miscellaneous

Important considerations for some activities include the following:

Family friendly: Many sports have options for children, with the age limit depending on the activity and/or the organiser.

Disability friendly: Some activities may not seem so easy to tackle for the disabled or handicapped, but many centres and organisers cater for the physically and mentally handicapped, and some national organisations have a special programme for the disabled or special centres. See **Contacts** under individual activities and the list of websites of organisations providing help for the disabled or handicapped in **Appendix B**.

Weight restriction: Some organisers impose a maximum weight limit (there may also be a minimum). This may vary between organisers and even, for example, between horses for pony trekking, so it's always worth enquiring. You may be surprised how heavy you can be and still take part in – for example – some aerial sport organisers set a weight limit of 220lb/100kg. If you're particularly large or heavy, it's advisable to check with the organiser rather than just turning up.

Water confident: Most organised water-based activities require a life jacket, but you may still need to be a good swimmer or at least be willing to be submerged in water and be comfortable in waves.

Autumn, Dartmoor National Park

2

IN THE AIR

- ❖ Paragliding
- ❖ Parachuting/Skydiving
- ❖ Hang Gliding
- ❖ Powered Hang Gliding
- ❖ Gliding
- ❖ Parascending
- ❖ Hot Air Ballooning
- ❖ Microlighting
- ❖ Paramotor
- ❖ Base Jumping

Y ou can fly! This weekend, tomorrow even, you can be airborne. This astonishing development in human evolution has arisen out of our greater understanding of thermals, and new lightweight gliding materials that allow us to ride them. Whichever method you use to get airborne, the thrill will stay with you for ever.

Warning!

Most adventure sports are inherently dangerous in some way, none more so than aerial sports, where if anything goes seriously wrong it can be potentially fatal. None of the activities in this chapter must be attempted without the supervision of a licensed operator and you should never try any of them alone until you're fully trained and qualified.

PARAGLIDING

AT A GLANCE

Accessibility Index: ❶❷❸④⑤

Fitness level: ❶❷③④⑤

Degree of Difficulty: ❶❷❸④⑤

White-knuckle rating: ❶❷❸❹⑤

Equipment: hire or medium cost

Season: year round

Disability programme: ✓

Weight restriction: ✓

📝 CONTACTS

- Airworks Paragliding Centre: ☎ 01273-858108, 🖳 www.airworks.co.uk

- British Hang Gliding & Paragliding Association/ BHPA: ☎ 01162-894316, 🖳 www.bhpa.co.uk/paraglide

- Flyability: ☎ 01768-773040, 🖳 www.flyability. org.uk (the disability initiative of the BHPA)

- Scottish Hang-Gliding & Paragliding Federation: ☎ 01313-336234 (Edinburgh area), 🖳 www.shpf.co.uk

The dream of our ancestors, to emulate the birds, has come to pass. Human beings can fly, these days. Not just 'plunge to earth at a slightly reduced velocity' but actually soar, float and swoop through the air like a bird, with a grandstand view of the British countryside. Yet how many of us pass hillsides filled with brightly-coloured wings and canopies without even considering the possibility of actually taking part in this exciting sport? While paragliding is certainly an extreme sport, with close attention to safety and learning about weather and the physics of flight, it's an affordable and accessible way of flying.

WHAT EXACTLY WILL I BE DOING?

Paragliders use a parachute-like canopy – though much lighter – to catch rising waves of warm air known as thermals, or the breeze rising over features such as hillsides. For a taster session, you can fly tandem with an instructor or take an Elementary Pilot certificate over a couple of days. To get a Club Pilot (CP) licence, which legally allows you to reach 'soaring' heights of up to 5,500ft (1,700m) – dictated more by air traffic control than by the laws of aerodynamics – you'll need to do a ten-day course.

Training begins with an explanation of the canopy and the controls. Then you'll venture onto a gentle slope to try a few short hops and learn the launching and landing techniques. Next, how to turn and control your height. As your confidence and proficiency increase, you move onto steeper hills and greater altitudes, as well as learning about the dynamics of flying, meteorology and air traffic control law.

With a paraglider weighing less than 22lb (10kg), once qualified and experienced this is a sport you can enjoy around the world. Compared to hang-gliding, paragliding equipment is cheaper to buy and more portable, it's quicker to learn and it's done sitting down, which some people find easier. You can also learn to paraglide from a flat field, using a winch, which has a quicker training process (see **Parascending** on page 45).

HAPPY MEMORIES?

Because you're using the same air currents as birds of prey, you'll occasionally find yourself flying next to a hawk or kestrel, sharing a thermal. The peace and silence of paragliding above a beauty spot is a rare chance to escape the trivia and stresses of everyday life for some real blue skies thinking.

WHAT SHOULD I BE WORRIED ABOUT?

Wind is the most fickle of mistresses, and you're at the mercy of it. Sudden thermals, storms, squalls and twisters can make paragliding a hazardous activity, even in Britain's (usually) relatively benign skies. You need to take particular care in changing wind conditions, and to be especially vigilant in popular areas when it isn't unknown for novices to crash into other paragliders. Wearing a parachute is a comfort, but it cannot always be deployed quickly enough in an emergency. It's one of the most dangerous of all aerial sports.

IN THE AIR

POPULAR LOCATIONS

Southeast: South Downs, Lewes; ☎ 01273-858108, 🖥 www.airworks.co.uk.

Southwest: Wiltshire; ☎ 07795-632710, 🖥 www.cloudbase paragliding.com.

Central: Staffordshire Scouts; ☎ 07941-115153, 🖥 www.staffordshirescouting.org.

North: Harrogate, Yorkshire Dales; ☎ 0845-389 3223, 🖥 www.yorkshiredalesandharrogate.com.

Wales: South East Wales Hang Gliding and Paragliding Club; ☎ 02920-710616, 🖥 www.sewhgpgc.co.uk.

Scotland: Scottish Highlands; ☎ 01463-244100, 🖥 www.visithighlands.com.

WHERE DO I START?

This is not, under any circumstances, an activity that you can teach yourself. However, there are plenty of UK paragliding schools, and you can be airborne by lunchtime on your first day of instruction.

WHEN'S THE BEST TIME FOR IT?

All year – however, conditions are better for beginners in winter, with fewer thermals and sea breezes, but require a cold-weather flying suit.

WHO CAN DO IT?

From the age of 14 at low level or from age 16 to 'soaring height' with parental consent. Most centres will take people weighing up to 18 stones (115kg), but some paragliders can (in theory) handle 30 stones (200kg).

WHAT WILL IT COST?

Taster days, including low-level paragliding, cost from around £100, but to get trained up to pilot level you should budget for around £1,000. New paragliders cost some £2,000 for a canopy, second (safety) parachute, harness and pack. More advanced (and wealthy) paragliders may wish to invest in an altimeter, variometer, windmeter and even a multi-function GPS unit.

CAMPFIRE GOSSIP

Ewa Wisnierska was caught by a thunderstorm in 2007 while paragliding in Australia at 2,500ft (765m). She was pulled by the storm up to 32,612ft (9,946m – much higher than Mt Everest) in just 15 minutes, surrounded by darkness and lightning, pelted by 6in (15cm) hailstones and coated in ice due to -45ºC (-49ºF) temperatures. She eventually passed out due to lack of oxygen and landed 35 miles (56km) away, still covered in ice, but alive.

PARACHUTING/ SKYDIVING

 **AT A GLANCE**

Accessibility Index: ❶❷❸④⑤

Fitness level: ❶❷③④⑤

Degree of Difficulty: ❶❷❸④⑤

White-knuckle rating: ❶❷❸❹❺

Equipment: hire or medium cost

Season: year round

Disability programme: ✓

Weight restriction: ✓

Free-falling is the ultimate thrill, plummeting to earth at 130mph (209kph) while looking death squarely in the face. "What did I do at the weekend? I stared death in the face at 12,000ft. And you?"

CONTACTS

- Accelerated Free Fall: 🖳 www.acceleratedfreefall.com

- British Parachuting Association: ☎ 0116-278 5271, 🖳 www.bpa.org.uk

- Dropzone: 🖳 www.dropzone.com

- Organisers: 🖳 www.aerial.org, www.londonparachuteschool. com, www.skydiving.co.uk, www.ukparachuting.co.uk, www.ukskydiving.co.uk, www.ukskydiving.com

You can descend fast, by freefalling before pulling the ripcord, or slowly, by using a static line. But either way, who amongst us with a brightly-coloured canopy above and a patchwork of fields below, could stop ourselves from humming the Battle of Britain theme tune? Most people parachute just once in their lifetime, if at all, which is a pity because it's an activity in which you can develop great skills, and offers thrills you'll never tire of.

WHAT EXACTLY WILL I BE DOING?

There are three ways to learn parachuting. The easiest and safest way is the tandem sky dive, where you're strapped to an instructor and experience freefall before the instructor pulls the rip cord and brings you safely in to land. It requires virtually no training and there's no upper age limit; hence, every summer, we see octogenarian veterans reliving D-Day.

The second and more traditional way is the static line, where your parachute is automatically deployed as you leave the plane, and you just steer your way gently to the drop zone. For this you'll need around six hours ground training and must be aged between 16 and 55 years old.

Then there's accelerated free-fall (AFF), where after extensive training you exit the plane with two instructors, all free-falling together for around 50 seconds, before pulling your own rip cord. This is normally done as part of a week's course of ten jumps, after which you're a partially qualified sky diver.

After around 30 jumps you should be a fully-qualified sky diver, ready to try formation sky-diving, freestyle freefalling and gymnastics, and landing accuracy where you attempt to land on a 6.5ft (2m) diameter target.

HAPPY MEMORIES?

Parachuting offers a smorgasbord of intense experiences: the take-off in a light plane, the delicious terror as you reach altitude and can see the drop zone far below. There's the ice-cold rush of wind as the door is opened, and the last-minute testing of your resolve. After that, plummeting to earth and the welcoming tug of the opening parachute is all pleasure.

WHAT SHOULD I BE WORRIED ABOUT?

When you combine light aircraft, high altitudes and trusting your life to an arrangement of string and material, whichever way you slice it you're operating at the extremes of human endeavour, with many exciting ways to hurt yourself. Although the mortality rate of one in 300,000 jumps may be comforting, experienced

POPULAR LOCATIONS

Southeast: Kent; ☎ 01622-890862,
💻 www.headcornparachuteclub.co.uk.

Southwest: Cornwall; ☎ 01872-553352,
💻 www.cornishparachuteclub.co.uk.

Central: Weston; ☎ 01869-343201, 💻 www.rafspa.com.

North: Yorkshire; ☎ 01262-228033, 💻 www.skydivegb.com.

Wales: South Wales; ☎ 01792-207035,
💻 www.skydiveswansea.co.uk.

Scotland: Perthshire; ☎ 0176-466 2572,
💻 www.skydivestrathallan.co.uk.

skydivers operating at the extremes say that one in 100 jumps goes wrong in some way (fortunately, usually minor).

WHERE DO I START?

There are around 25 British Parachuting Association (BPA) affiliated clubs in the UK. One phone call and you could be in the air tomorrow.

WHERE CAN IT LEAD?

The BPA runs skills workshops to help you develop as a sky diver. Sky divers form a close-knit and sociable community across the western world, with the US being the major centre with its huge expanse of empty skies.

WHO CAN DO IT?

The minimum age is 16, but you can experience freefall younger through 'bodyflying' in a wind-tunnel.

WHAT WILL IT COST?

Tandem sky dives cost from £150, static line from £200 and AFF from £350. Once trained, each jump can cost as little as £10.

CAMPFIRE GOSSIP

In 1943, US Airforce gunner Alan Magee exited his B-17 Flying Fortress without a parachute, and fell four miles before crashing through the glass roof of St Nazaire railway station in France. He survived. And was he put off flying? Not at all – after the war he became a pilot.

IN THE AIR

HANG GLIDING

 **AT A GLANCE**

Accessibility Index: ❶❷❸④⑤

Fitness level: ❶❷③④⑤

Degree of Difficulty: ❶❷❸❹⑤

White-knuckle rating: ❶❷❸❹⑤

Equipment: hire or medium cost

Season: year round

Disability programme: ✓

Weight restriction: ✓

Hang gliding was once the most lethal way to get down a hill (until someone invented cheese rolling), but safety has improved dramatically since the early days, and the latest models do more than just descend and can soar on rising winds and stay aloft for hours. Hang gliding is also about as close to recreating the experience of being a bird as you can get, as you lie headfirst like a bird, suspended from your wings (like a bird) and are able to swoop at speeds of up to 90mph (145kph), with superb control.

WHAT EXACTLY WILL I BE DOING?

To take off, you go to the top of a hill – there are also winch systems for when no slope is available – place the hang glider over your shoulders, strap yourself in and run down, just as if you were launching a kite. Wind will fill the sail and up you go. You then control the direction by moving your weight in relation to the control bar that you're hanging onto for dear life, and catch thermals to take you higher. Apart from allowing you to see the world from a very different angle, becoming a hang glider pilot means gaining expertise in predicting weather patterns, learning navigation and managing traffic in three-dimensions.

When training, you'll normally be in a two-person hang glider, but it's surprisingly easy to learn, roughly comparable to riding a bike or learning basic skiing. As your proficiency grows, you'll see that you don't even need wind to hang glide, but can rely on thermals and 'relative wind' – the movement of air over the wing to create lift. A hang glider can also be flown in stronger winds than a paraglider, due to its relatively robust aluminium structure and aerodynamic shape.

It's a great competition sport that the British excel at, and an exciting yet relaxing pastime that can be done anywhere in the world – and there's tremendous camaraderie amongst the hang gliding fraternity.

HAPPY MEMORIES?

In the past, hang gliders basically floated you down a hill. But modern models are able to circle upwards to astonishing heights, stay aloft for many hours and travel up to 155 miles (250km), the current UK distance record. Flying like this is a wonder of the modern age: only possible in the last few years.

WHAT SHOULD I BE WORRIED ABOUT?

Despite safety improvements, hang gliding still has an aura of sheer, devil-may-care lunacy, floating thousands of feet in the air suspended from a paper plane. And with good reason; it can be dangerous, with one in 116,000 flights ending in tragedy – almost double the rate of scuba diving, for example.

WHERE DO I START?

There are three main options: take a taster session and go tandem with an experienced pilot for a one-off trip, take a two-day 'taster' course with a small amount of low level flying, or do the full ten-day club pilot's course to become qualified at high altitude.

WHERE CAN IT LEAD?

Once you're expert at hang gliding, the next logical step is to attach an engine to the back of the glider, enabling you to take off without a slope, travel longer distances and be less reliant on the weather (see **Powered Hang Gliding** below). It requires only a few additional lessons after qualifying as a club pilot.

WHEN'S THE BEST TIME FOR IT?

It's possible to hang glide year round, although some training centres close for winter due to lack of demand.

WHO CAN DO IT?

You can fly solo from the age of 16 with parental consent. You must be fit enough to carry a 55-66lbs (25-30kg) glider while

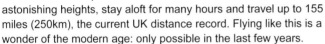

IN THE AIR

POPULAR LOCATIONS

Southeast: North Downs, Surrey; ☏ 01883-652666, 🖥 www.greendragons.co.uk.

Southwest: Devon and Somerset Condors; ☏ 01823-601202, 🖥 www.dscondors.co.uk.

Central: Thames Valley Hang Gliding Club; ☏ 01189-667512, 🖥 www.tvhgc.co.uk.

North: Northumbria Hang Gliding and Paragliding Club; ☏ 07890-276630, 🖥 www.nhpc.org.uk.

Wales: North Wales Hang Gliding and Paragliding Club; ☏ 01948-780378, 🖥 www.nwhgpc.org.uk.

Scotland: Lanarkshire and Lothian Soaring Club; 🖥 www.llsclub.org.uk

✎ CONTACTS

- The British Hang Gliding and Paragliding Association:
  ☏ 0116-289 4316,
  🖥 www.bhpa.co.uk/hangglide

- Flyability: ☏ 01768-773040,
  🖥 www.flyability.org.uk (the disability initiative of the BHPA)

- Scottish Hang-Gliding and Paragliding Federation:
  ☏ 01313-336234,
  🖥 www.shpf.co.uk

- Organisers:
  🖥 www.activeedge.co.uk, www.aerial.org

running downhill, though there are ways around this for disabled pilots.

WHAT SHOULD I TAKE?

As well as the hang glider, you'll require harness, helmet, flying suit, boots and gloves, as well as specialist equipment such as a parachute and altimeter. For novices, all this will be provided by the training centre.

WHAT WILL IT COST?

Around £90 for a taster day or some £900 to get to club pilot level. A basic new hang glider costs from around £2,000, plus at least £500 for the rest of the kit.

CAMPFIRE GOSSIP

The first hang glider flight was by a young Australian on the Clarence River in 1963, towed behind a speedboat. Only mid-flight did he realise that he had no idea how to land, and they were approaching a low bridge…

POWERED HANG GLIDING

The simplest form of 'real' flying (yet not officially an aircraft as it has no wheels), powered hang gliders use a small two-stroke engine to power a propeller situated behind the pilot's feet. You can launch from a flat field rather than a hillside and use it either to supplement the natural thermals or fly long distances when normal hang gliders are becalmed. Because it's cheaper and the training shorter than for a microlight (see page 48), interest is growing in this method of getting airborne; however, you can only train in the powered version when qualified in regular hang gliding.

CONTACTS

- British Hang Gliding and Paragliding Association: ☎ 0116-289 4316, 🖳 www.bhpa.co.uk/hangglidepower

IN THE AIR

GLIDING

 **AT A GLANCE**

Accessibility Index: ❶❷❸❹⑤

Fitness level: ❶②③④⑤

Degree of Difficulty: ❶❷❸❹⑤

White-knuckle rating: ❶❷❸④⑤

Equipment: hire or medium cost

Season: year round

Disability programme: ✓

Weight restriction: ✓

A Yorkshire aristocrat designed the first working glider in 1853, but he got his butler to fly it. More fool him, because flying gliders is a relatively comfortable, inexpensive and safe way to get amongst the birds. The British Gliding Association is keen to rid itself of its slightly fusty image, and is busily recruiting more women and youngsters through their club scheme, which also helps keeps costs down. Your local club – there are around 90 in the UK – will be delighted to see you, and all offer trial flights and full training.

WHAT EXACTLY WILL I BE DOING?

Gliders are single or two-seater aircraft with long wings, a small cockpit, virtually all-round visibility, but no engine (usually). You get airborne using a winch or a tow from an aircraft, although some gliders have an engine to get airborne, which is switched off when the craft is high enough. Once airborne, you stay aloft

by riding rising air currents, such as wind moving up over a ridge, or (columns of) rising warm air known as thermals. Modern gliders can stay up for hours, and the duration of a flight is only really limited by the hours of daylight, enabling gliders to travel up to 600 miles, as high as 50,000ft, and at speeds of hundreds of miles per hour.

To begin, the thrill of take-off, flying and landing in this almost noiseless environment is enough to concentrate on. Spotting potential thermals comes with experience, and you'll learn to fly the plane with maximum efficiency and economy, as well as coping with other gliders who could be sharing a thermal only a wingtip away from you. When you're ready for more advanced gliding you can go on to cross country racing, or maybe aerobatics. You can even loop the loop in a glider, experiencing weightlessness to 3G during the manoeuvre (the British have traditionally done well in competitive gliding).

Because gliders cost £10,000 to £30,000, and you usually need someone to give you a winch, this is the perfect club sport. Club membership costs from £200 per year, plus extra fees per flight. Many clubs offer free coaching but charge a fee per launch, and to go solo you'll need 40 to 100 flights.

WHAT WILL I REMEMBER?

Strapping yourself into the small cockpit of a glider is like strapping on your own wings. You'll feel every air current as you power up to the clouds at 1,000ft (300m) a minute and often find birds of prey catching a ride on the same thermal next to you. Yet, unlike hang gliding or paragliding, you're seated comfortably inside the aircraft in a proper seat.

WHAT SHOULD I BE WORRIED ABOUT?

Gliding may feel safe, it may look safe, they may tell you it's safe – so why do they give you a parachute? Bear in mind that like all aerial sports, gliding can be hazardous and is an extreme sport, but one you can do while sitting in a warm and relatively comfortable cockpit.

WHERE DO I START?

The British Gliding Association is extremely helpful and efficient, with a very informative website (see **Contacts**). Just book yourself in for a trial flight at your local club.

IN THE AIR

POPULAR LOCATIONS

Southeast: Ringmer, Sussex; ☎ 01825-840347, 🖳 www.sussexgliding.co.uk.

Southwest: Bath, Wilts and North Dorset Gliding Club; ☎ 01985-844095, 🖳 www.bwnd.co.uk.

Central: Nene Valley Gliding Club; ☎ 01487-813062, 🖳 www.nvgc.org.uk.

North: Trent Valley Gliding Club; ☎ 01652-648777, 🖳 www.tvgc.org.uk.

Wales: Black Mountains; ☎ 01874-711463, 🖳 www.black mountainsgliding.co.uk.

Scotland: Kinross; ☎ 01592-840543, 🖳 www.scottish glidingcentre.co.uk.

📝 CONTACTS

- British Gliding Association:
  ☎ 0116-289 2956,
  🖳 www.gliding.co.uk

- Junior Gliding:
  ☎ 0116-253 1051,
  🖳 www.juniorgliding.co.uk

WHEN'S THE BEST TIME FOR IT?

All year, but you generally cannot fly in rain, low cloud or high winds.

WHO CAN DO IT?

No legal minimum age, except for going solo (16), but most clubs' minimum age is 14. Over the age of 70, a medical certificate is required. It's an ideal sport for disabled people. Weight/height restrictions apply to some gliders, generally around the 6'3" (1.9m), 17 stones (110kg) level.

WHAT SHOULD I TAKE?

The only equipment you have to wear is a parachute.

WHAT WILL IT COST?

A trial lesson costs from £50 to £100.

CAMPFIRE GOSSIP

The 'Colditz Cock' was made by British POWs in Colditz Castle in 1944, with struts made from bunk-bed planking and sleeping bags for the skin. It was to be power-launched using a pulley attached to a bathtub full of concrete. The idea was to carry a man over the nearby River Mulde during an air raid black-out, but American soldiers liberated the castle before it was finished. Subsequent tests showed that it probably would have worked.

PARASCENDING

Parascending (also known as parasailing, parapenting and paraponting) involves wearing a harness that's attached by a 100-yard rope to the back of a Land Rover, winch or boat. If that sounds a little too much like a scene from Tom and Jerry, don't worry; you're also wearing a parachute, and as the vehicle gently moves off you rise into the air behind it.

You've probably seen this on a beach abroad (and maybe seen the scary YouTube recordings where dodgy operators have got it wrong) but you can also do it in the UK. Often it's part of an 'experience' package, including training in parachute landing falls (PLFs), to get youngsters interested in paragliding. As you progress, you learn to disconnect from the launch vehicle in mid-air, and parachute to a target. In ski resorts, there's a variation called parapenting (French), where you launch yourself off a mountain wearing skis.

For 'at a glance' ratings, see **Paragliding** on page 32.

CONTACTS

- British Hang Gliding and Paragliding Association:
  ☏ 0116-289 4316,
  🖥 www.bhpa.co.uk/parascend

IN THE AIR

HOT AIR BALLOONING

AT A GLANCE

Accessibility Index: ❶❷❸❹⑤

Fitness level: ❶②③④⑤

Degree of Difficulty: ❶②③④⑤

White-knuckle rating: ❶❷❸④⑤

Equipment: hire or very high cost

Season: spring-autumn

Family friendly: ✓

Weight restriction: ✓

Ballooning is the ultimate in genteel adventure. Because you're floating with the wind, it's totally silent and still (apart from the noise of the burners, which tends to spook livestock, etc.), and surprisingly warm without any wind chill. There's little to do but admire the view, but it can be scary if you allow yourself to think of all that space below the thin wicker floor. Children as young as five may be permitted to fly – but might not be able to see over the basket – and balloons don't allow wheelchair access.

When the ropes are released, the initial ascent can be alarmingly rapid. Once at a safe height above trees and power lines, however, things become distinctly relaxed. Flights are made in the early morning or evening because the wind is gentlest then, and they allow passengers to see the first stirrings of life in the countryside or the peaceful dusk.

The pilot cannot direct the balloon; it goes where the wind blows it, but by moving it up and down between air currents he can catch winds going in particular directions. When it comes to landing, however, ballooning hasn't developed much since a Frenchman (Montgolfier) came up with the idea some 230 years ago. You bounce along the ground in your basket, probably giggling with helpless hysteria and hoping that the basket remains upright. Hang on tight, as landings can be hard and potentially dangerous.

CONTACTS

- The British Balloon and Airship Club: 🖳 www.bbac.org
- British School of Ballooning: ☎ 01428-707307, 🖳 www.hotair.co.uk
- Bristol Balloon Fiesta: ☎ 0906-711 2191, 🖳 www. bristolballoonfiesta.co.uk

WHERE DO I START?

Balloon rides start from under £100, but anyone wishing to fly more cheaply should join a national or local club. There are training courses to qualify as crew and pilots, and by offering your services as volunteer crew or ground support, you should occasionally be invited for a free ride.

CAMPFIRE GOSSIP

Bristol hosts Europe's largest hot air balloon event (see **Contacts**) in August, attracting half a million spectators. Watching 150 balloons lift off simultaneously is quite a sight, and is absolutely free.

IN THE AIR

MICROLIGHTING

AT A GLANCE

Accessibility Index: ❶❷❸❹⑤

Fitness level: ❶②③④⑤

Degree of Difficulty: ❶❷❸❹❺

White-knuckle rating: ❶❷❸④⑤

Equipment: hire or high cost

Season: year round

Disability programme: ✓

Weight restriction: ✓

Microlight aircraft come in many speeds, shapes and sizes, not just those precarious-looking things you see buzzing slowly along overhead. Indeed many microlights look just like proper aeroplanes, and are rivalling light aircraft as the first step for budding pilots.

There are three types. The most basic, requiring relatively little training and no pilot's licence to fly them, are foot-launched microlights or FLMs (see **Paramotor** on page 50 and **Powered Hang-gliders** on page 41). A step up are 'flexwing', the hang glider-type machine with the engine and prop at the back, with you sitting in a breezy 'trike' suspended underneath. They're like riding a motorbike in the air, with a simple throttle control and a handlebar that you move around to go left and right or up and down. 'Fixed-wing' microlights look much like regular aircraft, with the propeller at the front, steering with a joystick and, sometimes, with a proper cockpit. They can go

up to 160mph (257kph), and some can reach the Mediterranean non-stop from the UK.

You can become a qualified (though restricted) pilot after just 15 hours' flying, seven of which must be solo, and fully qualified after 25 hours' flying (ten solo). Of course, that's the minimum, and given your precarious position 2,000ft (610m) in the air, it isn't worth rushing it. You'll usually need to weigh under around 15 stones (or around 100kg), and be aged 14 or over (16 to go solo). There's also

CONTACTS

- British Disabled Flying Association: www.aerobility.com

- British Microlight Aircraft Association (BMAA): ☎ 01869-338888, ⌨ www.bmaa.org

- The Microlight & Ultralight Aircraft Guide: ⌨ www.microlight.org.uk

- Nick's Micropages: ⌨ www.microlighting.com

- Walking on Air: ⌨ www.walkingonair.org.uk (Scottish charity for those with disabilities)

- Organisers: ⌨ www.activeedge.co.uk, www.aerial.org

classroom training to cover the principles of flight, aviation law, navigation and meteorology, and how engines, instruments and the human body perform in the air. You must pass an exam on this before you qualify.

The British Microlight Aircraft Association (see **Contacts**) reckons that full training costs around £3,000, and takes anything from a few weekends to a few years to complete. However, you can take it at your own pace, and the ground school theory is much easier if you can relate it to a couple of hours flying each week, and learn on the job rather than by just cramming.

If you just want to fly in a microlight, you can go as a passenger. Taster flights are available from as little as £20 and the club structure of British microlighting means that everyone is welcome.

WHERE DO I START?

Check the BMAA website (see **Contacts**) to find your nearest club.

CAMPFIRE GOSSIP

Organisers of Splash, the largest light aviation exhibition in the UK, have finally seen sense and renamed it The Flying Show (⌨ www.theflyingshow.co.uk), perhaps to reflect that not all planes come down in the sea.

IN THE AIR

PARAMOTOR

Also known as Powered Paragliders (PPG), you have a large fan strapped to your back below the paraglider canopy which gives you the thrust to take off from flat surfaces. You can turn the fan off, once airborne, or turn it on in mid-air to gain extra lift on a still day or to cover long distances cross country. With no airstrip, flying hill or licensing necessary, the paramotor is the hassle free route into the sky. When you're done for the day, it folds up small enough to be taken home on the bus or train. Training is straightforward and can be added to the normal paragliding training or you can try a one-off tandem flight.

📝 CONTACTS

- British Hang Gliding and
  Paragliding Association:
  ☎ 0116-289 4316,
  🖥 www.bhpa.co.uk/paramotor

- Paramotors UK:
  ☎ 01480-436805,
  🖥 www.paramotorsuk.co.uk

BASE JUMPING

 **AT A GLANCE**

Accessibility Index: ❶②③④⑤

Fitness level: ❶❷❸④⑤

Degree of Difficulty: ❶❷❸❹❺

White-knuckle rating: ❶❷❸❹❺

Equipment: hire or medium/high cost

Season: year round

Weight restriction: ✓

In the olden days, if you needed to prove a point by doing something insanely dangerous, you joined the French Foreign Legion. Nowadays, you take up base (or BASE) jumping and take a leap into the unknown. BASE is an acronym for Buildings, Antennae, Spans and Earth – the four fixed platforms that you jump from before opening your parachute with milliseconds to spare. Widely regarded as the most extreme of extreme sports, base jumping is actually increasing in popularity. Although there have been some 175 fatalities since it began 30 years ago, this is out of hundreds of thousands of jumps. It's comparable with extreme mountaineering, with its reputation based less on actuarial analysis and more from the fact that it looks absolutely terrifying (which it is – but also very cool).

WHAT EXACTLY WILL I BE DOING?

Base jumping grew out of skydiving, and you must usually be an experienced skydiver before you even contemplate base jumping. However, being an experienced skydiver won't equip you for the obvious differences between having thousands of feet to play with and just a few hundred. Therefore you'll need to do a first jump course (FJC), and find a mentor with base jumping experience. Your mentor will be the person who can (or may be able to) transform you from an overly-excited skydiver who knows how to pack a BASE rig and do a bridge jump, into a self-reliant BASE jumper with sufficient gear knowledge and site analysis skills to avoid certain death.

There are two bad things that can happen in base jumping – not deploying your parachute in time, and hitting the object you're jumping off on the way down. With so little time to react

IN THE AIR

to mishaps once you've jumped – literally a couple of seconds – every eventuality has to be planned for in advance. Hence 99 per cent of base jumping is in planning, as few base jumpers want to end up merged with the ground.

You'll need to plan your exit – where you'll jump from – and your landing, which you don't want to be among spiked railings or power lines! You'll need to know wind direction and be intimately aware of your parachute equipment and how to open and control it. You accelerate fast and don't have time to open a conventional chute in the limited space you have, so you use rapid activation devices. If you tumble and get tangled, there's no time to untangle yourself; if the chute opens with you facing the wrong way you could slam back into the platform, and you only have a split second to get your 'chute going in the right direction before setting yourself to land.

Contrary to popular opinion, base jumping isn't illegal: trespassing to get to a rooftop may be, but you won't generally be prosecuted for 'leaving' a building.

HAPPY MEMORIES?

Even experienced skydivers find jumping off a static object terrifying, a challenge so viscerally wrong that all manner of chemicals flood the brain both before and after the jump. All the senses are heightened and there's a sense of timelessness as you freefall, then the overwhelming euphoria as endorphins rush through the veins on landing. You'll want to go again.

WHAT SHOULD I BE WORRIED ABOUT?

The Splatula website (⌨ www.splatula.com/bfl) lists every death from base jumping since it started in around 1980, including that of Carl Boenish who invented the sport. Plenty to be worried about there!

Warning!

Base jumping is a highly dangerous sport that can easily injure and kill participants. Think long and hard before making a BASE jump. We do not recommend BASE jumping to anybody. You, and you alone, are responsible for your safety. (from ⌨ www.basejumper.com)

WHERE DO I START?

You'll need to be an experienced skydiver to prove you understand the principles of freefall, how to open your canopy correctly and control your drop-zone to within 100ft (30.5m).

WHERE CAN IT LEAD?

The logical next step is 'wingsuit base jumping' where you wear a special suit a lot like a flying squirrel to fly away from the platform before pulling the ripcord.

WHEN'S THE BEST TIME FOR IT?

You need calm and windless conditions.

WHO CAN DO IT?

Over 18s only.

WHAT WILL IT COST?

Once you have a parachute – which costs around £2,000 – the great benefit of base jumping is that it usually costs nothing but frayed nerves.

CAMPFIRE GOSSIP

The most tragic BASE jump was the first. Parisian tailor Franz Reichelt had invented a 'coat parachute' with which he hoped to make his fortune after demonstrating it from the Eiffel Tower in 1912. At the last moment, he did the first test flight himself instead of using the dummy. Er, it didn't work.

CONTACTS

- BASEjumper:
  www.basejumper.com,
  www.basejumper.org

- UKProBASE:
  www.ukprobase.com

IN THE AIR

3
ON
FOOT

- ❖ Hill Walking
- ❖ Scrambling
- ❖ Wild Camping
- ❖ Wildlife Safari
- ❖ Night Safari
- ❖ Trail/Fell Running
- ❖ Adventure Racing
- ❖ Orienteering
- ❖ Urban Adventure
- ❖ Geocaching
- ❖ Snake Spotting
- ❖ Canicross
- ❖ Foraging
- ❖ Coastal Foraging
- ❖ Parkour
- ❖ Endurance Events

Britain's countryside is perfect for enjoying on foot. Our (generally) mild weather is rarely uncomfortably hot or cold, the distances are small enough to find something interesting within walking distance of your home, and a network of National Parks and local nature reserves are stuffed full of amazing flora and wildlife.

HILL WALKING

 **AT A GLANCE**

Accessibility Index: ❶❷❸❹❺

Fitness level: ❶❷❸④⑤

Degree of Difficulty: ❶②③④⑤

White-knuckle rating: ❶②③④⑤

Equipment: low cost

Season: year round

Family friendly: ✓

We're a nation of walkers, brought up on tales of Captain Scott dragging his wardrobe across the frozen wastes, or of Ranulph Fiennes running seven marathons in seven days on seven Continents. Maybe it's because we have some of the most beautiful countryside in the world. Hill walking, known as fell walking in the Lake District and Yorkshire Dales, is one of the most popular participation sports in the UK. Since 2000, the 'right to roam' has been law, so there's no shortage of places to walk, with footpaths from every village clearly marked and specialist maps covering every hill in the land. There are also National Trails – long-distance walks – across the country.

WHAT EXACTLY WILL I BE DOING?

Walking can be a simple Sunday afternoon stroll or a week-long tour from coast to coast staying in bunkhouses and bothies. For more spectacular scenery, the UK has 15 National Parks and 47 Areas of Outstanding Natural Beauty (AONBs), but a 'greener' challenge is to find the hidden beauty spots within walking distance of your home.

There are many organisations offering ideas for routes and a network of people to walk with, including the Ramblers Association, the National Parks Authority and the Youth Hostelling Association. Hill walkers like nothing better than compiling lists of mountains and hills, checking them off as they're completed

– a good starting point is the eight English and 15 Welsh mountains over 3,000 feet, perhaps followed by 'The Wainwrights' (200 mountains and hills situated in the Lake District).

For some people, the pleasure is in the anticipation: unfolding the Ordnance Survey map and scanning it for points of interest – beacons, springs, tumuli, ancient coppices with medieval names – and planning the route; then comparing two-dimensional plans with the physical beauty as it unfolds. For others, it's the muscle-wrenching physical satisfaction and breathlessness of a long climb, followed by the joy of the downhill stretch with the sun in your face and the wind at your back. Whatever your preference, the simple pleasures of walking include wonderful views, coaxing cows to lick your hand, climbing fences and dry stone walls, and finding a comfortable hummock to sit on while enjoying a flask of tea.

HAPPY MEMORIES?

Hill walking releases the same endorphins as more energetic exercise (see **Trail Running** page 62), while still enabling you to have the breath to chat. The simple process of putting one foot after another is a proven aid to creating thinking, so not only can you listen to your favourite symphony while you walk, you may even be able to compose one.

WHAT SHOULD I BE WORRIED ABOUT?

Death by hill walking is surprisingly common. Four people died on Mount Snowdon in one weekend alone in February 2009, but even in spring and summer accidents can happen: the Duchess of Cornwall broke her leg in April 2010 while walking in Scotland. What to wear and take for your own protection will depend on where you're going, how far, the season, the weather forecast and your own abilities. If you're inexperienced or unsure about the conditions, check with the local park authorities or other experts to see what they recommend. Be sure to err on the side of caution, allowing for all eventualities, and let someone know where you're going.

WHERE CAN IT LEAD?

There are various 'Challenge Walks', with a set route to be completed within a certain period. For example, the Yorkshire Three Peaks Challenge (🖳 www.thethreepeakschallenge.co.uk), 23.5mi (37.8km) and 5,202ft (1,585m) in under 12 hours, and the TGO Challenge (🖳 www.tgochallenge.pwp.blueyonder.co.uk), a self-supported walk in May across the Highlands of Scotland.

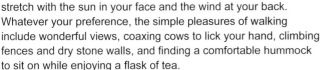

POPULAR LOCATIONS

Southeast: Leith Hill, Dorking; ☎ 01306-712711, 🖳 www.nationaltrust.org.uk.

Southwest: Thomas Hardy's 'Wessex'; ☎ 01305-267992 (Dorchester TIC), 🖳 www.westdorset.com.

Central: Thames to Cotswolds; ☎ 01865-810224, 🖳 www.nationaltrail.co.uk/thamespath.

North: Yorkshire coast and Moors; ☎ 01439-770657, 🖳 www.nationaltrail.co.uk/clevelandway.

Wales: Snowdonia; 🖳 www.walk-snowdonia.co.uk.

Scotland: Fife Coastal Path; 🖳 www.fifecoastalpath.co.uk.

📝 CONTACTS

- Areas of Outstanding Natural Beauty: ☎ 01451-862007, 🖳 www.aonb.org.uk

- Mountain Bothies Association: 🖳 www.mountainbothies.org.uk

- National Trust: ☎ 0844-800 1895, 🖳 www.nationaltrust.org.uk

- National Trails: 🖳 www.nationaltrail.co.uk

- Nordic Walking: 🖳 www.nordicwalking.co.uk

- Ramblers Association: ☎ 020-7339 8500, 🖳 www.ramblers.org.uk

- Walking & Hiking: 🖳 www.walkingandhiking.co.uk

- Youth Hostel Association: ☎ 0800-019 1700, 🖳 www.yha.org.uk

WHAT SHOULD I TAKE?

It depends on the conditions, but proper walking boots, and clothing that offers protection from the elements whether it's sun, snow or rain. For safety reasons, you should carry a fully-charged mobile phone for use in an emergency.

WHAT WILL IT COST?

Nothing, apart from the usual walking gear.

CAMPFIRE GOSSIP

The main risk to walkers is from cattle, which are responsible for the deaths of several walkers each year. The advice from the National Farmers Union is to avoid entering a field harbouring a bull and to avoid cows with young calves.

SCRAMBLING

Scrambling is a word that crops up in many outdoor sports, but for mountaineers (it's also known as alpine scrambling) it occupies the space between hill walking and climbing, where the going is difficult enough that you need to use your hands, but not so steep that you need to support your weight with your hands. It's a great way of getting into climbing, with scrambles in all major climbing areas, either as alternative routes to a summit (for example Crib Goch on Mount Snowdon) or as a stand-alone challenge similar to bouldering (see page 227). Scrambles are classified in difficulty from 1 (the easiest) to 3S (for serious) in England, and from 1 to 5 in Scotland.

CONTACTS

- The British Mountaineering Council: ☎ 0161-445 6111, 🖥 www.thebmc.co.uk

- Mountaineering Council of Scotland: ☎ 01738-493942, 🖥 www.mcofs. org.uk/scrambling.asp

- UK Scrambles: 🖥 www.ukscrambles.co.uk

- Walking & Hiking: 🖥 www.walkingandhiking. co.uk/scrambling.html

WILD CAMPING

AT A GLANCE

Accessibility Index: ❶❷❸❹⑤

Fitness level: ❶②③④⑤

Degree of Difficulty: ❶②③④⑤

White-knuckle rating: ❶❷③④⑤

Equipment: medium cost

Season: spring to autumn

Disability friendly: ✓

Family friendly: ✓

It's so simple, yet it feels so daring. By choosing to pitch your tent away from the 'official' sites, you're striking a blow for freedom and will feel part tramp, part explorer and all rebel. Basically, wild camping is simply pitching your tent in the countryside, rather than in an organised campsite. You could make it a weekend camping trip in its own right, or part of a cycle touring or even sea kayaking trip (see pages 118 and 152). In some beauty spots (for example Scotland's National Parks) you have a legal right to wild camping, but in most areas you should ask the landowner, both out of courtesy and to avoid having your tent run over by a sleepy/short-sighted/irritable farmer in his tractor in the morning.

ON FOOT

WHAT EXACTLY WILL I BE DOING?

You'll be taking a lightweight tent with you on your ramble, cycling trip or llama trek. When you reach a suitably secluded and sheltered spot, far from any road or property, you pitch your tent. There are many labour-saving devices to make your trip easier, from self-inflating mattresses to tents that almost pitch themselves. Although you're supposed to ask the landowner's permission, this isn't always possible. However, by pitching late and leaving early, staying in small groups and only for one night, using a camping stove rather than a camp fire, burying 'waste', and not damaging crops or disturbing livestock, you shouldn't offend anyone. Trespass is usually a civil not a criminal offence and you can only be told to leave if a farmer notices you there and objects.

The excitement of wild camping is in the freedom of doing it your way, and although you'll miss out on 'home' comforts such as running water and toilets, there are practical reasons to prefer this kind of camping. Even the smallest, most organic campsite carries the risk of shrieking teenagers, snorers, noisy lovers, or someone playing Heart FM very loudly – all of which will keep you awake and the wildlife away. Out in the 'wilds' you may see deer, owls and families of foxes playing in the twilight, the appearance – or at least the sounds – of nocturnal creatures, and curious cows peering into your tent at daybreak.

WHAT WILL I REMEMBER?

You'll relish the 'alive' feeling as you unzip your tent in the early morning and enjoy the satisfaction of having survived a night on your own. There are no hot showers, fast food or wi-fi facilities for the hardy wild camper. Buy who cares for the soft life – feel the dew and grass under your toes, have a good stretch and make yourself a nice cup of tea.

WHAT SHOULD I BE WORRIED ABOUT?

Feeling slightly vulnerable out on your hillside in the middle of the night is all part of wild camping's thrill. (What's that howling in the distance?)

WHERE DO I START?

You'll need to buy (or borrow) the equipment, but one quick trip to Blacks (🖥 www.blacks.co.uk) or Millets (🖥 www.millets.co.uk) later and you're ready. Books and websites list good wild camping sites, but this rather defeats the object. Your first expedition will make you feel very brave, but after that it comes easy – so find a spot you know, imagine you're just out for an evening stroll, and then don't go home when it gets dark. Simple!

🖥 CONTACTS

- Areas of Outstanding Natural Beauty: ☎ 01451-862007, 🖥 www.aonb.org.uk

- Bushcraft & Survival Skills magazine: 🖥 www.bushcraftmagazine.com

- Happy Campers: 🖥 www.thehappycampers.co.uk/campsites/wildcamping

- National Parks Authority: ☎ 029-2049 9966, 🖥 www.nationalparks.gov.uk

- Scottish Outdoor Access Code: ☎ 01463-725000, 🖥 www.outdooraccess-scotland.com

- Walking & Hiking: 🖥 www.walkingandhiking.co.uk/top-tips-for-wild-camping-uk.html

- World of Wild Camping: 🖥 www.worldofwildcamping.com

POPULAR LOCATIONS

Southeast: South Downs National Park; ☎ 0300-303 1053, 🖥 www.southdowns.gov.uk.

Southwest: Dartmoor National Park; ☎ 01822-890414, 🖥 www.dartmoor-npa.gov.uk.

Central: The Cotswolds; ☎ 01242-864171, 🖥 www.cotswolds.com.

North: Yorkshire Dales; ☎ 0300-456 0030, 🖥 www.yorkshiredales.org.uk.

Wales: Brecon Beacons; ☎ 01874-623366, 🖥 www.brecon beacons.org.

Scotland: Loch Lomond and the Trossachs; ☎ 01389-722600, 🖥 www.lochlomond-trossachs.org.

WHERE CAN IT LEAD?

When you're an experienced wild camper, you may prefer to ditch the tent (and other 'luxuries'), which in addition to reducing weight brings you closer to nature and the stars. However, most experienced wild campers opt for a 'bivi bag', a lightweight sleeping bag that offers (some) protection from wind and rain, and is used by mountaineers and soldiers as well as by wild campers. Otherwise, a good, stable, overhanging rock can provide shelter from wind, rain and dew. In remote and mountainous areas (particularly in Scotland) there are bothies (huts), which provide a free overnight refuge from the elements.

WHAT SHOULD I TAKE?

Lightweight tent (or bivi bag), self-inflating mattress, sleeping bag (or bivi bag) rated for the overnight temperatures you're

ON FOOT

expecting, head torch, multi-use knife, water (or water-purifying tablets or pocket filter), toilet paper, trowel, a good map and a mobile phone in case of emergencies.

WHAT WILL IT COST?

Nothing per night, although the equipment listed above costs from around £150.

CAMPFIRE GOSSIP

The National Camping Club, later the Camping and Caravanning Club, was formed in 1909 with Captain Scott as President. Ironically, although the club is a bit sniffy about wild camping, Scott died doing it.

WILDLIFE SAFARI

 **AT A GLANCE**

Accessibility Index: ❶❷❸❹❺

Fitness level: ❶②③④⑤

Degree of Difficulty: ❶②③④⑤

White-knuckle rating: ❶②③④⑤

Equipment: none

Season: year round (particularly spring)

Disability programme: ✓

Family friendly: ✓

In Africa, you can see the Big Five (buffalo, elephant, leopard, lion and rhinoceros) and much more, while down in the British countryside we have our own 'big beasts', from dormouse to deer; via hedgehog, stag beetle, seal, water rat, barn owl, adder, badger, great-crested newt, marsh harrier, otter, chalkhill blue butterfly, brown hare, puffin…

Wherever you are in the country, and in every season, there are creatures living wild lives within a few minutes of your home. As people have started to taking a renewed interest in their environment, so private companies and local authorities (such as the National Parks Authorities) are offering guided tours of the British countryside, with experts on hand to point out the signs of wildlife and track it down. There are weekend camping safaris

deep into the countryside, or you can simply download an app or buy a book and go exploring yourself.

Seeing a wild animal in its natural habitat is both thrilling and relaxing. Sitting by a river or lake on a summer's morning, watching a water rat swimming or a heron patiently waiting for prey, or at dusk in a meadow with fox cubs playing and a barn owl swooping past with a mouse in its mouth… is heavenly. Forget Africa's man-eaters, it's time to meet the neighbours.

WHERE DO I START?

There are 224 National Nature Reserves and 1,400 Local Nature Reserves in England alone, as well as thousands of Sites of Special Scientific Interest (SSSI). You'll find them all on the Natural England website (see **Contacts**), along with information on what you'll find where and when. There'll also often be organised events to help you see wildlife. Tracking wildlife, you'll learn about its habits and lifestyle, rediscovering knowledge that our ancestors took for granted. You can then start travelling to see the highlights in other areas, whether it's wildcats in Scotland or wild ponies on Exmoor or in the New Forest.

CAMPFIRE GOSSIP

Are there big cats in England? The Beast of Bodmin, the Fen Tiger, the Surrey Puma, the less imaginatively titled Hampshire Big Cat… Every county has its tales of a panther-like creature, but although there are dozens of sightings each year, there's never been any conclusive photographic evidence.

CONTACTS

- Wild About Britain:
  💻 www.wildaboutbritain.co.uk
- Natural England:
  ☎ 0845-600 3078,
  💻 www.naturalengland.org.uk
- Wildlife Trusts:
  ☎ 01636-677711,
  💻 www.wildlifetrusts.org
- Organisers:
  💻 www.safaribritain.com,
  www.scottishwildcats.co.uk, www.uksafari.com

ON FOOT

NIGHT SAFARI

 **AT A GLANCE**

Accessibility Index: ❶❷❸❹❺

Fitness level: ❶②③④⑤

Degree of Difficulty: ❶②③④⑤

White-knuckle rating: ❶❷③④⑤

Equipment: none

Season: year round (particularly spring)

Disability programme: ✓

Weight restriction: ✓

To see much of Britain's wildlife, you need to visit its habitat at night. Badgers, bats, otters, owls, polecats, stoats, foxes, hedgehogs, Scotland's wildcats, wild boar, adders and many more, are exclusively or mainly nocturnal. Organisations such as the National Trust arrange nature rambles after dark, and fans of particular species, such as the Badger Trust, will advise you on the best spots to see wildlife, and maybe let you join one of their own expeditions. Or you can go DIY, possibly as part of a wild camping expedition (see above).

Begin with an area you know well, on a night with a full-ish moon – that way you won't fall into a pond, or be frozen with terror by a ghost-shaped hedge. It's best to get settled into place before dusk, so that the animals don't know you're there, and let your eyes gradually become accustomed to the dark. Sitting with your back to a tree is a good way to boost your confidence (you can also use a hide) on what can be a scary excursion for first timers. Don't use a torch or you'll lose your night vision; however, a pair of 7x50 binoculars are useful, or even better a night-vision scope or goggles, which cost from around £200.

As well as keeping still and soundless, you'll see more if you can mask your smell by staying downwind of the area you're watching, or even by observing from the branches of a tree. Avoid wearing perfume or after-shave. It's a good idea to tell the landowner, as people have been shot by farmers mistaking them for foxes; and if you're you're around badger setts at night, you could be mistaken for 'poachers' catching badgers for baiting.

Wildlife set their own agenda, so don't be too surprised if nothing appears; but you can always take a planisphere with you and try some astronomy (see page 309) while you're waiting.

(see page 309)

TRAIL/FELL RUNNING

AT A GLANCE

Accessibility Index: ❶❷❸❹❺

Fitness level: ❶❷❸❹⑤

Degree of Difficulty: ❶②③④⑤

White-knuckle rating: ❶②③④⑤

Equipment: low cost

Season: year round

Disability programme: ✓

Family friendly: ✓

Anyone who remembers school cross-country runs may find trail running about as tempting as double maths, but maybe it's only when you have your own children that the idea of running far into the countryside suddenly begins to appeal. The old sport of fell running has left its northern roots (routes?) and become

CONTACTS

- Badger Trust:
  ☎ 08458-287878,
  🖥 www.badgertrust.org.uk

- National Trust:
  ☎ 0844-800 4642,
  🖥 www.nationaltrust.org.uk

- Wildlife Trusts:
  ☎ 01636-677711,
  🖥 www.wildlifetrusts.org

ON FOOT

trail running, both as a club and competitive event, and is a welcome relief from the tedium of gym treadmills. It's a growing sport in the UK, free, and offers a chemically-proven natural high.

WHAT EXACTLY WILL I BE DOING?

Once you've bought some proper trail-running shoes (£40 to £100), you can start running cross country. Don't expect to attain the same speeds as on the road, because you'll be clambering over gates and stiles, crossing streams, and possibly climbing and descending thousands of feet. You're running along country tracks, towpaths, bridle paths, or perhaps totally off-track and across fields. Trail running can be a solo activity, but to begin by joining a local club is a safe way to find new trails, build up fitness, and learn the particular skills of running over rough ground rather than on pavements. There are also plenty of organised competitions, over distances varying from 5 miles (8km) to over 100 miles (160km).

As you build up distances and seek out new challenges, navigation comes into play; and in severe conditions or remote areas, survival skills are essential. The thrill is in placing yourself in unfamiliar territory, against the elements and running.

HAPPY MEMORIES?

The 'runner's high' is well known anecdotally, and has now been proven in the laboratory to come from the release of endorphins, the natural opiates in the brain that are usually released when you're, for example, in love or listening to beautiful music. They're also released during prolonged hard exercise, making a legal 'high' and one which also eases the pain of running.

POPULAR LOCATIONS

Southeast: Mudman 10K, Camberley, Surrey; ☎ 020-8399 3579, 🖳 www.humanrace.co.uk.

Southwest: Forde Abbey 10K, West Dorset; ☎ 01460-30456, 🖳 www.acrossthedivide.com.

Central: Derbyshire; ☎ 01335-350333, 🖳 www.dovedale dash.acwager.co.uk.

North: Pennine Way; ☎ 01924-334500, 🖳 www.nationaltrail.co.uk/pennineway.

Wales: Snowdon 10-mile; ☎ 07867-976183, 🖳 www.snowdonrace.co.uk.

Scotland: Lowe Alpine Mountain Marathon; ☎ 01931-714106, 🖳 www.lamm.co.uk.

WHAT SHOULD I BE WORRIED ABOUT?

Running cross country may take you far from home, in thin clothing, perhaps a little bit lost, with a mist coming down and dusk not far behind it. But that's also part of the thrill of trail running…

WHAT SHOULD I TAKE?

Proper running shoes are essential, and women should wear a running bra. Beyond that, organised events will have a checklist of essential equipment; most trail runners run with a bum bag or small rucksack for longer events, to carry their essentials.

WHAT WILL IT COST?

A reasonable pair of trail running shoes costs from £40 to £100.

CAMPFIRE GOSSIP

The first recorded fell running race was at the Braemar Gathering in 1064, a time when wolves and bears still roamed Scotland – so you can see where they got the idea from.

CONTACTS

- British Open Fell Runners Association: ☎ 01535-634871, 🖳 www.bofra.org.uk

- Fell Runners Association: 🖳 www.fellrunner.org.uk

- National Trails: ☎ 0300-060 0507, 🖳 www.nationaltrail.co.uk

- Trail Running: 🖳 www.trailrunning.co.uk

ON FOOT

ADVENTURE RACING

 **AT A GLANCE**

Accessibility Index: **❶❷❸**④⑤

Fitness level: **❶❷❸❹❺**

Degree of Difficulty: **❶❷❸**④⑤

White-knuckle rating: **❶❷❸**④⑤

Equipment: medium cost

Season: year round

Confident swimmer: ✓

If one outdoor activity is enormous fun, then combining two will be twice the fun, yes? Well, not necessarily. Fun just isn't the word most associated with adventure racing. This is where Britain's toughest come to torture themselves. Adventure races are organised competitive events combining two or more endurance activities, often staged over a weekend. In the UK, it normally includes trail running, mountain biking and maybe kayaking, but it could also entail climbing and swimming, and can even include switching to inline skates. Many events also involve an element of navigation or orienteering (see page 71). In some events, competitors don't know the route or the activities until they turn up, with organisers springing surprises – such as a night navigation exercise just when you're about to climb into your sleeping bag.

WHAT EXACTLY WILL I BE DOING?

You'll be pinning on a number and following a course or trying to reach checkpoints, usually in wild country, maybe as an individual but more commonly as a team member, over a period of anything between a few hours and a few days. The basic rules of adventure racing are no engines, no GPS and no outside assistance – and you must carry mandatory safety equipment. It bears some resemblance to military training, and you'll be testing how far you can push yourself as well as trying to beat the other teams. The adrenalin kick of travelling fast over mountain and woodland tracks, fording rivers and leaping gates and fences is supplemented by the 'runner's high' from exercise, the thrill of competition and the mental kick from the achievement. And you do it all in the open air, usually in beautiful surroundings; so for endurance athletes it's a welcome relief from pounding the pavements.

There's rarely an upper age limit, and adventure racers continue well into middle age. Indeed, older competitors often do better, as a tortoise with good navigation skills may even beat a hare who loses his way (or has a nap on the way). There are also separate events for children.

WHAT SHOULD I BE WORRIED ABOUT?

Having to call the emergency services out to an organised outdoor activity isn't 'good form', therefore there's a huge emphasis on safety. However, events that take place across rugged terrain, in all weathers, at speed, on bikes, overnight – well, there's always the possibility of a mishap… Organisers try to keep track of competitors at all times, although obviously they cannot know exactly where people are for a lot of the time. A fell race in Wales (Snowdonia) in summer 2009 was abandoned due to atrocious weather conditions, and eight competitors were airlifted to hospital and another 25 helped to safety.

HAPPY MEMORIES?

What doesn't kill you makes you strong; no pain no gain; you'll hear a lot of this around adventure racing. All the same, the Monday after an adventure race, you'll walk a little bit taller (maybe with a slight limp). This is the closest you'll probably get to SAS training, and meeting that challenge will give you confidence, make you look good and keep you healthy.

WHERE DO I START?

You can practice until you feel fit and ready to make a good account of yourself, but sometimes the best option is just to scan the adventure activity press for an event this weekend and try

ON FOOT

CONTACTS

- Organisers: 💻 www.
  dynamicadventureracing.
  co.uk, www.mightcontainnuts.
  com/wordpress, www.
  openadventure.com, www.
  questars.co.uk, www.theomm.
  com, www.trailplus.com.

to get a late entry. There'll usually be someone slower than you, no matter how out of practice or unfit you are, and competing provides the motivation to work harder for the next one.

WHAT SHOULD I TAKE?

Organisers will provide a list of safety equipment, depending on the activity, which is checked before you're permitted to compete.

WHAT WILL IT COST?

One-day events cost from around £30 per person, but commercially-run, four-day events can cost £1,000 for a team of four.

CAMPFIRE GOSSIP

Adventure Racing was invented in the UK in 1968, when the Karrimor International Mountain Marathon was conceived to test orienteering skills. It's now called the Original Mountain Marathon (OMM, 💻 www.theomm.com), and takes place over two days with a maximum distance equivalent to two marathons.

ORIENTEERING

 **AT A GLANCE**

Accessibility Index: ❶❷❸❹❺

Fitness level: ❶❷③④⑤

Degree of Difficulty: ❶❷③④⑤

White-knuckle rating: ❶②③④⑤

Equipment: low cost

Season: year round

Disability programme: ✓

Family friendly: ✓

It began as an exercise for army officers, but has become a fast-moving, dynamic and exciting way to enjoy the countryside, learn valuable navigational skills and get super-fit. Orienteering is a competition where you use a map and compass to follow a cross country course. In Scandinavia and central Europe, it's a popular TV sport with fields of 15,000 in major competitions. In Britain, it's one of the most accessible of all cross country sports, with 120 UK clubs welcoming newcomers of all ages to events each weekend in every corner of the country. There are even special events for toddlers, who navigate by following a piece of string along a course.

You're given a special map, an electronic key and, for more advanced events, a compass. Competitors set off at intervals, and by reading the markings on the map – the contour lines, paths, gates, knolls, man-made features, woodlands, orchards, etc. – and using a compass, you navigate from control point to control point on a course that's generally 1.5-6.2mi (2.5-10km) in length. At each control point, you use the key to prove that you've found it. There are prizes for achieving the best times, but you can take it slowly and enjoy the views if you prefer.

It may sound technical but there are various grades of competition, so you can start on an easy course while you improve your map-reading and compass skills. There are competitions at local, regional and national level; and, if it takes your fancy, you can enter numerous competitions and climb up the league tables.

WHERE DO I START?

Orienteering requires no preparation or training. You can do it in a pair of old trainers or walking boots, or the most high-tech outdoor

ON FOOT

CONTACTS

- British Orienteering:
  ☎ 01629-734042, 🖳 www.
  britishorienteering.org.uk

- National Navigation Award
  Scheme: ☎ 01786-451307,
  🖳 www.nnas.org.uk (like
  orienteering but without
  the competitive element)

race gear. To enter competitions, you usually need to join a local club for £8 (free for children), and also the national organisation (£21.50). You start by finding your local club from the British Orienteering website (see **Contacts**) and giving them a call, and you could be competing this weekend. You may also need a red pen, compass and whistle, but you can usually rent/borrow these at an event if you're a beginner.

CAMPFIRE GOSSIP

There are as many variations to orienteering as there are points on a compass. There's ski orienteering, mounted orienteering, car orienteering, rogaining (long distance orienteering), night orienteering, ultrasprint, precision orienteering and many more.

URBAN ADVENTURE

CONTACTS

- Organisers: 🖥 www.adventurousactivitycompany.co.uk, www.ratracegreenbelter.com, www.urbanadventurechallenge.co.uk

AT A GLANCE

Accessibility Index: ❶❷❸④⑤

Fitness level: ❶❷❸④⑤

Degree of Difficulty: ❶❷③④⑤

White-knuckle rating: ❶❷❸④⑤

Equipment: low cost

Season: mainly summer

During your normal jogging route through urban streets, you may have imagined (like one does) hurdling the park benches, swimming the canal, or climbing the outside of a car park; here's where you get to do just that. Urban adventure racing has developed alongside parkour (see page 83) and 'boot camps' to help city dwellers escape the gym and reclaim the streets. You get the chance to run, cycle, kayak and climb around town, competing against other individuals or teams, and get fit in the process. Urban adventures are organised under a variety of names and formats, costing from around £40. Some have more emphasis on fun, and may include a space hopper section or a spot of pole dancing. Others are more serious: ex-SAS commander and explorer Ranulph Fiennes is a fan.

Courses usually start with a run, but can then move into cycling and possibly even kayaking down a canal. They may also involve climbing a lot of stairs in a high building and then abseiling down. Events can last all day or just a couple of hours, but most include a good 6mi (10km) of running. Sometimes, the course is through the everyday cityscape, running through crowded streets to reach a checkpoint; while others are essentially assault courses, but going over (and under) everyday objects such as bus shelters or walls, plus a few man-made obstacles such as a wall of haybales or a skidpan.

WHERE DO I START?

Events are held throughout the year, but primarily in summer, with several organisations staging events in Bristol, Cardiff, Edinburgh, London, Manchester and Nottingham. You take the normal gear for exercising outside, and if you need anything else, such as a mountain bike, the organisers will let you know.

ON FOOT

GEOCACHING

AT A GLANCE

Accessibility Index: ❶❷❸❹⑤

Fitness level: ❶②③④⑤

Degree of Difficulty: ❶❷③④⑤

White-knuckle rating: ❶②③④⑤

Equipment: low/medium cost

Season: year round

Disability friendly: ✓

Family friendly: ✓

If just walking around the countryside sometimes feels a little aimless, geocaching – geo as in geography and cache as in treasure – turns a stroll into a treasure hunt. There were over 1.2m geocaches hidden worldwide at the last count, everywhere from caves accessible only by divers, to suburban streets. There's probably one closer than you think – take a look at 🖳 www.geocaching.com and enter your postcode.

Your mission is to locate a cache, take the booty, note your presence in the logbook kept with the cache, and leave something for the next person. You find caches by logging onto a geocachers website and then entering the cache's latitude and longitude co-ordinates into a GPS (Global Positioning Satellite) device. Then you're off, tracking it down with the GPS like a bloodhound given a sniff of the runaway convict's socks.

Most handheld GPS devices, which cost from around £50, are accurate to within 16ft (5m), therefore a certain amount of hunting about may be required when you're in the general vicinity; but once you've found it (usually a plastic lunchbox-type container, discretely tucked away), written in the log book and replaced the treasure, you'll also want to mark your visit on the website.

As well as an exciting way of getting into the great outdoors, geocaching has a lively online community. You can hide your own caches too, record them online and see who sniffs them out.

WHERE DO I START?

Sound easy? Well it is quite easy, hence the value of the cache isn't very high. But some caches can be difficult to reach, in remote areas, high on cliffs or even underwater. The degree of difficulty will be shown on the website, but you can locate some caches even without a GPS, just by following website clues or the co-ordinates marked on an Ordnance Survey map. You can also buy an iPhone app.

CAMPFIRE GOSSIP

A 2009 Hollywood movie, *Splinterheads*, tried to make geocaching appear cool. It didn't really work and is easy to find in discount bins outside all the best DVD retailers. Maybe geocachers don't want to look hip anyway.

CONTACTS

- Geocaching Association of Great Britain: ☎ 033-3340 4242, ⌨ www.gagb.org.uk The Hornet's Geocaching page: ⌨ http://geocache.co.uk

- Official Global GPS Cache Hunt Site; ⌨ www.geocaching.com

- Open Geocaching: ⌨ www.opencaching.org.uk

SNAKE SPOTTING

AT A GLANCE

Accessibility Index: ❶❷❸❹⑤

Fitness level: ❶②③④⑤

Degree of Difficulty: ❶❷③④⑤

White-knuckle rating: ❶❷❸④⑤

Equipment: none

Season: spring to autumn

Family friendly: ✓

You can try and find British snakes yourself, but you'll probably see more on a snake safari led by an expert, or with one of the volunteer groups surveying snake populations at 'snake-friendly' areas such as Allerthorpe Common in Yorkshire and Wyre Forest in Worcestershire. Britain has three species; grass snake, smooth snake and adder. Grass snakes are the largest and most common, often found near water, green with black markings and a yellow spot behind the head. If threatened, they sometimes play dead, even squeezing blood out of their mouths to complete the look. Smooth snakes are also green, smaller and rarer. They

ON FOOT

✎ CONTACTS

- Allerthorpe Common:
  🖥 www.allerthorpe.org.uk

- Countryside Council for
  Wales: ☎ 0845-130 6229,
  🖥 www.ccw.gov.uk

- Natural England:
  ☎ 0845-600 3078,
  🖥 www.naturalengland.org.uk

- New Forest Reptile Centre:
  ☎ 01590-646600, 🖥 www.
  new-forest-national-park.com/
  new-forest-reptile-centre.html

- Wyre Forest:
  ☎ 01299-404740,
  🖥 www.wyreforest.co.uk

catch prey, constrict it to weaken it and then pop it into their mouth alive.

The adder is Britain's only poisonous snake, and grows to around 2ft (60cm), with a distinctive diamond pattern down its back and gorgeous silvery skin with iridescent blues and greens. Adders don't bite unless cornered and their bite is rarely dangerous even to young children. However, those who have experienced multiple bites, or with underlying health issues, could have a problem; therefore you should seek medical attention if you're unlucky enough to be bitten.

You can find snake habitats via the Natural England website or local wildlife trust. Walk quietly and slowly, because they can detect the vibration from your feet and will slink off. Snakes like heath and rough grass, and can be difficult to spot; but on the plus side, they tend to be diurnal (active during the day), and because they're cold-blooded they like to lie on a warm rock in the sun to catch some rays. Seeing two male adders 'dance' during the mating season in the warmer May days, when they rear up and try to push each other over in a trial of strength and to establish territory, is one of Britain's rarest and most beautiful natural sights.

CANICROSS

AT A GLANCE

Accessibility Index: ❶❷❸❹⑤

Fitness level: ❶❷❸④⑤

Degree of Difficulty: ❶❷③④⑤

White-knuckle rating: ❶❷③④⑤

Equipment: low cost

Season: year round

Family friendly: ✓

Weight restriction (for the dog!): ✓

Are you taking the dog for a walk or is it taking you? With canicross, the wackiest European sport to reach Britain since chess-boxing, the lines get blurred. But it's a great way to get a man and his dog fit and working as a team. Increasingly popular in the UK, there are canicross events most weekends. They're tightly controlled to protect the dogs (which must be at least one year old), marking it out from international dog-sledding events, some of which have a bad track record for valuing speed above doggy welfare.

WHAT EXACTLY WILL I BE DOING?

It's cross country running along forest tracks, with your dog. You can enter events with the dog on a normal collar and lead, but you'll compete much better with your dog wearing a proper canicross harness, from which is attached a 6ft (2m) bungee rope that fixes to your padded belt. This leaves your hands free, the stretchy rope prevents shocks, and your dog is pulling you up the hills with its whole body, not just its neck. Not every dog will pull, especially if it's been trained not to pull when on the lead, so it's perfectly acceptable to run alongside your dog rather than being pulled by it. Events organised by CaniX (see **Contacts**), the largest canicross club, are either 1.5 or 3mi (2.5 or 5km), which may not seem very far, but the dogs run fast and their owners try to keep up, meaning you'll be running fast along difficult trails. Events arranged by other organisations may be half-marathon length or more, and over mountainous country.

You can run with a maximum of two dogs, including assistance dogs (but not bitches in heat).

ON FOOT

CONTACTS

- European Canicross Federation:
  www.cani-cross.eu

- Organisers: www.canix.co.uk (largest UK club), www.canicross.org.uk

HAPPY MEMORIES?

Getting your dog to understand its role in the game isn't always easy. Many will want to wander off, sniff every tree in the forest and make really good friends with the other four-legged competitors. But once it does 'get' it, working as a team creates a new and exciting relationship between a man and his best friend, covering many more miles than walking, and getting you both fit in the process.

WHAT SHOULD I BE WORRIED ABOUT?

Running downhill being pulled by an excited dog (or two) can get very hairy, in more ways than one. Most belts have a quick release mechanism in case of emergencies.

WHERE DO I START?

Start by walking with your dog and adding in a few jogs along the way. They'll soon stop sniffing and catch on to what's required (or maybe not). Check out the rules governing how far each age and type of dog is permitted to run, recommended dog weights, and how much water they need – the rules are to protect the dogs, which would sometimes run themselves to death rather than let their owners down.

POPULAR LOCATIONS

There are events throughout the UK, often on Forestry Commission land. Check the websites listed below for your nearest event.

WHAT SHOULD I TAKE?

Doggy poo-bags are required. The organisers should provide a list of other requirements

WHAT WILL IT COST?

The harness for the dog and you costs less than £100. Entry to events costs £10 to £20, but you can do it independently for free.

CAMPFIRE GOSSIP

We're not saying our Continental friends are lazy, exactly, but many of their outdoor activities involve being pulled along by their dogs. There's 'skijoring', where a dog (or horse) pulls you skiing, and 'bikejoring' where a dog pulls your – yes, that's right – bike. Canicross was invented as a way of keeping the skijoring team fit during the summer season.

FORAGING

AT A GLANCE

Accessibility Index: ❶❷❸❹❺

Fitness level: ❶②③④⑤

Degree of Difficulty: ❶❷❸④⑤

White-knuckle rating: ❶②③④⑤

Equipment: none

Season: year round

Disability friendly: ✓

Family friendly: ✓

Heading into the woods to collect firewood and a bit of wild garlic to spice up your rabbit stew might sound like something from a fairy tale, but there's nothing 'Grimm' about the exciting new weekend foraging courses. It's the big new thing in weekend camping, learning to live off the land in Britain instead of a weekend of stress in the airport departure lounges of Europe. Residential courses usually involve a couple of days under canvas or even in a home-made bivouac, with sessions in how to recognise Britain's edible plants and cook them. There are plenty of day-courses available, and once you're confident of not poisoning yourself, you can go it alone, maybe doing a wild camping, wild-eating expedition.

ON FOOT

WHAT EXACTLY WILL I BE DOING?

You'll be walking through the countryside, being shown how to recognise the surprisingly large selection of food growing wild in our hedgerows and woodland. Not just mushrooms and nettles, but delicacies such as pig nuts, wood sorrel, rosebay willow herb and many others. Where's the meat? Our ancestors wouldn't have had the energy to invent the wheel on a diet of ox-eye daisies, so while some of these courses are a trifle New Age and vegetarian, others also include meat preparation. You could be learning to fish without a rod, or trapping, killing, preparing and cooking a rabbit. That sort of thing feels very elemental, 'red in tooth and claw', and is far more satisfying than buying it in a supermarket.

Hardcore foragers like to do the full Bear Grylls (British adventurer) bit, and arrive with nothing in their knapsack except a plate and a penknife – maybe a little butter for frying – and will only get to eat what they can forage. Let's face it, in an emergency you're rarely more than a few hours' hike from a corner shop.

HAPPY MEMORIES?

Making a fire and barbecuing your own trout, stuffed with fresh herbs and garlic, as the sun goes down, will make you feel part of the landscape and connected to the earth. It tastes even better when it's free. You'll also appreciate the sacrifice the trout made for your dinner and are more than likely to lose weight during your trip.

WHAT SHOULD I BE WORRIED ABOUT?

You may be wondering where pudding is coming from. The bad news is that nature abhors a pudding (apart from wild berries and fruit), so you may have to bring your own. It's important to know the difference between delicious mushrooms and deadly toadstools (the aptly-named Death Cap is best avoided).

WHERE DO I START?

There are books, videos and online courses, day courses from your local evening school, and long weekends available if you look online. Rather than looking for popular foraging spots, find your own special places – and then keep them to yourself!

WHEN'S THE BEST TIME FOR IT?

Late summer and autumn are the times of plenty in the countryside.

WHAT SHOULD I TAKE?

Normal seasonal clothing for a day out in the country.

WHAT WILL IT COST?

Day courses cost from £70.

CAMPFIRE GOSSIP

Beware what you eat and have a rescue plan. Christopher McCandless, who went into the Alaskan wilderness to forage, became trapped by the rushing waters from melting snow and eventually succumbed to starvation after eating the wrong type of Alaskan potato. Nevertheless, he's a folk hero to foragers, after his diaries were published as *Into the Wild* (also a film directed by Sean Penn). The golden rule is, if in doubt, leave it.

 **CONTACTS**

- Information/Organisers:
  www.bushcraftuk.com, www.eatweeds.co.uk, www.foragerangers.com, www.foragingcourses.com, www.mushroomdiary.co.uk, www.selfsufficientish.com

ON FOOT

CONTACTS

- Organisers:
  💻 www.bushcraftuk.com,
  www.coastalsurvival.com,
  www.eatweeds.co.uk,
  www.foragingcourses.com,
  ww.selfsufficientish.com

COASTAL FORAGING

AT A GLANCE

Accessibility Index: ❶❷❸④⑤

Fitness level: ❶②③④⑤

Degree of Difficulty: ❶❷❸④⑤

White-knuckle rating: ❶❷②④⑤

Equipment: none or low cost

Season: year round

Family friendly: ✓

Strandlopers were south-western African bushmen who foraged by walking (loping) along the beach (strand) subsisting on what they could find to eat. The died out (due to starvation?) many years ago, but there's something attractive about the lifestyle, and the sea is more consistently abundant than the land. Coastal foraging is the practice of gathering food from the seas and seashores, which can be combined with wild camping (see page 59) or a kayak trip (see page 152) from island to island. There are courses available to teach you what to look for and avoid possibly fatal mistakes, but the real joy will be in making your own expedition and living on your wits.

You'll be looking out for naturally occurring foods at the water's edge, or indeed in the water. Shellfish are the most easy to spot, with limpets and mussels easy to reach at low tide and cockles lurking in the mud. There are crabs and lobsters, crayfish and shrimps, all catchable without getting more than ankle deep. So that's the starter sorted. For the main course you could try fishing, and if rod and line feels a bit too normal, what about 'tickling' or spear fishing? For vegetables, there are edible seaweeds, beach mustard, samphire, seabeet, sea-lettuce, wild garlic and asparagus, berries and mushrooms. With wild food, you get what you get: there are no recipes and no store cupboard – so don't expect lemon with your fish; experiment with fennel seeds or some delicious wortleberries.

You'll inevitably have to kill something to eat it – never eat seafood that wasn't alive when you caught it – but if you're squeamish, bear in mind that you may be helping the environment. Large American signal crayfish, for example, have wiped out most of the native white-clawed crayfish, so feel free to eat as many as you like to save the indigenous ones, but make sure you know the difference (native crayfish are protected). It's also advisable to know about the seasons, as some shellfish are less edible at certain times of year.

WHERE DO I START?

Although you can glean useful information from books and websites, attending a course led by an expert is the safest and most enjoyable way to start, while learning what's available and safe to eat, and when. Any season will have food, but nature's larder is most abundant in summer and autumn.

CAMPFIRE GOSSIP

Marsh samphire, picked from the Norfolk coast on the Queen's Sandringham estate, was served at Charles and Diana's wedding reception.

PARKOUR

 **AT A GLANCE**

Accessibility Index: ❶❷❸④⑤

Fitness level: ❶❷❸❹⑤

Degree of Difficulty: ❶❷❸❹⑤

White-knuckle rating: ❶❷❸❹⑤

Equipment: low cost

Season: year round

When a young French naval officer went to the Congo, he was so impressed by the natural unschooled athleticism of the locals that he returned to France and developed a system of moves to get round a military obstacle course with the utmost efficiency. From the 'jungle' jungle to the urban jungle, parkour has gone

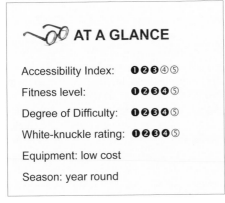

ON FOOT

CONTACTS

- British Parkour Coaching Association: 🖥 www. britishparkour.org

- Parkour Visions: 🖥 http://parkourvisions.org

- World Freerunning & Parkour Federation: 🖥 www.wfpf.com

- Organisers: 🖥 www.apexparkour.co.uk, www.parkourgenerations. com, www.urbanfreeflow.com

mainstream as a welcome relief from the tedium of jogging or waiting for a bus.

To be good at it you need acute spatial awareness, athleticism, balance, strength and a willingness to leap from obstacle to obstacle fearlessly and by the most direct route, rather than taking the stairs. Although it's now a competition sport (free running), purists dislike that element, because it promotes tricks that go against the concept of getting from A to B with the utmost simplicity, which is at the heart of parkour.

Basic moves involve lots of use of the hands for vaulting, quadrupedal movement like a cat, rolling after jumps to maintain momentum, converting horizontal energy to vertical movement and vice versa, learning to drop vertical distances usually considered dangerous, and lots of 'muscling up' – from hanging from an object to climbing over it.

Inevitably, after falling in love with parkour, the press changed its mind, and every burglary, act of vandalism and injured teenager was blamed on it. Nevertheless, it remains a skilful, efficient and fun way to get around town. You can 'learn' the moves from TV and YouTube, but it's advisable to attend a course and know exactly what you're doing before progressing to leaping tall buildings.

ENDURANCE EVENTS

Nettle Warrior and Tough Guy are two commercial events that take assault courses a soggy step further. You'll need to practice in advance to get into good physical shape, because these are seriously tough events which include such nasties as tunnels rigged with electric shocks; hill climbs and descents repeated over and over until you can barely stand; wading through bogs, swimming through tunnels, swinging into cargo nets and fighting your way through stinging nettles. Every muscle will be tested, and you'll be bloodied and battered by the end, say the organisers, who make you sign a death waiver before competing. You'll also be left with a huge sense of achievement, and new friendships formed in adversity. Only for the serious exercise nut.

CONTACTS

- Endurance Life:
  ☎ 01548-853524,
  🖥 www.endurancelife.com

- UK Endurance Events:
  ☎ 0787-743 3317, 🖥 www.ukenduranceevents.com

- Ultra Marathon Running:
  ☎ 07780-685538, 🖥 www.ultramarathonrunning.com

- Organisers: 🖥 www.toughguy.co.uk, www.triradar.com

ON FOOT

4

ON

HORSEBACK

Y ou'll never get bored riding a horse. When even conker fights have been
banned on safety grounds, every week thousands of us climb high onto the
back of a half-ton animal that barely tolerates our presence, which we then get to
run and jump about on. It's positively medieval and absolutely wonderful – but don't
let health & safety know!

PONY TREKKING

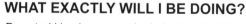 **AT A GLANCE**

Accessibility Index: ❶❷❸❹❺

Fitness level: ❶②③④⑤

Degree of Difficulty: ❶❷③④⑤

White-knuckle rating: ❶❷③④⑤

Equipment: hire/medium cost

Season: year round

Disability friendly: ✓

Family friendly: ✓

Weight restriction: ✓

A great introduction to riding and suitable for most ages and
abilities, including the disabled, pony trekking is the perfect way
to slow down and see Britain's countryside at a gentle
pace. The world looks better from the back of a pony. You
can see over hedges, you keep your feet out of the mud,
and it's a lot easier going uphill than walking. But pony
trekking also helps you get closer to nature than any
other mode of transport, and you should feel a strong
bond with your pony.

WHAT EXACTLY WILL I BE DOING?

Pony trekking is easy and relatively safe. You'll
usually go out in a group of riders with at least one
instructor and probably two. Younger riders can
be led, either by someone walking next to their
pony or by a more experienced rider with a leading
rope. Ponies are the steadiest and most reliable of

mounts; surefooted, unlikely to get over-excited and forgiving of novice riders.

So you'll amble along country lanes and trails, enjoying the views, the smells and the sounds of the countryside. You'll see more wildlife than when walking, as playful fox-cubs or basking adders will glance over, see four legs and continue their business oblivious to your presence on board.

Your trek may include a picnic or a pub lunch, and your route could include fording a stream or splashing along a beach. The instructor will be careful to judge the confidence of the group when deciding whether to stick with walking or to try trotting – and maybe even a little canter for those who have ridden before. Along with their reliability comes a tendency for ponies to plod along behind each other, so more confident riders could find it a little boring, though most will enjoy the sensation of seeing new countryside from an elevated height.

HAPPY MEMORIES?

It's the perfect family activity; mums can remember the riding lessons of their youth, dads can imagine they're Geronimo or Genghis Khan for a little while, and the kids can experience the real thrill of being in 'control' of an animal several times larger than them.

WHAT SHOULD I BE WORRIED ABOUT?

The challenges for new riders include nerves and balance; there's no footbrake and nothing very solid to hold on to. Because you can never entirely trust a pony, or other road-users, treks usually avoid both roads and large open fields, either of which can be hair-raising for novices.

WHERE DO I START?

You'll find pony trekking companies listed on tourist authority websites or can Google them.

ON HORSEBACK

POPULAR LOCATIONS

Southeast: New Forest National Park; ☎ 01590-646600,
🖥 www.newforestnpa.gov.uk.

Southwest: Devon Ponies; 🖥 www.devonponies.co.uk.

Central: The Cotswolds; ☎ 01386-837553,
🖥 www.cotswolds.info/equestrian.

North: Lake District; ☎ 015394-31999,
🖥 www.lakeland ponytrekking.co.uk.

Wales: Trans Wales Trails; ☎ 01874-711398,
🖥 www.trans wales.demon.co.uk.

Scotland: Trekking and Riding Society of Scotland;
☎ 01567-820909, 🖥 www.ridinginscotland.com.

CONTACTS

- Accommodation for horses:
  🖥 www.horseswelcome.org

- British Horse Society:
  ☎ 0844-848 1666,
  🖥 www.bhs.org.uk

- British Horse Society
  Scotland: ☎ 01764-656334,
  🖥 www.bhsscotland.org.uk

- British Tourist Authority:
  🖥 www.visitbritain.com

- The National Bridleroute
  Network:
  🖥 www.ride-uk.org.uk

- Pony Club: ☎ 02476-
  698300, 🖥 www.pcuk.org

- Riding for the Disabled:
  ☎ 0845-658 1082, 🖥 www.
  riding-for-disabled.org.uk

- The Trekking & Riding Society
  of Scotland: ☎ 01567-820909,
  🖥 www.ridinginscotland.com

WHAT SHOULD I TAKE?

Helmets are provided by trekking centres, but you should try to beg, borrow or steal jodhpurs and riding boots that fit; jeans can be uncomfortable for riding, and trainers are unsuitable footwear. A light windproof jacket is also desirable in all but the warmest weather, as you can get surprisingly cold ambling along at a slow pace.

WHAT WILL IT COST?

Trekking costs from £20 to £40 for two hours and £40 to £120 for a day.

CAMPFIRE GOSSIP

Ponies are smaller breeds of horses. They're fully grown – not to be confused with foals, which are young horses – and less than 14 hands high (58in/147cm) at the shoulder.

HORSE-RIDING WEEKEND

 **AT A GLANCE**

Accessibility Index: ❶❷❸❹⑤

Fitness level: ❶❷③④⑤

Degree of Difficulty: ❶❷❸④⑤

White-knuckle rating: ❶❷❸④⑤

Equipment: hire/high cost

Season: year round

Disability friendly: ✓

Family friendly: ✓

Weight restriction: ✓

If you're more used to trotting around a riding school or hacking through your local lanes, be prepared for the real thrill and sense of adventure that comes from making a proper expedition on horseback. You'll find as many varieties of horse holiday as there are riders in the Grand National. There are riding holidays at farmhouse B&Bs, racing stables, 'dude ranches', beaches and spa retreats. There are courses for horses involving horse whispering, holistic horsemanship, Reiki, agility, cross country, dressage and jumping – and riding every type of animal from Shetlands to heavy horses. There are also 'Horses Welcome' organisations promoting B&B accommodation, hotels and even country pubs where you and your horse can stay.

WHAT EXACTLY WILL I BE DOING?

The first choice is whether to take your own horse or to use one from the holiday centre. For the former, National Parks, riding magazines and tourist authorities list B&Bs offering accommodation for your horse, or try National Trails (see **Contacts**). Then you simply map out a route between them, following bridle paths (footpaths that horses are allowed to use) and quiet lanes. The British Horse Society has established the National Bridleroute Network to help keep bridle paths open, and to provide information on long distance routes.

ON HORSEBACK

Or you can stay in one area and explore it fully, for example the New Forest, with no need to set hoof on tarmac all the time you're there. Some equestrian centres offer this as an option, along with the chance to learn a new discipline or aspect of horsemanship. Perhaps you want to improve your dressage or make the leap from showjumping to cross country? You can also stay at a 'Pony Club for grown ups' and recapture the excitement of youthful riding adventures, but with extra consideration for the nerves (and good sense!) that comes with age.

There are also more relaxing holiday options, where you can enjoy the services of the hotel looking after your horse, and you just jump on board each morning to savour the views.

HAPPY MEMORIES?

The smell of leather and hot horseflesh, the quick responses of a well-trained animal, the fact that you don't have to walk… and if you've ever been trudging up a hillside on two feet when a troop of riders has come galloping past, you'll know that there's nothing more invigorating than being on a horse. An expedition, even a weekend trip, will forge a real bond between horse and rider that you won't forget in a hurry.

WHAT SHOULD I BE WORRIED ABOUT?

How can we put this? Horses are… not that intelligent. Wonderful creatures, full of instinct and a desire to please, but likely to be terrified of a litter bin or a funny-looking goat. And even the quietest horses will have their favourite spots to gallop, which you won't always know about until it happens.

POPULAR TRAILS

Southeast: The Ridgeway; ☎ 01865-810224, 🖥 www.nationaltrail.co.uk/ridgeway.

Southwest: The Three Downs Link; 🖥 www.ride-uk.org.uk.

Central: Sabrina Way, Oxfordshire to Derbyshire; 🖥 www.ride-uk.org.uk.

North: Newtondale Horse Trail; ☎ 01439-770657, 🖥 www.northyorkmoors.org.uk.

Wales: Radnor Forest Ride; 🖥 www.ride-uk.org.uk.

Scotland: Trail of the 7 Lochs; 🖥 www.southlochnessaccess.org.uk.

WHAT WILL IT COST?

Stabling or grazing for horses generally costs £5 to £15 per night, plus the cost of your own accommodation, and assume you'll muck out.

 CONTACTS

- Accommodation for horses: ☎ 01764-656334, 🖥 www.horseswelcome.org

- British Horse Society: ☎ 0844-848 1666, 🖥 www.bhs.org.uk

- The National Bridleroute Network: 🖥 www.ride-uk.org.uk

- National Trails: ☎ 0300-0600 507, 🖥 www.nationaltrail.co.uk

- Riding for the Disabled: ☎ 0845-658 1082, 🖥 www.riding-for-disabled.org.uk

- Scottish Horseriding: 🖥 www.scottishequestrianassociation.org

- The Trekking & Riding Society of Scotland: ☎ 01567-820909, 🖥 www.ridinginscotland.com

DRAG HUNTING

 **AT A GLANCE**

Accessibility Index: ❶❷③④⑤

Fitness level: ❶❷③④⑤

Degree of Difficulty: ❶❷❸❹⑤

White-knuckle rating: ❶❷❸❹⑤

Equipment: medium cost

Season: year round

Family friendly: ✓

Weight restriction: ✓

One of the most dangerous and exciting activities you can do in the countryside, drag hunting means sitting on a large horse, three metres from the ground, leaping obstacles at 40mph (65kph). The British countryside being relatively small and intensively farmed, riders rarely get the chance for a proper gallop before having to open a gate or negotiate a road. With drag hunting there's none of that nonsense, just all out speed

ON HORSEBACK

CONTACTS

- Horse & Hound:
  ☎ 01203-148 4564,
  🖳 www.horseandhound.co.uk

- Masters of Draghounds and Bloodhounds Association:
  ☎ 01252-703304,
  🖳 www.mdbassociation.co.uk

and adrenalin-pumpin' jumpin' – flying over every obstacle in your path.

WHAT EXACTLY WILL I BE DOING?

You'll be galloping mainly, with quite a lot of jumping – though generally anything over 30″ (80cm) is optional. Drag hunting is faster and more furious than traditional hunting, using either English foxhounds or bloodhounds. The hounds follow an artificial scent, either painted onto a horse's hooves and sent out before the hounds, or dragged by a running man who's given a head start of some 20 minutes. Meets are held on Saturdays from September to March and take three to four hours, divided into several legs or 'lines', each covering a distance of three to five miles. Don't assume that just because you aren't chasing foxes, etiquette goes out of the window: a rigid dress code of jacket, stock, hairnet, breeches or jodhpurs (etc.) applies – and let your horse tread on a hound or, heaven forbid, get ahead of the Master, and you'll be yelled at.

HAPPY MEMORIES?

There are few things more enjoyable than a long day in the saddle. Apart from all the speed and excitement, there's the bond between you and the horse – they really will go almost anywhere for you – and working hounds. And despite the obsession with etiquette, the camaraderie of your fellow riders is forged by the wintry conditions and the love of horses.

WHAT SHOULD I BE WORRIED ABOUT?

Where do you start? Each end of a horse carries its own risks, and that's before you even get on it. Horses can get thoroughly over-excited by the thrill of the chase and the sound of the horn, therefore only experienced riders should attempt drag hunting.

POPULAR LOCATIONS

Southeast: Kent and Surrey Bloodhounds; ☎ 01293-862235, 🖥 www.kentandsurreybloodhounds.co.uk.

Southwest: Southern Shires Bloodhounds; ☎ 01189-326028, 🖥 www.southernshiresbloodhounds.co.uk.

Central: Sandhurst Drag Hunt; ☎ 07831-251051, 🖥 www.sandhurstdraghunt.co.uk.

North: North East Cheshire Drag Hunt; ☎ 01782-511684, 🖥 www.necdh.co.uk.

Wales: Anglesey Drag Hounds; ☎ 01248-450089, 🖥 www.angleseydraghounds.co.uk.

Scotland: North of Scotland Drag Hunt; ☎ 01851-710218.

WHAT SHOULD I TAKE?

Check the dress code with the Master beforehand.

WHAT WILL IT COST?

Annual membership is generally £300+, with a 'cap' at each meet of at least £15.

CAMPFIRE GOSSIP

Foxhounds are deemed too slow when they reach eight years of age, and are put down because they don't adapt to life in a domestic setting; bloodhounds, however, which are frequently used by drag hunts, are usually re-homed.

ON HORSEBACK

COWBOY/WESTERN RIDING

AT A GLANCE

Accessibility Index: ❶❷❸❹⑤

Fitness level: ❶②③④⑤

Degree of Difficulty: ❶❷③④⑤

White-knuckle rating: ❶❷❸④⑤

Equipment: hire/high cost

Season: year round

Disability programme: ✓

Family friendly: ✓

Weight restriction: ✓

Riding Cowboy, or 'Western' style, doesn't mean you have to wear a Stetson or yell "Yeharr", although it's more fun if you do. It is, however, a more easy-going style of riding that feels safer than English style, so it's ideal for a nervous novice. Western riding developed from the need to spend long days in the saddle controlling cattle in a hostile environment; all very different from the jumping and dressage traditions of English riding. So the saddles are harder to fall out of, they're tougher – to support an unhappy cow on the end of a rope – with a high pommel to wrap a lariat (lasso) around – and the stirrups are worn longer, and held in place by tapaderos to protect the legs from thorny brush, while the reins are held in one hand leaving the other free to use the lariat.

WHAT EXACTLY WILL I BE DOING?

Riding cowboy-style means sitting snugly in a deep saddle, and relaxing. (It isn't obligatory to suck on a cheroot or spit chewing baccy into the dust.) Western riding feels very different from English style, and for new riders the most obvious difference is a feeling of safety. Western riding appeals to people returning nervously to riding after many years away. The depth of saddle and sturdy stirrups feels more secure than the flimsy saddle and flyaway stirrups of the English style. It also largely avoids

POPULAR LOCATIONS

Southeast: Surrey; ☎ 01306-628356,
🖳 www.cwwestern training.co.uk.

Southwest: Studland Stables in Dorset; ☎ 01929-450273,
🖳 www.studlandstables.com.

Central: Hertfordshire; ☎ 07939-890938,
🖳 www.western ways.co.uk.

North: South Yorkshire; ☎ 01226-767315,
🖳 www.rockys westernadventures.co.uk.

Wales: Pembrokeshire; ☎ 01437-541298,
🖳 www.sycamores ranch.com.

Scotland: West Highlands; ☎ 01852-500632,
🖳 www.lunga ridingstables.co.uk.

the need for expensive riding gear; jeans are fine on a western saddle, and the only necessity is a pair of boots with heels.

There are specific skills in western riding, such as barrel racing, neck reining and pole bending that developed from ranch work. Why not stay on a 'dude ranch', so-named because they were cowboy ranches offering a western experience to people from the east coast of America – known as dudes. Several organisers offer a similar experience in the UK.

HAPPY MEMORIES?

The kit, the clothing, the history, the hat, the Magnificent Seven theme tune playing in your head… if you don't find that exciting…

WHAT SHOULD I BE WORRIED ABOUT?

If you're used to English-style riding, then adopting the Western style of using only one hand and trusting the horse to know where

ON HORSEBACK

✏ CONTACTS

- The Western Equestrian Association: ☎ 01926-632916, 🖥 www.wes-uk.com

- The Western Horsemen's Association of Great Britain: ☎ 01366-727376, 🖥 www.whagb.co.uk

- Organisers: 🖥 www.cwwesterntraining.co.uk, www.themendipstud.com, www.rockyswesternadventures.co.uk, www.westernridinguk.co.uk

it's going takes some getting used to. Experts compare it to driving with power steering, as tiny movements are often enough to control the horse.

WHO CAN DO IT?

Most centres have a minimum age of five to nine, on a leading rein. Western saddles being chunkier and the horses often smaller, there may be a weight limit of around 14-15 stones (89-95kg).

WHAT SHOULD I TAKE?

Boots or shoes with a heel, to reduce the risk of your foot slipping through the stirrup.

WHAT WILL IT COST?

From £30 for an hour's ride and £100 for a full day's riding, with a lunch of barbecued pork and beans.

CAMPFIRE GOSSIP

Riding styles matter. A contributing factor to the collapse of the Roman Empire was because Roman cavalry didn't use stirrups while invading armies did, giving them better manoeuvrability and height in the saddle. It also meant the end of well-drilled infantry as the dominant military formation, and the rise of the heavily-armoured knight on horseback.

BEACH RIDING

CONTACTS

- Equine Tourism:
  💻 www.equinetourism.co.uk

- Organisers:
  💻 www.noltonstables.com,
  www.rideonthebeach.co.uk,
  www.studlandstables.co.uk

 **AT A GLANCE**

Accessibility Index: ❶❷❸❹⑤

Fitness level: ❶②③④⑤

Degree of Difficulty: ❶❷❸④⑤

White-knuckle rating: ❶❷❸④⑤

Equipment: hire/high cost

Season: year round

Family friendly: ✓

Weight restriction: ✓

Do you really want to live and die without ever galloping along a beach? It's the ultimate thrill; the thunder of hooves, manes and tails streaming, the smell of the sea, the wind rushing past, the splashing of the surf… Yet beach rides are reasonably accessible to experienced riders, with many seaside riding schools offering a ride along the beach as part of a trip. You'll need to hang on tight; regular beach horses will know what's coming and are likely to hit the sand at maximum revs, when even experienced riders may struggle to hold them back. However, although the wide open stretches are tempting to ride at high speed, they can also be fraught with hazards such as unexpected gullies, bits of flotsam and stray tourists. Beaches are often closed to horses in high summer.

After a gallop, most horses enjoy the water to cool off and they're good swimmers, so there may be an opportunity to take the saddle off and go for a deeper swim.

Prices for organised hacks usually start at £30, and riders need to be competent and confident to canter. Most riding stables have a minimum age of 12 and a maximum weight of around 14-15 stones (89-95kg).

ON HORSEBACK

CONTACTS

- Hawick Common Riding:
  ☎ 01450-378853, 🖥 www.
  hawickcommonriding.com

- Lauder Common Riding:
  ☎ 01835-822368, 🖥 www.
  laudercommonriding.co.uk

- Return to the Ridings:
  ☎ **01835-825060**, 🖥 www.
  returntotheridings.co.uk

- RideBorders: ☎ 01988-
  700974, 🖥 www.rideborders.
  com/common-ridings.html

COMMON RIDING

👓 AT A GLANCE

Accessibility Index: ❶❷③④⑤

Fitness level: ❶❷③④⑤

Degree of Difficulty: ❶❷❸④⑤

White-knuckle rating: ❶❷❸❹⑤

Equipment: hire/high cost

Season: summer

Family friendly: ✓

Weight restriction: ✓

Eleven Scottish border towns celebrate the ancient ritual of riding their boundaries, both to establish their independence and chase away anyone grazing livestock on common land without permission. In doing so, they created one of the most exciting riding events in the world – open to anyone, even the English whose encroachment led to the rides 500 years ago. The towns are Coldstream, Duns, Galashiels, Hawick, Jedburgh, Kelso, Lauder, Melrose, Peebles, Selkirk and West Linton. Each has its own traditions, but typically the day starts at 6am with a rousing Fife and Drum band parading around town to wake residents for the traditional breakfast of 'curds and cream' (rum and milk), a surprisingly pleasant tipple and the perfect settler for the riders.

Common riding involves long distance, cross country rides (that may include fording rivers) to various points marking the boundaries of the parish. Each ride can attract over 500 riders and thousands more foot followers. Cantering through the gorgeous Scottish countryside in summer as part of this huge mass of riders – immaculately dressed in tweed jacket, cream jodhpurs, long black riding boots and white silk neckerchiefs – is an exciting, memorable and occasionally terrifying occasion.

You'll need to provide your own horse, as riding centre horses will all be booked up, and organise accommodation a year in advance.

ENDURANCE RIDING

 **AT A GLANCE**

Accessibility Index: ❶❷③④⑤

Fitness level: ❶❷③④⑤
(horse) ❶❷❸❹❺

Degree of Difficulty: ❶❷❸④⑤

White-knuckle rating: ❶❷③④⑤

Equipment: hire/medium-high cost

Season: summer-autumn

Family friendly: ✓

Weight restriction: ✓

More fun than the name may suggest, endurance, or competitive long distance riding is a great way to build a rapport with your horse over a long distance and in an organised setting, as well as a wonderful day out in the countryside. It isn't about going as fast as you can, but neither is it an amble. The objective is to finish in a fast time but with your horse still in peak physical condition, as attested to by a vet both before, after and sometimes during the ride, by recording their soundness, heart-rate and hydration.

Almost any horse can compete, although Arabs tend to do best due to their stamina, but you'll need to practice and build up speed gradually for the longer events. When you register for a race, you're given a start time and a map. To keep your horse fighting fit throughout, you'll need to study the route with an Ordnance map or even walk it on foot for complicated sections. It's about tactics and navigation – don't just follow the horse in front, as they could also be lost. On the day, your horse will be checked over by the vet and then you're ready to go, usually with individual start times; but on the longer events, there's an all in one exciting mass start.

The longest events are for 100mi (160km), for which you'll need a back-up crew to meet you along the way and help look after the horse.

WHERE DO I START?

Beginners might want to start with Endurance GB's non-competitive rides (NCRs) or competitive rides (CRs). The former are 6-24mi (10-40km) and are ridden at 5-7mph (8-12kph), while competitive rides are usually 19-50mi (30-80km) travelling at 5 to

ON HORSEBACK

CONTACTS

- Endurance GB:
  ☎ 02476-697929, 🖥 www.endurancegb.co.uk

- Scottish Endurance Riding Club: 🖥 www.scottishendurance.com

- Sport Endurance:
  ☎ 01283-810011, 🖥 www.sportendurance.co.uk

11mph (8-18kph). These are easy to join without spending much money, and you can build up to the longer endurance rides. Look for a local group or event on the websites listed below.

CAMPFIRE GOSSIP

Like most equestrian sports, endurance riding grew from the needs of the cavalry. Their breeding programme was designed to produce horses that could carry a man and his equipment for 100 miles in 24 hours.

POINT-TO-POINT

AT A GLANCE

Accessibility Index: ❶②③④⑤

Fitness level: ❶❷❸④⑤

Degree of Difficulty: ❶❷❸④⑤

White-knuckle rating: ❶❷❸❹❺

Equipment: high cost

Season: winter-spring

Weight restriction: ✓

CONTACTS

- British Horseracing Authority: ☎ 020-7152 0000, 🖥 www.britishhorseracing.com

- Jumping For Fun: 🖥 www.jumpingforfun.co.uk

- Masters of Foxhounds Association (MFHA): ☎ 01285-653001, 🖥 www.mfha.org.uk

- The Point to Point Racing Company: 🖥 www.pointtopoint.co.uk

Today's riders can only imagine the thrill of an old-fashioned steeple chase; racing between village churches by the most direct route, ploughing through hedges with no barbed wire to worry about. Point-to-points are modern steeplechases, run by amateur jockeys on horses that have been out several times with the local hunt in the past season. The usual distance is three miles, over a temporary farmland course, with around 18 jumps up to 4′6″ (1.37m) high and a couple of ditches.

So it's local riders on local horses, generally the stars of the local hunting scene, on a local farm. They may be amateurs, but it's a far cry from the gymkhana, as there are always experienced riders and horses on the point-to-point circuit looking to mop up the silverware. Riders must obtain a certificate from the British Horseracing Authority (BHA), which costs around £50 for a single race and over £160 for a season. There are on-course bookmakers and sometimes The Tote, and these events attract large crowds.

To take part, you won't need to adhere to the harsh diet regime of professionals, but no horse is going to win over three miles with a fat jockey on board. Your horse will also need to be in peak condition and you may need professional coaching. Bear in mind that this is an extreme sport where jockeys can and do have serious accidents.

ON HORSEBACK

CARRIAGE DRIVING

AT A GLANCE

Accessibility Index: ❶❷❸④⑤

Fitness level: ❶②③④⑤

Degree of Difficulty: ❶❷❸④⑤

White-knuckle rating: ❶❷❸④⑤

Equipment: hire/high cost

Season: year round

Disability friendly: ✓

Family friendly: ✓

Weight restriction: ✓

"Chicks and ducks and geese better scurry, when I take you out in the surrey with the fringe, on top..." If you've ever hankered to take the reins of a coach and a pair of 'high steppin' strutters', you aren't alone. Driving horses in harness is a sport that's growing so much in popularity that the Forestry Commission in Wales has opened 20mi (30km) of extra off-road track to carriages, and in Scotland carriage drivers have a right of access similar to riders (🖥 www.outdooraccess-scotland.com).

You can learn the skills at equestrian centres up and down the country, and over the course of a weekend you should become confident in the basics – tack up, start, stop, turn, avoid bumping into large stationary objects. You don't even need to be 'horsey'; total beginners often do better than experienced riders, because you communicate with a horse in harness in a different way from one that you're sitting on – largely by voice commands. You can see the horse's ears flicker back at you sometimes, when it's expecting instructions.

Buying your own rig is an expensive business, and horses have to be specially trained – you can't just attach your daughter's riding pony to a cart and say 'giddee up'. But it can be well worth the investment for a skill that can be both a pleasant Sunday afternoon jaunt and a highly competitive sport. There's a huge range of competitive classes, from fast little scurries to teams of six pulling a western stage

coach. Carriage driving also has its own version of three-day eventing, and camping at a weekend event will bring back the camaraderie of Pony Club.

WHERE DO I START?

You can find activity centres offering lessons or experiences in carriage-driving via equestrian magazines or online.

CAMPFIRE GOSSIP

The Duke of Edinburgh is the public face of carriage driving, but don't let that frighten you – it's far from being an elitist sport, and is beloved by people from all walks of life, including the travellers' community. A sign on a busy dual-carriageway in Sussex states: 'No Racing by Horsedrawn Vehicles' in response to competitions held along it.

 CONTACTS

- British Driving Society:
  ☎ 01473-892001, 🖳 www.britishdrivingsociety.co.uk

- British Horse Driving Trials Association:
  ☎ 0845-643 2116, 🖳 www.horsedrivingtrials.co.uk

- Driving with Disabilities:
  🖳 www.cdsg-dd.co.uk

ON HORSEBACK

CONTACTS

- Organisers: Wiltshire,
  ☎ 01672-851119, 🖥 www.
  whitehorsegypsycaravans.
  co.uk

GYPSY CARAVAN

For a really slow holiday, but one that won't be boring, you can hire an old-fashioned gypsy caravan from around £100 per day, and a horse to pull it. It's a popular holiday option in Ireland, and one you can also do in Britain. You spend the first evening at or close to the home farm, learning how to catch, feed, groom, tack up and get your horse to move in the right direction. The next day, once you've shown that you're capable, you'll be let loose, normally to follow a route set by the holiday company, with accommodation for the horse pre-booked while you stay in the caravan. You'll probably have to help pull the cart up any steep hills, and some people also take a spare horse with them so that they can ride alongside. You're also learning age old skills, making a new friend and discovering a new landscape. Children will learn that not all excitement has to be powered by batteries or electricity!

EVENTING

- British Eventing Ltd:
  ☎ 0845-262 3344, 🖥 www.britisheventing.com
- Local Riding: 🖥 www.localriding.com/ equestrian-eventing.html
- Riding Diary: 🖥 www.ridingdiary.co.uk

AT A GLANCE

Accessibility Index: ❶❷③④⑤

Fitness level: ❶❷❸❹⑤

Degree of Difficulty: ❶❷❸❹❺

White-knuckle rating: ❶❷❸❹⑤

Equipment: high cost

Season: spring-autumn

Family friendly: ✓

Weight restriction: ✓

There are an estimated one million horses and ponies in Britain today, more than in medieval times apparently, and it can be a problem to get them properly exercised with our roads so busy with traffic. One way to give you and your horse a good workout is with the equine equivalent of a triathlon: eventing, where you compete in the three main riding disciplines – dressage, cross country and showjumping – over one to three days.

Eventing is based on the skills that a cavalry officer needed to master; control of the horse, courage and speed across country, and jumping obstacles such as banks, farm carts and gates. The sport in the UK is well regulated and organised (like most equestrian activities), with youth and novice entry levels, right up to Olympic level. To compete at the lowest level (BE80), you'll

ON HORSEBACK

need to be able to canter over grassland, jump 31.5in (80cm) fences and open ditches, and take your pony through a water splash. You can start in eventing at age 11, while your horse or pony must be five years old (four for novice events). There are some 200 competitive events held annually throughout the country, or you can do the three disciplines individually and tackle a combined event later when you're ready.

WHO CAN DO IT?

Eventing isn't something you want to try after a couple of weekends at the local riding school, as it involves a high degree of trust between horse and rider, and a solid grounding in all aspects of horsemanship – otherwise you can expect some crashing falls. The best route into eventing is via sponsored rides, followed by One Day Events, where you can learn the ropes over smaller fences.

DRESSAGE

People tend to either love or hate dressage. The advantage is that wildly differing breeds and sizes of horse and pony can compete on more or less equal terms. While it may not be the most exciting spectator sport, riders learning dressage gain a much better understanding of their horse and vice versa, which benefits them in all the riding they do, especially while hacking on the roads.

A dressage arena has four letters at fixed positions where the different movements must start and end, with the judges awarding marks of between one and ten for accuracy and obedience. At its most basic, you may just have to show that you can walk and trot; but at all levels, turnout must be impeccable, both for horse and rider. Competitors perform individually, riding a sequence of movements with bewildering names such as flying changes, half passes, pirouettes, piaffes, and extended and collected gaits. In its highest form, as demonstrated by the Spanish Riding Schools in Jerez and Vienna, it's truly horse ballet.

CONTACTS

- British Dressage: ☎ 024-7669 8830, 🖥 www.britishdressage.co.uk

- Classical Dressage: 🖥 www.classicaldressage.co.uk

- Local Riding: 🖥 www.localriding.com/equestrian-eventing-dressage.html

CROSS COUNTRY

 CONTACTS

- Local Riding: www.localriding.com/equestrian-eventing-cross-country.html

- Organisers: www.jumpcross.com, www.rideborders.com, www.wildwoodsriding.co.uk

This is the exciting and dangerous part of eventing – the one that the crowds come out for. The course is over three to four miles of open countryside and woodland, with between 12 and 40 jumps; the more jumps, the higher the level of the competition. They're mainly natural-looking obstacles such as fallen trees, hedges or agricultural fencing, but supplemented by banks, drops, streams, ponds and combinations of several of these. The emphasis is on courage and speed, so between jumps the riders canter or gallop.

There were grave safety concerns after 18 eventing riders died between 2006 and 2008. The solid jumps and the speed they're taken at meant horses hitting them somersaulted over on top of their riders. However, collapsible jumps and new technology in protective clothing (such as air bag vests) is improving safety, and for both horse and rider this is as exciting as riding gets.

ON HORSEBACK

CONTACTS

- British Show Jumping:
  ☎ 024-7669 8800, 🖳 www.
  britishshowjumping.co.uk

- Local Riding: 🖳 www.
  localriding.com/equestrian-
  eventing-showjumping.html

SHOWJUMPING

You don't see so much showjumping on the TV any more, outside of the Olympics, but at grass roots level it's still the most popular competitive activity for amateur riders. It's also one of the most frightening; but don't worry, you can start with very small jumps of just a few inches and go higher as your confidence grows. Competitor and horse enter the ring and jump a course of around 15 to 20 jumps in sequence, and usually within a certain time. Penalty points or 'faults' are awarded for refusals or for knocking parts of a fence down, and the horse with the fewest faults wins, or there may be a jump-off against the clock.

Show jumping fences are brightly coloured, highly creative and, unlike cross country obstacles, are composed of different elements that can be knocked down, such as railings, fence panels and 'bricks'. There may be combinations of two or three jumps, which can have a long spread as well as height. An 'open water' fence is also quite common, and in high level competitions you may also see the very scary 'Irish bank', which feels like leaping off a cliff.

5

ON

WHEELS

- ❖ **Mountain Biking**
- ❖ **Trail-Centre/ Downhill Biking**
- ❖ **Cycle Touring**
- ❖ **Night Riding**
- ❖ **Quad Biking**
- ❖ **4X4 Driving**
- ❖ **Go Karting**
- ❖ **Land Yachting**
- ❖ **Parakart/Kite Buggy**
- ❖ **Skateboarding**
- ❖ **Mountain Boarding/ Dirt Surfing**
- ❖ **Inline Skating**
- ❖ **Roller Skiing**
- ❖ **Dirt Buggy**
- ❖ **Dirt Biking**
- ❖ **Green Laning**

Ramp up the thrill-factor and see the countryside as a passing blur by letting some wheels speed you along. Whether on two wheels or four (or three when land yachting), motorised or propelled by wind or gravity, Britain's most beautiful places are criss-crossed with amazing trails suitable for every kind of wheeled vehicle.

MOUNTAIN BIKING

AT A GLANCE

Accessibility Index: ❶❷❸❹❺

Fitness level: ❶❷③④⑤

Degree of Difficulty: ❶❷③④⑤

White-knuckle rating: ❶❷❸④⑤

Equipment: hire/medium cost

Season: year round

Family friendly: ✓

It's the most accessible adventure activity of them all. Your bike will get you to the 'mountains', over the mountains and to a refreshing hostelry, all without the need for public transport, petrol, change for parking or a bag of oats. Mountain bikes may have only hit the shops some 25 years ago, but they've quickly become the most popular mode of transport for Britain's long distance trails. Brake and suspension technology has taken some of the shake, rattle and roll out of the experience, while full body protection gear can give you the added confidence to try tricks, jumps and top-speed downhills without breaking your neck (usually). Mountain bikes enable you to feel the contours of the land intimately, while getting from A to B ten times quicker than walking – and it's great for all-round fitness.

WHAT EXACTLY WILL I BE DOING?

The same bike can take you for a gentle cruise along a country lane or a full-on tear-up through rough single-track downhills. For longer trips, you can use the bike as a packhorse to carry your picnic and water, or maybe your wild camping (see page 59) equipment. Mountain biking is a part of most adventure races (see page 114), and it's a sport you can do any time, any season and in any weather, even at night (see **Night Riding** on page 121).

You can use bikes on bridleways, byways, restricted byways and green lanes – all clearly marked on Ordnance Survey maps. Allow for extra time to read maps, get lost, stop for food, take pics and fix punctures; 25mi (40km) a day is a conservative target for off-road cycling. There are dozens of bike-friendly, long-distance trails in Britain, including the 101-mile (162km) South Downs Way, the 212-mile (343km) Southern Upland Way in Scotland and the new 171-mile (277km) Way of the Roses (Morecambe to Bridlington).

Your riding experience will be enhanced if you get some basic bike maintenance under your belt, such as varying your tyres according to the terrain, changing brake pads or tightening spokes – you'll be surprised how quickly your performance improves.

WHAT SHOULD I BE WORRIED ABOUT?

A small downside to mountain biking is that the uphills bring you out in a hot sweat and the downhills a cold sweat. Rapid descents are a test of nerve and skill; requiring animal-like awareness and lightening reflexes to avoid slippery tree roots, spoke-crushing rocks, loose stones that take out the front wheel and soft mud that stops the bike dead (but not you).

HAPPY MEMORIES?

You'll probably fall in love with your bike. A decent one costs from £500, but is a thing of timeless beauty: simple to understand, easy to fix, with no computers, batteries, wires or fuel; just clean, sparkling metal. You can even buy special bike bivouacs that use the handlebars as a tent pole and fit over you and your machine.

WHERE DO I START?

You can hire a bike at many outdoor adventure centres from around £10 per day, or buy a cheap one from £200. Mountain bike tours and group skills' courses cost from around £20 per hour.

WHERE CAN IT LEAD?

"It's like riding a bike." Really? Don't believe that there's nothing to add to your riding skills. Courses at trail centres (see **Contacts**) will introduce you to dynamic weight shift, core body position,

ON WHEELS

POPULAR LOCATIONS

Southeast: South Downs Way; ☎ 01243-558716, 🖥 www.nationaltrails.co.uk/southdowns.

Southwest: Weston to Frome, Mendip Way; ☎ 01761-462338, 🖥 www.mendiphillsaonb.org.uk.

Central: The Ridgeway from Wiltshire to Buckinghamshire; ☎ 01865-810224, 🖥 www.nationaltrails.co.uk/ridgeway.

North: Leeds to Chesterfield; ☎ 01226-772574, 🖥 www.transpenninetrail.org.uk.

Wales: Trans-Cambrian Way; 🖥 www.imba.org.uk.

Scotland: Borders; ☎ 01644-430015, 🖥 www.southern uplandway.com.

CONTACTS

- Bike magic:
  🖥 www.bikemagic.com

- Bike Radar:
  🖥 www.bikeradar.com

- British Cycling:
  🖥 www.britishcycling.org.uk

- Forestry Commission:
  🖥 www.forestry.gov.uk/mtbwales, www.forestry.gov.uk/mtbscotland

- International Mountain Biking Association UK:
  🖥 www.imba.org.uk

- MTB Britain:
  🖥 www.mtbbritain.co.uk

- National Cycle Network:
  🖥 www.sustrans.org.uk

- National Parks:
  🖥 www.nationalparks.gov.uk

- Rough Stuff Fellowship:
  🖥 www.rsf.org.uk

cornering skills and controlled descents without overdoing the brakes, while also looking pretty cool.

WHAT SHOULD I TAKE?

A helmet, padded shorts and repair kit are a minimum. You should also consider survival gear if you're cycling in remote areas.

CAMPFIRE GOSSIP

Forget what you've heard, Californians didn't invent mountain biking. A bunch of Brits formed the Rough Stuff Fellowship in 1955, and you can still ride with them. And a guy called Geoff Apps developed the tough, rugged, lightweight mountain bike that we see today, in the mud of the Chilterns.

TRAIL-CENTRE & DOWNHILL BIKING

📝 CONTACTS

- Forestry Commission: 🖥 www.forestry.gov.uk, www.forestry.gov.uk/mtbwales, www.forestry.gov.uk/mtbscotland

- FlyUp: 🖥 www.flyupdownhill.co.uk

- The Hub: 🖥 http://thehubintheforest.co.uk

- MTB Britain: 🖥 www.mtbbritain.co.uk

- Skills Courses: 🖥 www.mountainbikeskillscourses.co.uk

- Scottish Cross Country Association: 🖥 www.sxc.org.uk

 **AT A GLANCE**

Accessibility Index:	❶❷❸❹⑤
Fitness level:	❶❷❸④⑤
Degree of Difficulty:	❶❷❸④⑤
White-knuckle rating:	❶❷❸④⑤

Equipment: hire or medium cost

Season: year round

Family friendly: ✓

Extreme mountain biking is such a hit (and a danger to hikers) that private companies, the Forestry Commission and landowners are creating specialist centres with challenging downhill courses, and (at some centres) a lift back uphill. They often include jumps, obstacles (some with elevated sections on ramps, known as 'north shore' riding), and mud and rock-hopping sections, as well as the long, sweeping downhills – where you're encouraged to go as fast as you like. Best of all, some of the more extreme downhill routes are on ski slopes (in Scotland) during the summer months, with the lifts operating: all the adrenalin but without the lung-bursting uphills. There may even be refreshment facilities, bike repair shops and medical help (!) provided. There will certainly be other extreme cyclists to compare bikes and bruises with.

Trails are classified like ski routes from green (easy) to black (severe), plus orange routes which include 'big-air' jumps and very serious slopes, so there should be something for every mountain biker, from young families to extreme sports' fanatics. If the trails expose any shortcomings in your technique, many cycling centres offer skills courses to help you get even more thrills with fewer spills.

ON WHEELS

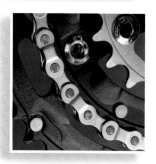

CYCLE TOURING

 **AT A GLANCE**

Accessibility Index: ❶❷❸❹❺

Fitness level: ❶❷❸④⑤

Degree of Difficulty: ❶❷③④⑤

White-knuckle rating: ❶❷③④⑤

Equipment: hire or high cost

Season: year round

Family friendly: ✓

On a modern, lightweight, touring bicycle you can eat up the miles while enjoying the countryside at a leisurely pace, which allows far more appreciation of its beauty than from the inside of a car. Cycle touring generally means taking the tarmac option and using roads instead of mountain tracks, although there are a few off-road routes that suit touring bikes, such as the Great Glen Way and West Highland Way. No household should be without a decent bike, but for a weekend away without the bother of taking your bike on the train, you can hire a road bike in most cycling areas.

In recent years, tourist authorities have been falling over themselves to develop long-distance cycling routes, such as the new 171-mile (277km) Way of the Roses, a coast-to-coast route from Morecambe to Bridlington. You can get ideas for touring routes in all areas from Sustrans (see **Contacts**), and buy detailed maps from their online shop.

WHAT EXACTLY WILL I BE DOING?

You can go it alone or take a supported trip. The advantage of the former is that it's cheaper; you can travel at your own pace, choose your route and stop where you like. However, you'll have to carry all your gear, which can be a major disadvantage. Supported holidays are where a tour company chooses and plans a route, and may even rent you a suitable bike. They'll even organise a picnic on the way, and are the local experts in planning a good, traffic-free route that will suit your fitness and wishes. Best of all, your bag will be waiting for you when you reach your overnight stop, along with a nice hot bath to ease your aching muscles.

Cycling is a great way to get outdoors, have some serious exercise and travel from A to B efficiently and

POPULAR ROUTES

Southeast: London to Brighton, via Ditchling Beacon.

Southwest: West Country Way;
🖥 www.westcountryway.co.uk.

Central: Mercian Way; 🖥 www.ncr45mercianway.co.uk.

North: The Way of the Roses, Morecambe to Bridlington;
☎ 01756-753868, 🖥 www.wayoftheroses.co.uk.

Wales: 🖥 www.routes2ride.org.uk/wales.

Scotland: Lochranza to Blackwaterfoot, Isle of Arran;
🖥 www.routes2ride.org.uk/scotland.

cheaply. Arriving at your destination by bike is a joy, as you feel your tyres skimming across the road; a quick step on the pedal to speed past the queuing traffic, and freewheel to a stop outside your hotel.

HAPPY MEMORIES?

The pleasure of a cycling holiday is boosted by the release of endorphins from exercise, the sense of achievement from completing a long route, and the beautiful sights you see on the way. And there's no nicer way of arriving at your holiday destination than by bike – you'll already feel at home.

WHAT SHOULD I BE WORRIED ABOUT?

Heavy traffic can be a worry, especially when travelling with young people, and there's also the danger of pollution in towns and

ON WHEELS

CONTACTS

- British Cycling: 🖥 www.britishcycling.org.uk/clubs
- Cyclists Touring Club (CTC): 🖥 www.ctc.org.uk
- Cycle Tourer: 🖥 www.cycletourer.co.uk
- National Cycling Network: 🖥 www.cycle-routes.org
- Routes to Ride, Scotland: 🖥 www.routes2ride.org.uk
- Sustrans: 🖥 www.sustrans.org.uk
- Organisers: 🖥 www.bikeadventures.co.uk, www.countrylanes.co.uk, www.cycle-n-sleep.co.uk

cities (wear a mask). However, cycling around cities can be an enervating experience, with every sense working at full capacity.

WHERE CAN IT LEAD?

The Big One is Lands End to John O'Groat's – 10 to 14 days on the road, covering around 875mi (1,407km). However, it should be noted that John O'Groats recently 'won' an award as Scotland's most dismal town.

WHAT WILL IT COST?

Unless you're planning on going superfast, a perfectly good touring bike needn't cost more than £500.

CAMPFIRE GOSSIP

The Cyclists Touring Club (se **Contacts** below) is the oldest tourist organisation in the UK, founded in 1878. In those days, members had to wear a green uniform with knickerbockers and a pith helmet, and had a bugler in front.

NIGHT RIDING

Trying daytime activities at night makes for a weirdly different experience: scuba diving at night is like space walking, wildlife spotting at night feels like SAS manoeuvres, and night cycle riding is like a race against the darkness. You won't know this unless you go out in the woods at night, but night riding has caught on in a big way in the UK. It's the new black, literally, with both organised rides and ad hoc adventures. It's simple to do, requires no training or supervision, and what's more it's free! You should, however, always do it in groups of two or more, as the risks of injury are far greater, and you won't be able to explain to a 999 operator where you are if you're unconscious.

WHAT EXACTLY WILL I BE DOING?

It's best to start off with routes you already know, especially wide flat forest paths. They'll look a lot different at night, and even the simplest will be a totally new challenge. Navigating by the beam of an ultra-bright light feels like you're travelling fast down a narrow tunnel, with little time to react to sudden bumps and turns that you would have processed from a distance in the daytime. The speed of the bike won't be impaired by the dark, but your perception of it will be heightened, so it's like riding a supercharged bicycle. With no horizon to guide you, your balance will be affected, while obstacles such a slippery tree roots, potholes and bogs may be disguised by the shadows cast by your lights, although the benefit of riding in pairs is that the leader can shout warnings. As your eyes become used to the dark and your instincts improve, you can push faster and harder, and tackle tougher routes for a bigger adrenalin buzz and an even more extreme experience.

Because of the need to night ride with other cyclists, organised clubs and internet forums are good ways to find local groups.

ON WHEELS

POPULAR LOCATIONS

Southeast: Stanmer Park, Brighton, Sussex;
☎ 01273-290000, 🖥 www.brighton-hove.gov.uk.

Southwest: Quantock Hills, Somerset;
🖥 www.quantockonline.co.uk.

Central: Thetford Forest, Norfolk; ☎ 01842-816010,
🖥 www.forestry.gov.uk/thetfordforestpark.

North: Dalby Forest, Yorkshire; ☎ 01751-472771,
🖥 www.forestry.gov.uk/dalbyforest.

Wales: Afan Forest, South Wales; ☎ 01639-850564,
🖥 www.afanforestpark.co.uk.

Scotland: Glentress Forest, Peebles, organised events;
☎ 01721-721736, 🖥 www.thehubintheforest.co.uk.

WHAT WILL I REMEMBER?

Cycling at night is a rush in every sense; an intense and exhilarating experience quite unlike most cycling. Without the distractions of a view, the focus comes back onto you and your ability to get the most out of your bike. The uphills may seem easier; the downhills infinitely steeper. Within your little arc of light, you'll be buzzed by low-flying owls and bats, and struggle to avoid hitting slow-moving rabbits and toads. Sleep after a night ride may be hard to come by.

WHAT SHOULD I BE WORRIED ABOUT?

Whose are those eyes being picked out by your helmet-light in the dark? Fox? Badger? Gamekeeper? Or worse…? No matter how you rationalise it, being out in the woods at night is scary. It's easy to get lost, and when you stop to check a map the dark will creep up on you. At least you won't have to worry about man-eating nocturnal wildlife.

WHERE DO I START?

You could start by riding around your hometown at night – with empty roads and few pedestrians, it's a liberating experience in itself and you can go on your own. When you're ready to go off-road you'll need a companion; there are companies which organise group night rides, for a fee, which is a good way to make contacts among like-minded cyclists.

WHAT SHOULD I TAKE?

As well as the usual safety gear of helmet and fluorescent clothing, you'll need a powerful handle-bar-mounted light and a head torch (they run for around three hours on high beam and 36 hours when flashing).

WHAT WILL IT COST?

Assuming you have a mountain bike, lights cost from £50 to as much as £600.

CAMPFIRE GOSSIP

For a nocturnal challenge, why not try the South Downs Way? You leave the twinkling promenade of Eastbourne at sunset and attempt to cycle the 80-mile (129km) off-road route to Petersfield in Hampshire before the rising sun breaches the horizon.

 **CONTACTS**

- Forestry Commission:
  🖳 www.forestry.gov.uk

- International Mountain Biking Association:
  🖳 www.imba.org.uk

- MTB Britain: 🖳 www.mtbbritain.co.uk

- National Parks: 🖳 www.nationalparks.gov.uk

ON WHEELS

QUAD BIKING

 AT A GLANCE

Accessibility Index: ❶❷❸④⑤

Fitness level: ❶②③④⑤

Degree of Difficulty: ❶❷③④⑤

White-knuckle rating: ❶❷❸④⑤

Equipment: hire or high cost

Season: year round

Disability friendly: ✓

Family friendly: ✓

They're like an iron pony. Small, stout, tough, sometimes difficult to get started, sure-footed in the toughest conditions yet liable to throw you off if mishandled. Quad bikes, also known as All Terrain Vehicles (ATVs), are four-wheeled (usually) vehicles of between 49 and 1,000cc, originally developed for farmwork. They have a seat in the middle and handlebars like a motorcycle, with low-pressure off-road tyres to travel cross country through deep mud, water and rough terrain.

WHAT EXACTLY WILL I BE DOING?

Most people's first experience of quad biking is at an outdoors centre as part of a stag/hen weekend or team-building experience, where you ride the machines around a course, through obstacles and over terrain of varying degrees, from soft springy turf to deep mud to terrifying inclines. There are few opportunities for off-road riding, except on private land; because quad bikes can have a highly damaging effect on tracks and trails, they're banned on bridleways. However, they're legal on 'green lanes' (see page 147). For competitive racing, quad biking comes in many classes: grass track, enduros, moto cross, desert and beach racing, to name but a few.

Quad biking is a lot of fun, but it also tests your driving ability. You learn to stand up in the saddle much like on a horse, and flex the knees to take the shock as you bounce

POPULAR LOCATIONS

Southeast: Essex Quad Academy; ☎ 07984-777110, 🖳 www.essexquadacedemy.com.

Southwest: Off Road Experience; ☎ 01749-679945, 🖳 www.ore-events.co.uk.

Central: Oxfordshire; National Off Road Racing Association (NORA); 🖳 www.nora-mx.org.uk.

North: Cumbria: ☎ 01768-483561, 🖳 www.rookinhouse.co.uk.

Wales: Denbighshire: Dragon Quad Racing; 🖳 www.dqracing.co.uk.

Scotland: Dunkeld, Perthshire; 🖳 www.scottishquads.co.uk.

over ruts. You'll need to judge speeds to ensure you get over dunes and through bogs – being left floundering and needing a push from a passer-by isn't cool – but without going so fast as to become airborne. Indeed, the skills of quad biking have a lot in common with cross country horse-riding.

HAPPY MEMORIES?

A day on a quad bike is one of those 'out there' experiences that can give you a whole new outlook on life: the machinery, the noise, the power beneath you controlled by the flick of your wrist, the speed as you bomb through the undergrowth or up a hill that would take you all day to climb… how can this be so much fun and why aren't you doing it every weekend?

WHAT SHOULD I BE WORRIED ABOUT?

Quad bikes may look stable, but it's all too easy to find you've tipped over and have the all-terrain in your face. A 440lb (200kg) quad bike sitting on top of you is no way to spend a weekend.

ON WHEELS

CONTACTS

- Quadnation: 💻 www. quadnation.co.uk
- Quad Racing Association: 💻 www.quadriding.com
- Quad Racing Association UK: 💻 www.qrauk.com

Sadly, a few people die on quad bikes in the UK each year and many more are seriously injured, so judgement and risk-assessment are essential.

WHERE CAN IT LEAD?

The Weston Beach Race is one of the most exciting races in the world of quad biking, taking three hours over a man-made course of sand dunes and bog in the Somerset town of Weston-super-Mare.

WHO CAN DO IT?

Over 16s can ride a (road-legal) quad bike on the road when insured, and children aged under 16 may ride a quad bike on private land. Many activity centres will take kids as young as six.

WHAT WILL IT COST?

New 49cc quad bikes start at around £1,000, while a 1,000cc bike can set you back over £10,000.

4X4 DRIVING

 **AT A GLANCE**

Accessibility Index: ❶❷❸❹⑤

Fitness level: ❶②③④⑤

Degree of Difficulty: ❶❷③④⑤

White-knuckle rating: ❶❷❸④⑤

Equipment: hire

Season: year round

Disability friendly: ✓

This is where your 'Chelsea tractor' (4WD vehicle) starts to earn all that extra tax you pay on it. Or alternatively, those stuck driving a small family car every day can get behind the wheel of a behemoth for a change. You can either take your own car along to see what all those gear settings are really for or use one from an off-road centre. You'll get to drive through rivers, over ravines and up terrifying slopes. You definitely won't want to be driving your own car if you're trying 'mudbugging', where you attempt to drive through a large patch of wet clay mud without getting stuck, or 'rock hopping', both of which require specialist tyres.

Courses cover the basic safety issues and the many ways you can damage your car, then how to tackle steep ascents, descents, ruts, ditches and long grass; assessing the risks and driving through deep water; use of power and momentum; and coping with brake, engine and other mechanical failures. There'll be advice on how to avoid getting water in the engine, the use of specialist tyres and maybe also the use of a skid pan.

The governing body for off-road driving is the British Off Road Driving Association (BORDA), and most centres base their training on half-day BORDA Basic, full-day BORDA Standard or two-day BORDA Higher Level certificates.

WHERE DO I START?

You can learn off-road skills as an 'experience' at an activity centre or at a specialist off road centre, all of which are easy to find online (see **Contacts**). Some country fairs also provide the opportunity to have a go. If you fancy a go without the training, the network of green lanes (see page 147) are legally roads but are unpaved.

ON WHEELS

CONTACTS

- British Off Road Driving Association (BORDA): www.borda.org.uk

- Countryside Recreational Access Group (CRAG): www.crag-uk.org

- Land Rover Experience: www.landrover.co.uk/experience

- UK Off Road: www.ukoffroad.com

CAMPFIRE GOSSIP

When driving through water, the bow wave is your friend – keeping water out of the engine. The important thing is to take it steady, not so slow that the wave falls back into the engine and not so fast that you run into it. If you have second thoughts and reverse, the water will flood back into the exhaust. Well, no-one said this would be easy…

GO KARTING

AT A GLANCE

Accessibility Index: ❶❷❸❹❺

Fitness level: ❶②③④⑤

Degree of Difficulty: ❶❷③④⑤

White-knuckle rating: ❶❷❸④⑤

Equipment: hire or high cost

Season: year round

Disability programme: ✓

Family friendly: ✓

Weight restriction: ✓

Didn't go karts used to be things you made out of orange boxes and pram wheels and launched down a hill (before spending the rest of a summer's afternoon in the casualty department)? Not any more. These days they can reach speeds of up to 160mph (260kph). Okay, they're rare, and called Superkarts – the ones you'll come across at a kids' activity centre are usually limited to 15mph (24kph). But they still offer children their first taste of motorised driving, while higher-powered karts give adults a chance to recreate race track conditions – though with more chance of overtaking than in most Grand Prix.

There are two kinds of karts – amusement-park-type karts with a four-stroke or electric engine, and racing karts with a two-stroke engine. Both types have an extremely low risk factor (though there have been recent fatalities due to scarves getting caught in the wheels), and electric karts can be stopped remotely by a track attendant in the event of an accident.

At the higher levels, karts are fast, powerful and feel like a racing car, with dramatic braking and acceleration, and greater steering-wheel forces than a Formula One car, according to Michael Schumacher. Yet you can ride them with very little hassle or training – isn't driving a racing car a better option for Sunday afternoon than watching it from the sofa? You'll have to wear a helmet, driving suit, gloves and boots, and most circuits are outside, so if it rains you'll get wet. But that generally adds to the excitement – just like bombing down your road in a converted orange box.

ON WHEELS

CONTACTS

- UK Go Karting: 💻 www.uk-go-karting.com

- UK Karting: 💻 www.karting.co.uk

- Motor Sports Association (MSA): 💻 www.msauk.org

- National Association of Schools & Youth Group Karting (NatSKA): 💻 www.natska.co.uk

- National Karting Association: ☎ 01206-322726, 💻 www.nationalkarting.co.uk

- Scottish Karting: 💻 www.scottishkarting.co.uk

- Organisers: ☎ 01935 83713, 💻 www.claypigeonraceway.com

WHERE DO I START?

Kids can start out with 'bambino karting' from six years of age. For competitive go karting, you must be aged at least eight and have a competition licence. For details of both, contact the MSA (see **Contacts**) and obtain a 'Go Karting' pack for full details.

CAMPFIRE GOSSIP

Lewis Hamilton isn't the only world champion motor racing driver to have started on go karts – Nigel Mansell, Prost, Senna and Michael Schumacher all did. It's where F1 champions are born. But it's also where champions recover their skills – Schumacher and Felipe Massa (after his injury) both went karting on their way back to Formula One.

LAND YACHTING

 **AT A GLANCE**

Accessibility Index: ❶❷❸❹⑤

Fitness level: ❶❷③④⑤

Degree of Difficulty: ❶❷❸④⑤

White-knuckle rating: ❶❷❸④⑤

Equipment: hire/medium to high cost

Season: year round

Disability programme: ✓

Family friendly: ✓

Weight restriction: ✓

One of the first adventure sports invented, land yachting's (also called land sailing) roots are among the most serious attempts to get from A to B before the invention of the internal combustion engine. It's now a high-adrenalin thrill ride, but you'll need to be able to read a tide-table. Wind power on land is, ironically, more efficient than at sea due to wheels having less drag than water, and land yachts reach speeds even motorboats can only dream of. They're used for recreation from any age, and can be used on grass and tarmac as well as the beach. There's also a lively racing scene, both in Britain and on the Continent.

WHAT EXACTLY WILL I BE DOING?

Land yachting involves sitting in a low-slung, three-wheeled vehicle like a go kart, except it has a windsurf-like sail attached. You use the traditional principles of sailing, but to speed along the beach instead of the water. Land yachts don't have brakes, so the first lesson is how to stop. Next is turning, and the difference between the relatively gentle 'luff' turn and the faster, flashier 'gype' turn. Now you're ready to build up speed and manoeuvrability and go racing.

It's usually a single-person sport, but two-seater yachts are sometimes used for training and for 'experience days', and yachts are raced in a range of classes, with sails varying in size from 6 to 26ft (2 to 8m) high. The largest generally raced in the UK are class 3, which reach a top speed of 70mph (113kph). Beginners start with class 5, with a 59ft² (5.5m²) sail, travelling at

ON WHEELS

speeds of up to 50mph (80kph). For a simple and fun experience, and for children, there are miniyachts and class 7s, which are basically skateboards with a sail.

HAPPY MEMORIES?

The laws of physics allow land yachts to travel at three times the average wind-speed, so even a steady 20mph (32kph) breeze will see you moving at 60mph (96kph), just an inch or two above the ground. Harnessing the power of the wind feels better than driving a Ferrari (so they say).

WHAT SHOULD I BE WORRIED ABOUT?

Being a natural surface, beaches may have humps, bumps, dips, debris and large pools of standing water. Landyachters fly into and over these at speeds of up to 70mph (113kph), while trying to prevent their craft tipping over. You also need to avoid people, dogs, seagulls and other landyachts.

WHERE CAN IT LEAD?

Once you understand the principles of wind power you can move on to bigger and faster yachts with larger sails, over a wider range of surfaces including grass. You can also try racing, which is particularly popular on the Continent.

POPULAR LOCATIONS

Southeast: Greatstone Beach, Kent. Contact: Mark Serejko; ☎ 07727-826373, 🖳 www.landyachting.co.uk.

Southwest: Weston super Mare, Somerset; ☎ 07847-015155, 🖳 www.windandwheels.org.uk.

Central: Mablethorpe Beach, Lincolnshire; 🖳 www.mablethorpe.info/entertainment/clubs-landyacht.htm.

North: Hoylake, Wirral Sand Yacht Club; ☎ 07988-413662, 🖳 www.wsyc.org.uk.

Wales: Newborough, Anglesey.

Scotland: St Andrews Sands, Fife; ☎ 07784-121125, 🖳 www.blownawaylandyachts.co.uk.

WHAT SHOULD I TAKE?

Depending on the season, some people use wetsuits, but standard safety equipment is helmet, goggles and gloves.

WHAT WILL IT COST?

From £60 for a taster session that should get you moving and understanding the principles. Land yachts cost from £1,500 to £40,000.

CAMPFIRE GOSSIP

The land speed record for a wind-powered vehicle was set by a young British engineer Richard Jenkins, in 2009. His land yacht *Greenbird* reached a top speed of 126mph (203kph), in winds of 30-50mph (48-80kph).

 **CONTACTS**

- British Federation of Sand & Land Yacht Clubs: www.bfslyc.org.uk

- International Land & Sandyachting Federation: www.fisly.org

- Manufacturers: Seagull, www.landyachting.com; Mini Land Yachts www.minilandyachts.co.uk

- Tides: www.bbc.co.uk/weather/coast/tides, www.pol.ac.uk/ntslf/tidalp.html

- Organisers: www.landyachting.co.uk

ON WHEELS

PARAKART/KITE BUGGY

AT A GLANCE

Accessibility Index: ❶❷❸❹⑤

Fitness level: ❶❷③④⑤

Degree of Difficulty: ❶❷❸④⑤

White-knuckle rating: ❶❷❸④⑤

Equipment: hire or medium cost

Season: year round

Disability friendly: ✓

Family friendly: ✓

Advances in kite technology have taken these activities from being a fun pastime on a windy hillside to a high-powered propulsion method taking 'pilots' at speeds of over 75mph (120kph) over fields, beaches, ice or tarmac. Parakarts, also known as kite buggys, have many similarities to land yachts (see above) – indeed you may also see it advertised as Class 8 landyachting – but instead of a fixed sail you're holding onto a kite. Like many wind-powered sports, it's a dynamic experience where you never stop learning, yet you can do it at any fitness level or even from a wheelchair.

WHAT EXACTLY WILL I BE DOING?

You sit on a three-wheel vehicle much like a flattened baby buggy, with big fat wheels, widely spread for stability. You usually hold two handles or a single bar, with four lines leading from them to the power kite, sometimes known as a traction kite, which leaves you with foot-pedals to steer with. You launch the kite and use its power to propel you along the surface.

The same power that can carry you along at high speeds can also drag you into danger, therefore proper training is essential, usually through the club structure of landyachting (see Contacts). The first thing you'll need to learn is how to control your kite and your speed. You'll quickly have to master gybing and turning, know the rules of the road to avoid colliding or tangling strings with other karts, and learn how to obtain maximum speed in the

available wind. As your expertise improves, you can try freestyle, which can include jumps, spins and wheelies.

Although it can be a highly technical activity, beginners shouldn't be put off, because it starts with the fairly straightforward proposition of flying a kite, which you can learn in minutes. The size of the kite (and wind speed) determines your power, so you can start slowly and build up your speed along with your confidence.

HAPPY MEMORIES?

Travelling at high speed just inches from the ground is a thrilling and eco-friendly experience. It's also a great workout, as you enjoy the feel of controlling a bucking and powerful kite with incredible potential power.

WHAT SHOULD I BE WORRIED ABOUT?

You may be worried that you could be taken up and away by a strong gust. Fortunately, there are devices called 'kite killers' which attach to your wrists, and if it all gets too powerful you just let go of the handles and the kite killer collapses the kite. Even so, it's an extreme sport where accidents and collisions are fairly commonplace.

WHERE CAN IT LEAD?

The technology for all power kite sports is basically the same, with the kite attached to the person instead of the board or buggy, therefore once you're proficient at one power kite sport you can use the same techniques for riding mountainboards, snowboards or kitesurfing (see page 172), for jumping and floating up to dizzying heights.

ON WHEELS

POPULAR LOCATIONS

Southeast: Greatstone Beach, Kent.

Southwest: Brean, Somerset.

Central: Clacton, Essex.

North: Hoylake, Wirral.

Wales: Westshore, Llandudno.

Scotland: The Isle of Barra, Outer Hebrides.

CONTACTS

- British Federation of Sand & Land Yachts: 🖥 www.bfslyc.org.uk
- British Power Kitesports Association: 🖥 www.bpka.co.uk
- The Kite Society of Great Britain: 🖥 www.thekitesociety.org.uk
- Kiting events: 🖥 www.kitecalendar.co.uk
- Parakart Association: 🖥 www.parakartassociation.co.uk
- Scottish Power Kite Association: 🖥 www.spka.co.uk
- Organisers: 🖥 www.paracademyextreme.co.uk, www.uggitt.co.uk

WHAT SHOULD I TAKE?

Parakarters wear full protective equipment including helmets, goggles, knee and elbow protectors and sometimes also back supports. However, for your first training session all you need to bring is warm clothing.

WHAT WILL IT COST?

There are dozens of kite festivals throughout Britain where you can try power parakarting for nothing (see 🖥 www.thekitesociety.org.uk). For parakarting/kite buggying, you can book a taster session via the Parakart Association (see Contacts) for around £50. Beginner's kites cost from as little as £30, but you should look to spend £100 for a good kite and £500 for the whole rig.

CAMPFIRE GOSSIP

We could be about to see a lot more of kites. The golden age of kiting was the 50 years prior to 1910, with amazing advances in their use for leisure, travel and even military purposes. Advances were choked off by the arrival of the petrol engine, but now they're coming back. There are even plans to float kites fitted with wind turbines at 30,000 feet to harvest sustainable energy from the jet stream, which has ten times the power of low-altitude winds.

SKATEBOARDING

 **AT A GLANCE**

Accessibility Index: ❶❷❸❹❺

Fitness level: ❶❷③④⑤

Degree of Difficulty: ❶❷❸④⑤

White-knuckle rating: ❶❷❸④⑤

Equipment: low cost

Season: year round

Family friendly: ✓

Skateboarding became a global phenomenon in the early '70s as an extreme sport for kids, and some of its earliest fans (now approaching middle-age) are starting to look fondly at the skate parks that their council tax has paid for and thinking, why not…? In the last few decades, skateboards have been joined in the park by (push) scooters, which are a middle ground between skateboards and BMX bikes, and most of the information below applies equally to scooters.

Skateboards are inexpensive and easy to carry around when not being ridden. They're small compared to surf and snowboards, at just 7-8in (17-30cm) wide and around 30in (76cm) long, with small polyurethane wheels to reduce the weight. They're extremely manoeuvrable, the basic move being to stand on the board and steer by shifting your weight across the width of the board. To turn sharply you put the weight on the back of the board to lift the front up and swivel round.

You can skateboard just to get around town – the wheels are only suitable for pavements and roads, although mountain boarding (see below) takes the sport into the countryside – or in specially designed skate parks which include ramps, pipes and slides for trick skating. Basic safety equipment is flat-soled boots/shoes with ankle support, knee and elbow pads and a helmet; although most skateboarders manage without any of these, they can increase your confidence when a beginner.

It's an exciting and challenging sport that's cheap, keeps you fit and you can do it in your local park or even your own street. No surprise then that this '70s fad has refused to die, and is attracting a wider audience each year,

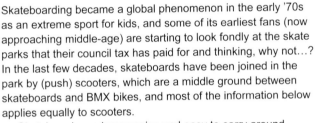

ON WHEELS

CONTACTS

- Go Skateboarding Day: ⌨ www.goskateboardingday.org
- United Kingdom Skateboarding Association (UKSA): ⌨ www. ukskate.org.uk
- UK Skateboarding: ⌨ www.skateboarduk.com

despite it remaining resolutely 'street'; there are very few clubs or courses – you just get out there and do it.

WHERE DO I START?

You can buy a good skateboard for around £50 to £60. Find your nearest bit of (quiet, traffic-free) tarmac, balance on the board and learn to push off, steer and stop. There's no shame – well, not much – in holding onto something while you get your balance. If you're worried about looking a bit old to be skateboarding, wait for Go Skateboarding Day (see **Contacts**), on June 21st 2011, when everyone is encouraged to give it a go.

Warning!

Skateboarding is an extreme sport and isn't without its dangers. You should never do it without protective clothing, including a helmet, wrist guards, elbow and knee pads and appropriate footwear. Minor injuries are *de rigueur* for skateboarders, but you can help avoid serious injury by always wearing protective gear and observing safety rules.

CAMPFIRE GOSSIP

The 'ollie' is that trick you see skateboarders doing where they leap in the air, somehow flipping the board in the process, and hopefully land on the correct side of the board with a satisfying thwack. Its official name is a 'no hands aerial', which was invented by Alan 'Ollie' 'No Hands Aerial' Gelfand in 1978.

MOUNTAIN BOARDING/DIRT SURFING

 **AT A GLANCE**

Accessibility Index: ❶❷❸❹⑤

Fitness level: ❶❷③④⑤

Degree of Difficulty: ❶❷❸④⑤

White-knuckle rating: ❶❷❸④⑤

Equipment: hire or low cost

Season: year round

Family friendly: ✓

The principles of mountain boarding (also known as dirt surfing) are the same as for most boards (e.g. snowboarding); you stand with both feet on the deck, and steer by shifting your weight forwards and backwards. The difference with mountain boarding is that (a) we invented it and (b) it's perfectly suited to our green and verdant hills.

Mountain boards look just like a snowboard, about 3ft (1m) in length and usually made of laminated wood. But they have chunky 8-10in (20-25cm) pneumatic wheels and your feet fit securely into bindings, allowing for more confident jumping and for them to be ridden over grass and rough country – hence their other name – dirt surfing. There are mountain board centres throughout the country, offering tuition and freestyle obstacles such as rails, jumps, pipes and slalom courses. The sport is yet to attract an audience far beyond school age, but it seems to be the obvious answer for all those middle-aged parents who secretly long to join their kids in the skate park.

WHAT EXACTLY WILL I BE DOING?

Learning mountain boarding is relatively easy, and most people can confidently go down a hill by the end of an introductory lesson. It's even easier if you've done snowboarding. The first thing you'll learn is stopping: some mountain boards are fitted

ON WHEELS

POPULAR LOCATIONS

Southeast: Redhill, Surrey; ☎ 0845-094 4360,
🖥 www.ridethehill.com.

Southwest: South West Mountain Board Centre, Devon;
☎ 01237-472366, 🖥 www.thebigsheep.co.uk.

Central: Herefordshire; ☎ 01886-880099,
🖥 www.outtograss.co.uk.

North: Lake District; ☎ 07740-861019,
🖥 www.surf-the-turf.co.uk.

Wales: Gower Peninsula; ☎ 07856-152540,
🖥 www.brdsports.co.uk.

Scotland: Galloway; ☎ 01557-840217,
🖥 www.lagganoutdoor.com.

with brakes, but the proper way to stop is with a cool-looking powerslide.

There are several competition disciplines, which closely mirror snowboarding: downhill is a timed event along a longish course, past natural and man-made berms, ramps, jumps and steep inclines. Freestyle includes tricks, both on slopes and rails (slopestyle), and Big Air, where the rider attains maximum height off a jump to perform aerial acrobatics. Boarder X is where four riders head down a track together, and the first to the end wins.

But that's all for later: beginners will just want to get out and get riding – what's known as freeriding – over hills, fields and natural obstacles. You can easily attain fast speeds on a mountain board, therefore helmets and kneepads are essential.

HAPPY MEMORIES?

Boarder-X is the most exciting discipline in mountain boarding. It pitches four riders down a track at the same time in a breakneck race for the bottom. Suddenly you realise just how boring the municipal skate park is…

WHAT SHOULD I BE WORRIED ABOUT?

You're easily getting up to speeds of 30mph (50kph) and getting big air, which can be a dangerous combination if you land awkwardly on grass. Hence some centres have created foam-padded pits for riders to practice their freestyle moves.

WHERE DO I START?

You don't need to learn at an activity centre (although it isn't very expensive), and can just buy a board and learn the basics from YouTube, or even better, experiment with friends. Many centres close for the winter, and most only open at weekends and school holidays, even during the season.

WHAT WILL IT COST?

You can buy a decent mountain board for around £100. Lessons at a mountain boarding centre cost from around £10 per hour for a group lesson, including hire.

CAMPFIRE GOSSIP

The British own this sport. At the 2010 World Downhill Championships, held on a Winter Olympics course in Italy, British men took all three podium positions, led by Pete Tatham.

CONTACTS

- All Terrain Boarding Association (ATBA): www.atbauk.org

- International Mountainboard Association: www. mountainboardworld.org

- Remolition: www. remolition.com

- UK Dirt Surfing: www. ukdirtsurfing.com

ON WHEELS

CONTACTS

- UK Inline Skating Association (UKISA): 🖥 www.ukisa.org

- Organisers: 🖥 www. citiskate.co.uk, www.thefns. com, www.inlineonline. co.uk, www.rollerstroll. com, www.skatefresh.com

INLINE SKATING

AT A GLANCE

Accessibility Index:	❶❷❸❹⑤
Fitness level:	❶②③④⑤
Degree of Difficulty:	❶❷③④⑤
White-knuckle rating:	❶❷③④⑤

Equipment: low cost

Season: year round

Family friendly: ✓

It's still the coolest way to get along a beachfront on a hot summer's day, a snappy way of getting from A to B and an excellent cardio-vascular workout. And it's fun. Inline skating has had its ups and downs as a fashionable activity, but has so many natural advantages that it keeps on bouncing back, and you can sign up for a course in many cities. You wear a pair of skates with between two and five wheels in a line – hence the name – mimicking traditional ice-skates. They provide great manoeuvrability and speed compared to old-fashioned roller-skates, allowing skaters to use them for sports such as hockey, skate parks, tricks and even off-road.

Inline skating burns as many as 700 calories per hour, while also toning the legs, thighs, back and shoulders. It's one of those activities where you're so busy having fun that you don't realise what a vigorous workout you've had until the next morning. Once proficient in the basics – starting, stopping (being able to stop is useful), turning, remembering to look where you're going instead of down at your skates – you can think about doing some tricks, starting with a simple heel or toe roll leading to a one-legged glide. Next there's 'aggressive skating', which may not sound too friendly but is really just freestyle skating over ramps and obstacles, much like skateboarding. You can also try sports such as rollerhockey or rollersoccer, and there are leagues in many towns – not all filled by youngsters; inline skating has been around long enough to have plenty of mature fans. It's also one of the most sociable outdoor activities, with mass skates in London, including the Friday Night Skate (FNS, 🖥 wwww.lfns. co.uk) and the Sunday Roller Stroll (🖥 www.rollerstroll.com), which starts at 2pm every Sunday from Hyde Park.

ROLLER SKIING

📝 CONTACTS

- Organisers: 🖥 www.rollerski.co.uk, www.rollerskiing.co.uk, www.skikeuk.com

👓 AT A GLANCE

Accessibility Index: ❶❷❸❹⑤

Fitness level: ❶❷③④⑤

Degree of Difficulty: ❶❷❸④⑤

White-knuckle rating: ❶❷③④⑤

Equipment: hire or medium cost

Season: year round

Family friendly: ✓

People sometimes refer to 'reinventing the wheel' as if that was a bad thing. But we're living in an amazing age of discovery right now, and wheels are constantly being reinvented to startling effect. Take rollerskis. They've been around for decades as longish metal strips with skateboard-type wheels on the end but were largely ignored as a dull exercise activity that had to be done on flat tarmac. But now roller skis have gone high-tech, with a racier look and an off-road, all-terrain style that allows for much more exciting downhills.

Each is the length of a foot, with bindings for your normal trainer to fit in, plus two pneumatic tyres on each end. You use them just like normal skis, with two poles, but due to their shorter length you can add an element of skating too, with a running motion on the flat and uphill sections. Learning to use rollerskis usually takes a matter of minutes, especially if you've cross country skied before, and having poles to hang onto is certainly a comfort. There are some differences, though. Some rollerskis have brakes at the back wheel or the calf, to help beginners stay in control, and because the 'snowplough' method of stopping doesn't work so well on tarmac (although there's a version of it). For similar reasons, users tend to wear a helmet, knee- and elbow-pads.

The new rollerskis, usually under the brand-name Skike, can be used in much the same way as mountainboards, downhill on grass, over and around obstacles, or even for jumps and tricks. Prices are around £150 to £200 for the rollerski and pole set.

ON WHEELS

CONTACTS

- Southern Dune Buggy Club: ⌨ www.sdbc.co.uk

- Web's Dune Buggy: ⌨ www.dune-buggy.co.uk

- Suppliers: ⌨ www.ragemotorsport.com

- Organisers: ⌨ www.dirtbuggyracing.com, www.team-action.co.uk

DIRT BUGGY

AT A GLANCE

Accessibility Index: ❶❷❸④⑤

Fitness level: ❶②③④⑤

Degree of Difficulty: ❶❷③④⑤

White-knuckle rating: ❶❷❸❹⑤

Equipment: hire or high cost

Season: year round

Disability friendly: ✓

Family friendly: ✓

A cross between a Jeep and a go kart, dirt buggies are 4x4's for those with smaller pockets; rough 'n' tough all-terrain vehicles, with a better power-to-weight ratio than a supercar. They come under many trade names: dune buggy, dirt buggy, Rage buggy, Apache buggy, Honda Pilot buggy… and though largely replaced by quad bikes, they still have many advantages over quads. They're safer for a start, because you're seated in a proper bucket seat and have roll bars and seat belts. Boring? Not really – how does 0-60 in three seconds sound? And those safety features allow you not only to go faster but do manoeuvres such as 'drifting', where you slide into a turn like a rally driver, sending a spray of dust and dirt up. You're just a few inches from the ground, and outside too, without windscreen or door; so it's noisy, windy and can get a bit dirty. Marvellous!

Originally, they were modified vehicles – such as a Volkswagen Beetle, as the engine in the back increased rear-wheel traction – with the bodywork removed to reduce weight. You can still make

your own or buy a kit, but most people buy them complete. At an activity centre you'll probably be taken out for a drive as a passenger first, then be let loose to go along trails, over muddy banks, skidding and sliding over gravel and burning rubber along the straights.

WHERE DO I START?

To use them at their full capacity you need a lot of space – hence they're popular in the deserts of California. So you're best to start at an activity centre (Google 'Rage Buggy' or 'Honda Pilot Buggy') that offers buggy driving on a suitable dirt track.

CAMPFIRE GOSSIP

Special Forces use dune buggies that are dropped with them by parachute into Afghanistan to operate in remote desert areas. They're light but seriously rugged little vehicles.

DIRT BIKING

 **AT A GLANCE**

Accessibility Index: ❶❷③④⑤

Fitness level: ❶❷③④⑤

Degree of Difficulty: ❶❷❸④⑤

White-knuckle rating: ❶❷❸④⑤

Equipment: hire or high cost

Season: year round

Weight restriction: ✓

Dirt biking is riding a motorcycle cross country. One aspect of dirt biking is trail riding along green lanes (see below), minor roads and byways, which isn't off-roading, because these are legally classified roads where all the usual road rules apply. The other side of dirt biking is properly off-road, on private land and in competition, which may include scrambling, enduro events and rallies.

Trail riders like to think of themselves as motorised pony-trekkers, but this implies a quiet plod. Dirt biking is more like three day eventing: noisy, rugged and dangerous – taking your vehicle to places it may not want to go, but also learning close control of a bike built to go much faster than the conditions allow. You'll be learning how to handle a motorcycle in mud, over rocks, through water, and both up and down steep inclines. The countryside is your obstacle course, and the power to get round it is literally in your hands; in the throttle you control with your right hand, the gears and the courage you get from all the leather protection.

Riding along a high sweeping pasture, you may feel as cool as Steve McQueen in *The Great Escape*, and then you'll have to get off the bike and push it through a bog… For this reason a certain

ON WHEELS

CONTACTS

- Byways: 🖥 www.byways.org
- Green Lane Association: 🖥 www.glass-uk.org
- Green Lane Users: 🖥 www.glu.org.uk
- Trail Riders Fellowship: 🖥 www.trf.org.uk
- Trail World: 🖥 www.trailworld.co.uk
- Yamaha in Wales: 🖥 www.yamaha-offroad-experience.co.uk

level of fitness is advisable. Many centres accept children from 12 or even younger.

WHERE DO I START?

There aren't a huge number of activity centres offering dirt biking, so you'll need to contact one of the organisations listed below (see **Contacts**) to find a local organiser. It normally costs around £200 for a day's trail with the use of a bike. You could also go DIY along green lanes (see page 147) if you're confident enough.

CAMPFIRE GOSSIP

The Trail Riders Fellowship is a peaceful-sounding name for an organisation whose members dress up like Star Wars Imperial Stormtroopers to make a big noise in the countryside. But as well as helping to keep historic rights of way open, they promote good conduct such as switching off engines for horse-riders, and it's a good way to meet fellow dirt bikers.

GREEN LANING

 **AT A GLANCE**

Accessibility Index: ❶❷❸❹⑤

Fitness level: ❶②③④⑤

Degree of Difficulty: ❶❷③④⑤

White-knuckle rating: ❶❷❸④⑤

Equipment: none

Season: year round

Disability friendly: ✓

Family friendly: ✓

Green Lanes are ancient country lanes that were never tarmaced. Their official titles are 'unsealed unclassified roads' or 'Byways Open to All Traffic' (aka BOATs), and there are some 2,800mi (4,500km) of them in England and Wales, often going through the wildest rural countryside. They're normally used as footpaths and bridlepaths, but you're entitled to drive along them in your car or motorbike as on any other road. They're beloved by 4x4 drivers, quad bike riders and dirt bikers because they're free to use, but often a challenge to drive along, far from the madding traffic crowd.

Green lanes tend to represent a problem for landowners and groups such as the National Parks authorities, however, who don't want motor vehicles driving through their beauty spots. There's a constant battle to keep them open. A fringe benefit of the struggle is the action of many groups and websites in publicising green lanes in an effort to keep them open.

These campaign groups are trying to get all vehicle users of green lanes to abide by a code of conduct, such as turning off your engine when encountering horseriders and avoiding routes that are already churned up, i.e. not seeing them as a wonderful challenge to speed along as fast as possible. They are country lanes, not skid pans for people to test their off-road driving skills in the deepest mud possible (see **4x4 Driving** on page 127).

All the same, you may end up fording streams or bogs, hacking your way through brambles, and tackling steep inclines and tricky ruts. That's because so many green lanes have been neglected; by getting out there and using them responsibly, you're doing fellow nature lovers and yourself a favour. You may even enjoy cleaning the car after a weekend trip, while reliving what a great time you had.

ON WHEELS

📝 CONTACTS

- Byways: 💻 www.byways.org
- Countryside Recreational Access Group:
  💻 www.crag-uk.org
- Four by Four Clubs:
  💻 www.4x4-clubs.co.uk
- Green Lane Association:
  💻 www.glass-uk.org
- Green Lane Users:
  💻 www.glu.org.uk
- Land Rover Experience:
  💻 www.landrover.co.uk/experience
- Trail Riders Fellowship:
  💻 www.trf.org.uk

WHERE DO I START?

Look at the websites and campaign groups for local green lanes or on an Ordnance Survey map where they're shown as a thick green line made up of small crosses. Take a mobile phone and try not to go alone until you know the route well, as you could get stranded.

CAMPFIRE GOSSIP

4x4 users often get blamed for churning up green lanes, but according to the government minister responsible: "We have found no compelling evidence of widespread problems being caused by the recreational use of motor vehicles on byways, and have concluded there is no case for a general ban."

Send someone you love over the edge.

If you're looking for a gift for someone who loves driving, a Land Rover Experience voucher could be perfect. On our off-road course they will tackle exhilarating slopes, obstacles and challenges at the wheel of the latest model Land Rover and Range Rover vehicles. It's so much fun, maybe you should treat yourself too…

To give someone you love a muddy great day call us on 0800 110 110 or visit www.landrover.co.uk/experience

LAND-ROVER

experience

6

ON WATER

- ❖ Kayaking
- ❖ Canadian Canoeing
- ❖ Dinghy Sailing
- ❖ Barging and River/ Canal Cruising
- ❖ Surfing & Bodyboarding
- ❖ Bore Surfing
- ❖ Windsurfing
- ❖ Kite Surfing
- ❖ Yacht Crewing
- ❖ Tall Ship Crewing
- ❖ Whitewater Rafting
- ❖ Stand Up Paddle Boarding
- ❖ Waterskiing & Wakeboarding
- ❖ Kneeboarding
- ❖ Hydrofoil Waterskiing
- ❖ Jetskiing
- ❖ Float Tubing/River Bugging
- ❖ Storm Watching
- ❖ Whale Watching
- ❖ Skiff Camping

Britannia still rules the waves! We've topped the last three Olympic sailing medals tables, we're blessed with the largest canal system in the world, some of the cleanest rivers and most beautiful lakes, and you're never more than an hour or so drive from the sea. (Just don't mention the America's Cup.)

Warning!

Although most organisers provide a life jacket and safety equipment, it goes without saying that you need to be a confident swimmer to participate in most watersports.

KAYAKING

AT A GLANCE

Accessibility Index: ❶❷❸❹❺

Fitness level: ❶②③④⑤

Degree of Difficulty: ❶❷③④⑤

White-knuckle rating: ❶❷③④⑤

Equipment: hire or medium cost

Season: year round

Disability programme: ✓

Weight restriction: ✓

Wherever there's water, there'll be a version of kayaking. Whether on sea, lake or whitewater, for fishing or for exploration, for sport or for recreation, kayaking is simple to learn at any age and one of the safest ways of getting onto the water. Kayaking is the light, fast-moving version of paddling, where you face forward and use a double-bladed paddle. Kayakers used to distinguish themselves from canoeists by sitting legs forward in a 'cockpit', with a spray-skirt to keep the water out. However the growth of sit-on-top and inflatable versions has muddied the distinction.

WHAT EXACTLY WILL I BE DOING?

It's best to get some training in safety and technique (and maybe navigation) before getting into a kayak for the first time. In closed cockpit versions especially, you'll need to practice a 'wet exit', i.e. bailing out of the kayak when it's upside down with you in the water. Once you're expert at that, the world's your oyster. Sea kayaks can be used for long-distance touring, with your supplies and camping equipment safely stored in water-tight bulkheads, perfect for wild camping expeditions (see page 59). You can even get a sail attachment to reduce the strain on your muscles.

Sit on top kayaks require less training, as there's no risk of getting trapped underneath it – you simply fall off – and they're fun for a day at the seaside, maybe a bit of fishing, or for crashing through the waves. Whitewater kayaking is a popular choice at outdoor activity centres, but requires more technical skill. The kayak's short length (as little as 4.5ft/1.2m), and width barely more than your hips, allows you to slip along narrow creeks and streams. Fitted out correctly, your kayak can cope with waves and strong surf, with a snug waterproof 'skirt' that keeps the water out.

Kayaks are available in a wide range of sizes; you can even get one that's small and light enough to carry down to your nearest stream, where you can launch it from the bank and paddle away. When you run out of water, hop out and bring the kayak home on the bus.

HAPPY MEMORIES?

You can get up close and personal with seals, dolphins, basking sharks and even whales. Kayaks being a sleek, aquatic sort of shape, the wildlife below won't realise that you're human, and kayaks have the kind of nimble steering you'll want when that huge tail comes looming out of the water next to you.

ON WATER

POPULAR LOCATIONS

Southeast: River Medway, Kent.

Southwest: Falmouth, Cornwall.

Central: River Wye, Herefordshire.

North: Farne Islands, Northumberland.

Wales: 'The Bitches', tidal swell off the Pembrokeshire Coast.

Scotland: Outer Hebrides, Scotland.

CONTACTS

- British Canoe Union:
  ☎ 0845-370 9500 or 0300-011 9500, 💻 www.bcu.org.uk

- Canoe & Kayak magazine:
  💻 www.canoekayak.co.uk

- Scottish Canoe Association:
  ☎ 0131-317 7314, 💻 www.canoescotland.com

- Welsh Canoeing Association:
  ☎ 01678-521199, 💻 www.welsh-canoeing.org.uk

- Organisers: 💻 www.seakayakingcornwall.com, www.seakayakinguk.com, www.ukriversguidebook.co.uk

WHAT SHOULD I BE WORRIED ABOUT?

You'll feel pretty small in your little kayak when you're tackling big water around the rocky coasts of the Hebrides or the Pembrokeshire coast, with whirlpools and waves two metres high, or tumbling down whitewater rapids in a Welsh river (see **Whitewater Rafting** page 178).

WHERE CAN IT LEAD?

For the super-fit, kayaking is an element in many adventure races and ultra-marathons. For those who like expeditions, kayaking offers the freedom of paddling out to remote islands as part of survival and coastal foraging (see page 82) trips.

WHO CAN DO IT?

Anyone confident in the water can kayak after instruction, but children must a wear a life jacket.

KUSHI ADVENTURES

Based in Inverness in the Scottish Highlands, we offer part, full and multi-day adventures...

- Half a day kayaking on Loch Ness, a gentle day canoeing down the River Beauty, or why not a 5-day guided trip across Scotland via the Great Glen?

- We also offer a full canoe and kayak hire service including all equipment and, if needed, a shuttle service.

- Also guided mountain walks, climbing, abseiling, gorge walks and navigation training.

Inverness is very accessible by train, road and air, and is a fantastic base for a Scottish Adventure.

Contact - Russell ☎ 07833-462707
✉ info@kushiadventures.co.uk 💻 www.kushiadventures.co.uk

WHAT WILL IT COST?

Inflatable and sit on top kayaks start at £250, including pump, paddles and life-jacket.

CAMPFIRE GOSSIP

Kayak means 'man's boat' in the Inuit language, and they've been used for hunting for 4,000 years. They were originally made from driftwood and animal skins, to a size determined by three times a man's outstretched arms for length, and his hips plus two fists for the width. The 'eskimo roll', where you roll over in the boat without falling out, was developed because the Inuits never learned to swim, the water being too cold.

ON WATER

CANADIAN CANOEING

 **AT A GLANCE**

Accessibility Index: ❶❷❸④⑤

Fitness level: ❶②③④⑤

Degree of Difficulty: ❶❷③④⑤

White-knuckle rating: ❶❷③④⑤

Equipment: hire or medium cost

Season: year round

Disability friendly: ✓

Family friendly: ✓

Confident swimmer: ✓

Weight restriction: ✓

If kayaks are the sports cars of the paddling world, canoes are the Range Rovers. You can take the whole family on a canoeing expedition, and maybe your dog also. Canadian canoes are the double-ended, open-decked boats (originally made from strips of bark) that you may associate with paddling down the Great Lakes hunting for beaver and trying to avoid falling over Niagara Falls.

WHAT EXACTLY WILL I BE DOING?

Sometimes referred to as 'open canoes', you sit or kneel, facing forwards, generally using a single-bladed paddle on alternate

POPULAR LOCATIONS

Southeast: Bosham Harbour, West Sussex.

Southwest: Wimblehall Lake, Exmoor.

Central: Source of the Thames, nr Cirencester.

North: Derwent Water, Cumbria.

Wales: Dee Valley and Llangollen, Denbighshire

Scotland: River Lochy, Fort William.

sides of the boat to begin with, until you develop the special 'J-shaped' paddling technique that allows you to paddle only on one side without going in circles.

Far less suited to rough water and inherently unstable due to their smooth bottom, canoes are mainly used on lakes and slow moving rivers, rather than at sea or in whitewater. A capable canoeist travels at around 3 knots (3.5mph/5.5kph), therefore distances of 20-30mi (32-48km) per day are perfectly achievable.

For many people, canoeing is about serenity. All you can hear is the gentle dip and pull of each paddle stroke and it's the perfect get-away-from-it-all pastime. For others it's about exercise, as both an aerobic work-out and a way of building your upper body strength (Hilary Swank used paddling to bulk up for her role as a female boxer in *Million Dollar Baby*.) Many activities can get you hot, bothered and stressed, but canoeists simply jump over the side whenever they feel like cooling off, and Britain's rivers are now the cleanest they've been for over a century.

HAPPY MEMORIES?

Travelling the entire length of a river from source to estuary – or vice versa – is more than a simple test of endurance; it's also a geographical exploration with a hint of the Dr Livingstones about it, likely to provoke all manner of philosophical meanderings along the way. Try the Thames Path National Trail, which follows the 180mi (290km) from the Thames Barrier to its source near Cirencester (Glos.).

WHAT SHOULD I BE WORRIED ABOUT?

Don't rock the boat! With the canoe's justified reputation for instability, effective canoeing requires you to remain still with your centre of gravity low. Open canoes are also far less safe for white-water, as there's generally no cover to stop the water coming in (although covers are now available).

ON WATER

CONTACTS

- Canoe England:
  ☎ 0300-011 9500, 💻 www.canoe-england.org.uk

- Canoe Man: 💻 www.thecanoeman.com

- Canoe Union: ☎ 0845-709500 or 0300-011 9500, 💻 www.bcu.org.uk

- The Scottish Canoe Association: ☎ 0131-317 7314, 💻 www.canoescotland.org

- Welsh Canoeing Association:
  ☎ 01678-521199, 💻 www.welsh-canoeing.org.uk

- Equipment: 💻 www.kayaksandpaddles.co.uk

- Organisers: 💻 www.songofthepaddle.co.uk, www.thecanoeman.com

WHERE CAN IT LEAD?

You can cross a whole continent by canoe, by paddling from the estuary to the source of one river, then pick up another river heading from the same source but flowing in another direction. Catch fish en route (see Coastal Foraging on page 82) and pitch your tent by the river bank (see Wild Camping on page 59), and you'll never have to go back to the office again…

WHO CAN DO IT?

Anyone, including children wearing a life jacket

WHAT SHOULD I TAKE?

Children and poor swimmers must wear a life jacket (indeed, it's sensible for everyone to wear one). For rapids and whitewater, you'll need a helmet.

WHAT WILL IT COST?

Canoes were traditionally more expensive than kayaks because their construction is altogether more complicated and expensive, from canvas stretched between wooden struts. However, there are now cheaper aluminium and Kevlar versions. A 14-16ft (4.3-4.9m) canoe costs from around £500.

CAMPFIRE GOSSIP

War canoes as developed by African and Maori tribesmen would be hollowed out from a tree trunk so massive that when finished they could carry well over 100 warriors. They were dug out of the tree trunk – usually Totara or Silk Cotton – by lighting the wood and scooping out the ashes.

DINGHY SAILING

>  **AT A GLANCE**
>
> Accessibility Index: ①②**❸❹**⑤
>
> Fitness level: **❶**②③④⑤
>
> Degree of Difficulty: **❶❷❸**④⑤
>
> White-knuckle rating: **❶❷❸**④⑤
>
> Equipment: hire or medium cost
>
> Season: year round
>
> Disability friendly: ✓
>
> Family friendly: ✓
>
> Confident swimmer: ✓

Dinghy sailing is inexpensive and fun, and can be done on rivers, lakes or at sea. Dinghies can be stored in a garage and towed behind a car, making it the most versatile way of getting onto the water without getting your feet wet. A dinghy is a small boat – usually 6 to 20 feet (2 to 6m) – that you usually sail, but can also row or use with an outboard motor. For ease of storage, the mast will often fold down. For landlubbers, the processes of sailing can seem mysterious – how do you sail into the wind, for heaven's sake? Why doesn't the boat blow over? Why does that large wooden beam keep hitting me on the head? But learning on a dinghy is how all the great sailors started, as you learn the principles of sailing on the relative safety of a lake or river.

WHAT EXACTLY WILL I BE DOING?

Sailing is surprisingly easy to grasp once you get going. There are two sails – a large one at the back and a smaller one at the front, which can switch sides to catch the wind from either direction. A 'daggerboard' below the water keeps you stable and, with the rudder, enables you to travel in almost any direction apart from directly into the wind.

After just a few hours training with an experienced instructor, you should be able to go solo in light winds. From there you can start competing, move onto larger boats and yachts, and improve your technique to include a trapeze which allows you to shift your weight outboard to balance the boat, and a spinnaker, a large sail which enables you to go faster. You can also use your boat to reach islands or go on camping trips.

ON WATER

POPULAR LOCATIONS

Southeast: Whitstable Bay, Kent.

Southwest: Poole Harbour, Dorset.

Central: Edgbaston Reservoir, Birmingham.

North: Hartlepool Marina.

Wales: Menai Strait, Anglesey.

Scotland: Oban Sailing Club, Argyll.

Dinghies can be beautiful pieces of equipment, crafted from wood, able to be rowed or paddled, and can be used for a relaxing family outing, a quiet day's fishing or a frantic dash for the finishing line.

HAPPY MEMORIES?

When sailing, you're right in the moment, harnessing the elements and coping with the forever changing conditions. Sailing your own dinghy is pure, literal, escapism that you can do sitting down. It's a popular sport for disabled people and has been used in treating conditions such as autism. Sailing also has a lively social side (clubs stage a wide programme of events), and it's a great way to widen your circle of friends. Splice the mainbrace!

WHAT SHOULD I BE WORRIED ABOUT?

The reality of any watersport is that the calmest river, lake or sea is a frightening place when you're out on a small boat and things start going wrong. You may find yourself blowing into bridges or beaches, or becalmed while watching a storm heading towards you.

WHERE DO I START?

The Royal Yacht Association-approved courses, levels 1 and 2, take five days to complete and cost around £200. You won't need to buy a boat at first, as most clubs will allow you to hire one.

WHO CAN DO IT?

You can start sailing at any age, but most training centres start children at around the age of eight. There are also sailing schemes for the disabled.

WHAT WILL IT COST?

Around £500 is enough to buy a second-hand dinghy and all the equipment a beginner should need.

CAMPFIRE GOSSIP

The Mirror Dinghy (see **Contacts**), promoted by the Daily Mirror newspaper, was a highly successful attempt to bring sailing within the budgets of ordinary people. Since 1962, 70,000 have been made and they have been sailed all over the world. Secondhand Mirror Dinghies cost from a few hundred up to a few thousand pounds.

CONTACTS

- Dinghy Sailing: 💻 http://dinghysailing.net

- Mirror Dinghies: 💻 http://ukmirrorsailing.cz.cc

- Royal Yachting Association (RSA): ☎ 023-8060 4100, 💻 www.rya.org.uk

- RSA Sailability: 💻 www.ryasailability.org.uk

- Welsh National Watersports Centre: 💻 www.plasmenai.co.uk

- Weymouth and Portland National Sailing Academy: ☎ 01305-866000, 💻 www.wpnsa.org.uk

- The Wheelyboat Trust: 💻 www.wheelyboats.org (boating for the disabled)

- Yachts & Yachting magazine: 💻 www.dinghysailingmagazine.co.uk

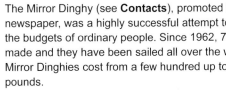

ON WATER

BARGING & RIVER/ CANAL CRUISING

 AT A GLANCE

Accessibility Index: ❶❷❸❹❺

Fitness level: ❶②③④⑤

Degree of Difficulty: ❶❷③④⑤

White-knuckle rating: ❶②③④⑤

Equipment: hire

Season: year round

Disability friendly: ✓

Family friendly: ✓

In recent years barging has become an increasingly popular activity on Britain's inland waterways. It may be a weekend adventure without a drop of whitewater – except what you're splashing into your scotch once the sun's over the yardarm – but the combination of relaxation and the ever-changing landscape has made cruising along Britain's rivers and canals one of the UK's most appealing activities.

Although it's commonly referred to as barging, the actual boats used are called narrowboats, which refers to the original working boats built to transport goods on Britain's network of narrow canals from the 18th-20th centuries.

There are many ways to get aboard, including 31,000 narrowboats (more than during the Industrial Revolution) – especially designed for Britain's 2,200 miles of narrow canals (narrowboats are also designed for relatively narrow people – you will probably have to shuffle sideways to negotiate the aisles). There are also barges (technically distinct from narrowboats, as not all barges are narrow) and cabin cruisers, all of which have enjoyed a major surge of interest in the past decade. Maybe that's because cruising combines several things that people really value in a holiday – it's intensely relaxing, yet you've got something to do; you're arriving in a

new place every day, but you're in a cosy little home of your own.

WHAT EXACTLY WILL I BE DOING?

What you're mainly doing is steering a boat through canals, slow moving rivers or Norfolk Broads. Controlling a narrowboat of 7ft (2.1m) wide and up to 70ft (21.3m) in length, you'll need to concentrate when manoeuvring; however, with a maximum speed of around walking pace, you're unlikely to get a speeding ticket. Nevertheless, until you get the hang of it, it's very easy to crash into river banks, bridges and other boats!

You'll need to leap on and off the boat to tie up and to get through the lock systems – shifting tons of water may seem mildly daunting the first time, but most people quickly get to grips with it. However, opening and closing some locks can be hard work, and there can be many in quick succession, such as the 29 Caen Hill Locks on the Kennet & Avon Canal at Devizes – a daunting prospect! Canals are sociable places where people chat and banter as they quietly chug past each other, and you'll rarely be far from a country pub. Children generally love a barge holiday – the boats move so slowly that they can play on the canal bank and walk alongside, and although canals aren't deep, most kids enjoy wearing a life-jacket and soon forget they have it on.

Narrowboat design may be based on Victorian commercial traffic, but today's models are modern with all mod cons. They must be less than seven foot wide to get into the locks, but they have flush toilets, showers (baths even), TVs, comfortable double beds and fitted kitchens.

On other, wider, waterways, such as the River Thames or the Norfolk Broads, you have the option of using a 'cabin cruiser' instead – a wider, more modern-looking boat.

WHAT SHOULD I BE WORRIED ABOUT?

Once you've mastered steering and locks, there's nothing to worry about on a river cruising holiday. You don't need a licence,

ON WATER

POPULAR LOCATIONS

Southeast: Regents Canal, London.

Southwest: Kennet and Avon Canal.

Central: Four Counties Ring – Shropshire, Staffordshire, Cheshire and Worcestershire.

North: Bridgewater Canal, Manchester.

Wales: Llangollen Canal and the Pontcysyllte aqueduct (a World Heritage site).

Scotland: Forth and Clyde Canal and the Falkirk Wheel.

they're easy to use and have modern diesel engines. However, although barging is generally very safe, you need to be nimble as there's a lot of scrambling about on slippery decks; you need to be particularly careful when opening and closing locks, as falling in can prove fatal.

HAPPY MEMORIES?

River holidays take you into the deepest countryside while enjoying all the comforts of a luxurious self-catering apartment. You can usually tie up for the night where you like, free of charge, and sit out on deck for an evening meal in a rural setting teeming

with wildlife, including the otters that are making a come-back on Britain's waterways. Or see one of our cities – Bath, Birmingham, Edinburgh, Glasgow, Oxford and London – from a totally fresh perspective.

WHERE DO I START?

Visit the British Waterways website (see **Contacts**) for a list of Britain's canals and rivers, and just pick where you fancy. Don't aim to do too many miles a day – remember that you only travel slowly and need to allow time to negotiate the locks (and stop at pubs for coffee, lunch, tea, dinner, etc.).

WHO CAN DO IT?

Anyone can go on a narrowboat or river cruising holiday, although children should wear a life-jacket, and you may wonder how relaxing a time you'll have with a toddler on board. Dogs are welcome on many boats, but you'll need to check with the operator.

WHAT SHOULD I TAKE?

Just take what you'd normally take on holiday, plus trainers, swimming togs and waterproofs (the latter may be provided). You probably won't be tempted to swim in a canal, many of which aren't very clean, but on a river you may be (see **Wild Swimming** on page 207).

WHERE CAN IT LEAD?

If you like canals and waterways, you can become a volunteer with British Waterways or one of the many groups helping with the intensely satisfying (and dirty) task of clearing lost waterways, repairing locks and restoring narrowboats.

WHAT WILL IT COST?

Cruisers sleeping four cost from £450 to £1,200 per week to rent, and narrowboats usually a little more. Mooring is usually free, and fuel is included in the rental cost (enough for at least a week).

CAMPFIRE GOSSIP

The simple pleasures of a barging holiday can even attract Hollywood royalty, with Harrison Ford and Calista Flockhart tackling the Llangollen Canal, and Kevin Spacey taking on the Kennet and Avon and its many pubs.

 **CONTACTS**

- The Barge Association: www.barges.org
- British Waterways: ☎ 01923-201120, www.waterscape.com
- Canal Junction: www.canaljunction.com
- The Inland Waterways Association: www.waterways.org.uk
- Scottish Canals: www.scottishcanals.co.uk
- Hire: www.black-prince.com, www.drifters.co.uk, www.hireacanalboat.co.uk, www.waterwaysholidays.com

ON WATER

SURFING & BODYBOARDING

AT A GLANCE

Accessibility Index: ❶❷❸④⑤

Fitness level: ❶❷③④⑤

Degree of Difficulty: ❶❷❸④⑤

White-knuckle rating: ❶❷❸❹⑤

Equipment: hire or medium cost

Season: year round

Disability friendly: ✓

Family friendly: ✓

Confident swimmer: ✓

The British surf scene is big and growing, expanding well beyond its traditional base in Cornwall to every corner of the land, from Kent to the Hebrides. Even Yorkshire's got a surf school: surf's oop! You don't need to be able to hang ten – standing at the front of the board with all your toes over the edge – or even stand up at all. You can bodyboard, where you lie on your tummy, from any age: the thrill of catching a wave is just the same as if you're riding the big waves at Waimea Bay (Hawaii). However, it isn't such a thrill in winter, when even the hardiest surfers need a wetsuit (and possibly at other times also).

WHAT EXACTLY WILL I BE DOING?

In surfing, the board is powered by the movement of the wave into the beach, as opposed to kitesurfing (see page 172), where wind provides the propulsion. You start by lying on the board and paddling out to beyond where the waves break. Then you spin yourself round on the board – still lying down – to face the shoreline. When you see a big wave approaching from behind, you (panic?) start paddling like mad until it catches you, then ride the face of the wave as it breaks towards the beach. Depending on the size and shape of the wave, you can attempt to stand on the board and execute manoeuvres such as turning or riding inside the tube created by the breaking wave. When you 'wipe out' (i.e. fall off), the buoyancy of your wetsuit will help to keep you afloat, while being able to rest on your board between rides means you'll feel at home in waves that would normally be terrifying.

You don't need huge waves to surf, and Britain is a great place to do it.

HAPPY MEMORIES?

Feeling your body being swept along by thousands of tons of water is such an intoxicating and addictive thrill that a whole language and lifestyle has built up around it, and thousands of normally sensible people drop out of society to become full-time surf dudes and surf chicks each year.

WHAT SHOULD I BE WORRIED ABOUT?

Even in the UK, 15-20ft (4.5-6m) waves make surfing an easy way for inexperienced adventurers to drown themselves. Add to that the risk of encountering rip tides and currents or colliding with reefs, sandbars, other surfers or your own surfboard – but at least in the UK we don't have to worry about shark attacks.

Warning!

If you're an inexperienced surfer, you should try to surf only at beaches patrolled by lifeguards, shown by a red and yellow flag (see ⊑ www.rnli.org.uk), while black and white chequered flags indicate an area designated for watersports such as surfing (NOT bodyboarding) and kayaking.

WHERE DO I START?

The British Surfing Association (see Contacts) lists around 40 approved surf schools, most of which are in north Cornwall and Devon. But these assume you want to look good standing up – you can bodyboard with no training and a cheap board from the bucket and spade shop at almost any beach. However, it's important to check for any warnings about odd local tidal effects, rips or undertows, and not to surf on beaches without lifeguards until you're experienced.

WHERE CAN IT LEAD?

For the monster surf of California and Hawaii with waves of 50ft (15m), surfers catch a tow from a jetski to help them catch the waves.

ON WATER

POPULAR LOCATIONS

Southeast: Viking Bay, Margate, Kent; ☎ 01843-577577, 🖳 www.visitkent.co.uk.

Southwest: Newquay, Cornwall; ☎ 01637-854020, 🖳 www.visitnewquay.org.

Central: Scratby, near Great Yarmouth, Norfolk; ☎ 01493-846346, 🖳 www.great-yarmouth.co.uk.

North: Scarborough, Yorkshire; 🖳 www.yorkshiremoors andcoast.com.

Wales: Hell's Mouth, Llyn Peninsula; 🖳 www.llyn.info.

Scotland: Tiree, Inner Hebrides; ☎ 01879-220510, 🖳 www.isleoftiree.com.

📝 CONTACTS

- British Surfing Association: ☎ 01637-876474, 🖳 www.britsurf.co.uk

- Daily Surf: 🖳 www. dailysurf.net

- Global Surfers: 🖳 www. globalsurfers.com

- Lifesavers: 🖳 www.

- Lifesavers.org.uk (Royal Life Saving Society)

- Scottish Surfing: 🖳 www. visitscotland.com

- Surf Directory: 🖳 www. thesurfdirectory.co.uk

- Surf Life Saving Great Britain: 🖳 www.slsgb.org.uk

- Surf UK: 🖳 www.surf-uk.org

WHAT SHOULD I TAKE?

You'll need a surfboard, a leash and generally in the UK, a wetsuit. Young children should wear a life jacket.

WHAT WILL IT COST?

Lessons cost from £20 for two hours with the use of a board and wetsuit; hire alone may be half that. Bodyboards cost from under £10, surfboards from £100.

CAMPFIRE GOSSIP

Captain James King, one of Captain Cook's subordinates, wrote in the 1770s of the 'astonishing velocity' attained by men riding the swell on planks in Hawaii, so it has taken a while to catch on in his home town of Clitheroe.

BORE SURFING

Who says you need a beach to go surfing? The Severn Bore is a tidal surge along the River Severn that's the ultimate challenge for UK surfers. It creates a surge wave travelling at up to 10mph (16kph) for mile after mile down the River Severn to the sea. It happens up to 30 times a year, and attracts surfers trying to break the current record of riding it for 5.7mi (9km), set in 1996. It's a hard wave to catch as the crest moves from side to side, but a lifetime thrill if you get it right.

For 'at a glance' ratings, see **Surfing** above.

CONTACTS

- Seven Bore: 🖳 www.severn-bore.co.uk

ON WATER

WINDSURFING

AT A GLANCE

Accessibility Index: ❶❷❸❹⑤

Fitness level: ❶❷❸④⑤

Degree of Difficulty: ❶❷❸④⑤

White-knuckle rating: ❶❷❸④⑤

Equipment: hire or medium cost

Season: summer

Family friendly: ✓

Confident swimmer: ✓

Walk along Brighton's Palace Pier during a storm and marvel at the vast grey waves crashing onto the beach. Thank heavens you aren't out in that! But hang on, what's that brightly-coloured sail flying over the waves at 50 miles per hour... When the sea is at its stormiest and any normal person stays indoors, that's when windsurfers get their adrenalin fix. They're using a modified surfboard with a sail in the middle of it, to catch the wind and move over the water. You don't start out that extreme, of course, and can windsurf in the relative peace of a lake or lagoon; but once expert you have a choice of disciplines including wave jumping, speed, slalom and freestyle. It's also an Olympic sport.

Windsurfing is cheap (with board hire from £10) but it isn't easy; you need to master both balancing on a moving board, albeit with something to hold onto, while also learning how to sail, including tacking and gybing. You'll normally learn either on a static board or on a quiet lagoon in winds of under 5 knots. Once you're able to stand on the board, balance and pull up the sail, you'll find you're moving slowly through the water and can

POPULAR LOCATIONS

Southeast: Brighton Beach, Sussex.

Southwest: Weymouth, Dorset.

Central: Rutland Water, Leicestershire.

North: Salford Quays, Manchester.

Wales: Bala Lake, Merioneth.

Scotland: Tiree, Hebrides.

then experiment with direction control. As you gain confidence in stronger winds, the board will start 'planing', riding above the waves at much greater speed. This is where the real buzz begins, zipping along and getting some 'air' (height) off the waves.

WHERE DO I START?

The RYA runs courses at centres throughout the UK, including on lakes and inshore waters. You can just buy your own board and teach yourself, albeit taking all due safety measures, but this is a technical sport where lessons are usually necessary. One day taster courses start at under £100.

CAMPFIRE GOSSIP

The world speed record for windsurfing is an average of 56.49mph (90.91kph), set in France on a canal specially constructed to catch the Mistral wind. However, this is slightly slower than the kitesurfing record of 58.16mph (93.6kph), set off Namibia.

CONTACTS

- Royal Yachting Association:
  ☎ 023-060 4100,
  🖥 www.rya.org.uk

- UK Windsurfing Association:
  🖥 http://ukwindsurfing.com

- Weymouth and Portland National Sailing Academy:
  ☎ 01305-66000,
  🖥 www.wpnsa.org.uk

- Windsurf magazine:
  🖥 www.windsurf.co.uk

ON WATER

KITESURFING

AT A GLANCE

Accessibility Index: **❶❷❸**④⑤

Fitness level: **❶❷❸**④⑤

Degree of Difficulty: **❶❷❸**④⑤

White-knuckle rating: **❶**②**❸❹❺**

Equipment: hire or high cost

Season: year round

Confident swimmer: ✓

In November 2009 on a blustery day, two kitesurfers flew over Worthing Pier, using a giant wave as a springboard to lift them to 100ft (30m). By all accounts, it was the most exciting thing to happen in Worthing since VE Day. Kitesurfing (sometimes written as 'kite surfing' and also called kiteboarding – or fly surfing in France) is one of several adventurous activities that you can do using a powerkite as a means of propulsion. From total novice, it takes just three days tuition/practice to become a reasonably proficient kitesurfer, making it the ideal activity for a long weekend by the sea. And once skilled, you can also use the same kite to power you along on your snowboard, mountainboard or kite buggy.

WHAT EXACTLY WILL I BE DOING?

The 'pilot' wears a harness attached to a kite, and stands on a type of surfboard. The kite isn't connected to the board, so the only connection is via the pilot, who places his feet in footstraps on the board. The wind provides the power and the board is the platform, from which the pilot can do jumps, acrobatics, high speeds or a leisurely cruise. Best conditions are winds of between 10 to 50mph (16 to 80kph), depending on your skill level, and you can ride on all kinds of seas from calm to choppy to rough.

Kites are specially constructed around an inflatable support for ease of launching in the water. They have four lines leading to a kind of handlebar which you use to control the kite, rather than the two handles on a normal stunt kite, where the bar allows for one-handed

POPULAR LOCATIONS

Southeast: Worthing area, West Sussex; ☎ 01903-600149, 💻 www.lancingkitesurfing.co.uk.

Southwest: Weymouth, Dorset; ☎ 01903-600149, 💻 www.paracademyextreme.co.uk.

Central: Hunstanton, Norfolk; ☎ 01485-534455, 💻 www.hunstantonwatersports.com.

North: Ainsdale Beach, Merseyside; ☎ 07913-017925, 💻 www.westcoastkiteboarding.co.uk.

Wales: Newgale Sands, Pembrokeshire; ☎ 07816-169359, 💻 www.bigbluekitesurfing.com.

Scotland: Troon, Ayrshire; ☎ 01294-312100, 💻 www.extreme-zone.co.uk.

control. The lines then carry on down to your harness, to spread the load of the kite. Boards are 3 to 6ft (1 to 2m) in length and are usually ridden with footstraps. There are two kinds of boards; two-directional boards (a bit like snowboards) and mono-directional, which are more like surfboards.

At competition level, kitesurfing combines gymnastics and sailing, with competitors judged on style, performance and technical manoeuvres. But most people just go for fun, speed and jumping. 'Hangtime' is the way to impress spectators, using waves as the springboard for massive jumps, and then using the power of the kite to stay airborne for as long as possible.

HAPPY MEMORIES?

The best feeling is the amazing contrast when jumping, between the exhilaration of splashing across the surface of the water at top speed, and the silence and peacefulness when you're in the air; just you and the board with the waves far below.

WHAT SHOULD I BE WORRIED ABOUT?

Just two months before the pier leap, a 49-year old was killed kitesurfing in Worthing when he was carried onto rocks. Controlling a large kite in winds of 50mph (80kph) is dangerous and unpredictable, and a kite can easily be pulled out to sea in high winds. You also need to be vigilant in popular areas, when it isn't unknown for novices to crash into other kitesurfers.

WHERE CAN IT LEAD?

Kickers and Sliders are the latest buzz in kitesurfing, where ramps and rails are securely placed in the water and kitesurfers use

ON WATER

CONTACTS

- British Kitesurfing Association (BKSA): 🖥 www.britishkitesurfingassociation.co.uk

- British Power Kitesports Association: 🖥 www.bpka.co.uk

- Kitesurf magazine: 🖥 www.kitesurf-magazine.co.uk

- Organisers: 🖥 www.forces-of-nature.co.uk, www.kiteboardinguk.com, www.kitesurfwales.co.uk, http://ukkitesurfing.com

them as the springboard for tricks and freestyle. For a similar buzz, but dryer, why not try Land yachting (see page 131).

WHAT SHOULD I TAKE?

Most clubs insist on wetsuits, helmets, boots and a life jacket, but will supply these for beginners.

CAMPFIRE GOSSIP

Ancient Chinese armies are reputed to have attached people to massive kites in order to spy on enemy positions.

YACHT CREWING

 **AT A GLANCE**

Accessibility Index: ❶❷❸④⑤

Fitness level: ❶❷③④⑤

Degree of Difficulty: ❶❷③④⑤

White-knuckle rating: ❶❷❸④⑤

Equipment: hire or high cost

Season: spring to autumn

Disability programme: ✓

Family friendly: ✓

Confident swimmer: ✓

Yachts are a glorious combination of climbing frame, fairground ride and motorhome; a wonderful way to spend a day or a weekend, or even sell up home and live at sea permanently, moving between the marinas and pretty fishing villages of Britain. Yachts are expensive, but before rushing out and buying one, there are cheaper alternatives. You could buy a share of a yacht, since few of us use our yachts every weekend, and sharing the initial cost and the marina fees brings it within the pocket of many more people.

You can join a yacht club, or you can often cadge a free trip on someone else's yacht in return for helping to crew it. Start by taking a 'competent crew' course from the RYA, and once you know your port from your starboard, make yourself available to yacht owners by putting a note on the notice board at a yacht club. You may be invited to help crew around the world or just around the marina, as you help steer, organise the sails, tack and jibe, tie up, ferry passengers to shore, and maybe cook, clean and maintain the yacht in exchange for your trip.

Sailing often feels like an activity on the edge of disaster; your first storm, your first night sail, your first realisation that you can't see the land any more – every stage in your development as a sailor will have its thrills and its fears. And the lively social side (an important part of being a yachty) will widen your circle of friends.

WHERE DO I START?

Unless you can find a friendly boat-owner to help you learn, the RYA runs a five-day 'competent crew' course where you live

ON WATER

POPULAR LOCATIONS

Southeast: Brighton Marina, Sussex.

Southwest: Falmouth Harbour, Cornwall.

Central: Levington, Suffolk.

North: Liverpool Marina, Merseyside.

Wales: Cardiff Bay.

Scotland: Dunstaffnage Marina, Argyll.

aboard while learning the essential techniques of yacht crewing. It costs around £480. The Start Yachting course lasts two days and costs £210, and is 'credited' towards a 'competent crew' course if you choose to go further.

CAMPFIRE GOSSIP

Hilary Lister is a quadriplegic Oxford graduate who can only move her head, due to an agonising muscle-wasting disease. Nevertheless, she has broken many sailing records, including sailing around the coast of Britain solo, controlling the sails and steering of her 20ft (6m) yacht by blowing down three tubes.

 **CONTACTS**

- Royal Yachting Association (RYA): ☎ 023-8060 4100, 🖥 www.rya.org.uk, www.ryasailability.org.uk

- Yachting & Boating World magazine: 🖥 www.ybw.com

- Yachting Monthly magazine: 🖥 www.yachtingmonthly.com

- Yachts & Yachting magazine: 🖥 www.dinghysailingmagazine.co.uk

- Organisers: 🖥 www.go-sail.co.uk, www.intotheblue.co.uk

TALL SHIP CREWING

 **AT A GLANCE**

Accessibility Index: ❶❷③④⑤

Fitness level: ❶❷③④⑤

Degree of Difficulty: ❶❷③④⑤

White-knuckle rating: ❶❷❸④⑤

Equipment: hire or medium cost

Season: spring to autumn

Disability friendly: ✓

Family friendly: ✓

Confident swimmer: ✓

CONTACTS

- Sailing for the disabled: 🖳 www.jst.org.uk, www.ryasailability.org.uk

- Organisers: 🖳 www.adventureundersail.com, www.tallships.org, www.classic-sailing.co.uk, www.schoonersail.com

A tall ship needs a large crew – up to 70 for a sea crossing – to climb rigging, stow sails and pull ropes (which you'll soon know as sheets), all on a rocking ship on the ocean. Could this be the most 'braggable' weekend of all? There are hundreds of tall ships still sailing, preserved to maintain traditional sailing skills, and many of them are either based in Britain or call here regularly. You can get a weekend trip on a brig, barque, brigantine or schooner from around £200, and each summer the Tall Ships Races (various venues – 🖳 see www.tallships.org) bring together some 100 ships, half the crew of which must be young people in sail-training.

You're unlikely to forget your turn at steering a three-masted brig, with thousands of square foot of sail under your command, but climbing the rigging is usually both the high point, literally, of your trip and the scariest. Once on the yard, you'll be clipped on with a safety harness so you have both hands free to stow the sail, but you have to get up there first. And that means climbing the mast on a swaying ship, negotiating the 'futtock shrouds' and stepping out onto a thin rope slung under the yard, then shuffling along to the end. Oh, and the reason you need to do this is because the wind's getting up. Tall ships have as many as 40 sails, so there's plenty of opportunity to get aloft.

ON WATER

WHITEWATER RAFTING

AT A GLANCE

Accessibility Index: **❶❷❸**④⑤

Fitness level: **❶**②③④⑤

Degree of Difficulty: **❶**②③④⑤

White-knuckle rating: **❶❷❸❹**⑤

Equipment: hire or medium cost

Season: spring/autumn

Disability friendly: ✓

Family friendly: ✓

Confident swimmer: ✓

Weight restriction: ✓

Remember the Water Cycle from school geography? Seawater evaporates, forms a cloud, is blown over land, hits a mountain, ascends higher, cools, falls as rain and runs off the mountain as fast-flowing rivers – which is where you and rafting come in… Whitewater rafting is done in groups of up to 12 in an inflatable raft, navigating down a turbulent, fast-flowing river full of rocks, obstacles, rapids and waterfalls. The raft is steered by the passengers of the boat under the command of a helmsman at the rear who controls the rudder. There are international grades of white water from Grade 1 – very small rough areas which require only basic skill – up to Grade 6, which is effectively unnavigable and can only be completed with a large dose of luck, even if you can find a raft operator willing to risk it. There are also single person and kayaking versions (see **Float Tubing** on page 190 and **Kayaking** on page 152).

WHAT EXACTLY WILL I BE DOING?

You'll be kitted out with helmet and life jacket, maybe even a wetsuit, and given an oar to hold onto (even if you'll be too busy holding on for dear life to actually use it). The length of trips varies, but usually there'll be time to learn how to a paddle the boat as a team before you hit the rapids, and an opportunity to enjoy the scenery while getting your breath back afterwards.

POPULAR LOCATIONS

Southwest: River Meavy, Plymouth.

Central: National Water Sports Centre, Nottinghamshire.

North: Teesside White Water Centre, Stockton-on-Tees.

Wales: Afon (river) Tryweryn, River Dee.

Scotland: River Spey, Tay, Orchy and Findhorn.

It's the wildest white knuckle ride in the world. No car, horse or machine (okay, maybe a jet fighter) has anything remotely approaching the power and force of the river that you're sitting on, in a flimsy raft. In the UK, operators are strictly licensed to ensure maximum safety. This isn't, however, always the case abroad, and there have been cases of operators deliberately capsizing boats and videoing the results to sell to the occupants.

HAPPY MEMORIES?

Yes, it's scary, but you're all in the boat together, so along with speed, excitement and water – lots of water – you'll be learning teamwork, all pulling together, which is why so many companies use it as a teambuilding exercise (and it's good fun).

WHAT SHOULD I BE WORRIED ABOUT?

You approach the rapids and hear the thunderous roar of thousands of tons of water flowing over the rocks below. This isn't a fairground ride; there's enough water to drown you all 1,000 times over, whirlpools to get trapped in, rocks to dash your flimsy bones against. Whole expeditions have been lost doing this. Want to get out? Sorry, it's too late, we're at the faaaaalllllssss…

WHERE DO I START?

You'll need to go through a private company when rafting in the UK, so just get Googling. But you could start to get comfortable in fast-flowing water by trying kayaking, river bugging or coasteering.

WHERE CAN IT LEAD?

The British Raft Team competes against other rafters all over the world, and they're keen to develop

ON WATER

✏ CONTACTS

- British Raft Team:
  ☎ 07710-410453, ⌨ www.britishraftteam.co.uk
- International Rafting Federation: ⌨ www.internationalrafting.com
- National Watersports Centre: ⌨ www.nwscnotts.com
- Organisers: ⌨ www.rafting.co.uk, www.skylinerafting.co.uk, www.ukrafting.co.uk, www.waterbynature.com

rafting into a sport in which Britain excels. They organise rafting competitions throughout the year around the country, including at the National Watersports Centre in Nottingham (see **Contacts**).

WHO CAN DO IT?

This depends on the raft owner and their insurance policy, but children under 13 or those weighing below 6 stones (3kg) or over 19 stones (120kg) should check with the organiser.

WHAT SHOULD I TAKE?

Everything essential will be provided, but you should take a waterproof bag to put your things in and a change of clothes.

WHAT WILL IT COST?

Single trips from £20 and a half-day's activity from £45.

CAMPFIRE GOSSIP

A bit of rafting lingo: a 'dump truck' is where the passengers are thrown out but the raft remains upright; a 'rock splat' is where the passengers throw themselves to the back of the raft, enabling the raft to hit a rock and ride over it smoothly; and a 'taco' is where the raft curls up like a, well, taco. The latter is marginally less alarming for the passengers than a reverse taco!

STAND UP PADDLE BOARDING

AT A GLANCE

Accessibility Index: ❶❷❸❹⑤

Fitness level: ❶②③④⑤

Degree of Difficulty: ❶❷③④⑤

White-knuckle rating: ❶❷③④⑤

Equipment: hire or high cost

Season: year round

Family friendly: ✓

Confident swimmer: ✓

Combining punting, kayaking and surfing, paddleboarding is a versatile new way to get on to the water, whether you're looking for a quiet amble along a river or a thrilling ride over the waves. You stand on a large, wide, relatively stable surfboard and propel yourself over the water with a long-handled paddle. Stand Up Paddleboarding (SUP for short) is simple enough that you can learn the basics in minutes, and is easily the most civilised way to get onto the river. At sea, it's known as paddlesurfing, and allows you to bypass the tricky process of standing up on a moving board when riding a wave.

There are three bits of kit: a board, which is longer and heavier than most surfboards at 10-12ft (3m-3.6m) in length and around 30in (76cm) wide, a paddle that's a little taller than you, and a leash if you're using it at sea or in rough water. Boards cost from £600 and paddles around £100 for a good, strong, lightweight model, but kayak and surfing centres will rent you the lot from as little as £10 per hour.

The technique is simple; you stand half to two-thirds of the way along the board – further back for faster speed and further forwards to turn – and paddle on alternate sides just like a canoe. The tricky part is getting on and off without a soaking, and learning to balance and paddle.

WHERE DO I START?

Most kayak and windsurf centres now offer SUP as an alternative, either as a hire-only option or for a whole weekend including

ON WATER

POPULAR LOCATIONS

Southeast: River Hamble, Hampshire.

Southwest: Watergate Bay, Cornwall.

Central: Norfolk Broads.

North: Cayton Bay, Yorkshire.

Wales: Freshwater West, Pembrokeshire.

Scotland: Linlithgow Loch, West Lothian.

CONTACTS

- British Stand Up Paddle Association: 🖳 www. bsupa.org.uk

- Stand Up Paddle Boarding UK: 🖳 www. standuppaddlesurf.co.uk

- SUP Scotland: 🖳 www. standuppaddlescotland.co.uk

surfing training. You can even do it instead of punting at Cambridge and Oxford.

CAMPFIRE GOSSIP

The sport developed when surfing instructors needed to keep an eye on their pupils, and take photographs of them. They began standing on their boards to get a better view and avoid getting the camera wet.

WATERSKIING & WAKEBOARDING

 **AT A GLANCE**

Accessibility Index: ❶❷❸❹⑤

Fitness level: ❶②③④⑤

Degree of Difficulty: ❶❷❸④⑤

White-knuckle rating: ❶❷❸④⑤

Equipment: hire or medium cost

Season: year round

Disability friendly: ✓

Family friendly: ✓

Confident swimmer: ✓

Being towed behind a speedboat, attached by a cable and skimming over the surface of the water has been a summertime highlight for Brits abroad since we first started going on package holidays to Benidorm. But you can also do it in the UK and at any time of year, although it's wise to use a wetsuit at any time.

Waterskiers use two separate skis or a monoski, while wakeboards are more like kiteboards than surfboards, with pockets for your feet. You'll normally start in the water wearing a life-jacket, lining your skis or board up with the direction of the boat and keeping your knees close to your chest. As the boat speeds up, you keep your arms straight out, but relaxed, and allow the skis to reach the surface and start planing as you're pulled. Keep your back straight and your legs will naturally straighten up. And you're off! However, beginners often find it difficult to stand up, so some new variations have arisen, including kneeboarding, riding an inner tube, banana boat and disc, or just going barefoot. Waterskiing and wakeboarding are more active and technically tricky, requiring skill and training, while tubing and banana boats are exhilarating white-knuckle rides along the beach or lake, where you simply hold on tight and enjoy.

Either way, once you're moving comfortably across the water, the extra thrills come from making it bumpy, usually by crossing the speedboat's own wake or zigzagging from side to side. To make the sport even more accessible without the need for a

ON WATER

POPULAR LOCATIONS

Southeast: Lydd, Kent.

Southwest: Exmouth, Devon.

Central: Tallingford Lakes, Lincolnshire.

North: Windermere, Cumbria.

Wales: Lleyn Peninsula, Gwynedd.

Scotland: Town Loch, Dunfermline.

CONTACTS

- British Water Ski & Wakeboard: ☎ 01932-560007, 💻 www.britishwaterski.org.uk Wakeboard: ☐ 07958-617121,

- 💻 www.wakeboard.co.uk

- Waterski Scotland: ☎ 01383-620123, 💻 www. waterskiscotland.co.uk

speedboat, there are now several cable tows in the UK, where skiers go in groups of up to ten at a time at a fraction of the cost of boat-towing.

WHERE DO I START?

There are some 120 waterski and wakeboard clubs in the UK, affiliated to British Water Ski and Wakeboard, offering inexpensive access to the sport. Commercial cable ski operators charge from around £13 per hour, plus the hire of a wetsuit.

CAMPFIRE GOSSIP

Doubt you can waterski? Be inspired by Twiggy, the original waterskiing squirrel as featured on dozens of 'and finally…' news reports. Orphaned in a Florida hurricane in 1978, Twiggy was rescued by Chuck and Lou Ann Best, loving to join in with family games in the pool. The Twiggy performing today is actually the fourth Twiggy, but by tragic irony, Chuck Best drowned in 1997 while rescuing his father-in-law.

KNEEBOARDING

The days of being humiliated by your waterskiing failures in front of a crowded beach are over. There's now a variation on waterskiing that anyone can master – and you look pretty cool doing it. With kneeboarding, you're still being pulled by a speedboat and can still do all the tricks, but with the distinct advantage that you don't need to stand up. You start off lying on the round convex board, with your elbows in two divots. As the boat starts moving, you pull yourself onto the board and put your knees in the holes where your elbows were, pull the strap tight over your knees, and you're off. By moving your weight on the board you can slide in either direction, jump the wake, do a backflip, a 360 degree turn or even try standing up. Or just kneel there and enjoy the ride.

For 'at a glance' ratings, see **Waterskiing** above.

CONTACTS

- British Water Ski & Wakeboard: ☎ 01932-560007, 🖥 www.britishwaterski.org.uk

- UK Kneeboarding: 🖥 www. kneeboarding-uk.com

ON WATER

CONTACTS

- British Water Ski & Wakeboard: ☎ 01932-560007, ⬜ www.britishwaterski.org.uk

- Foil Addiction: ⬜ www.foiladdiction.com

HYDROFOIL WATERSKIING

It's the craziest action sport you'll ever see, riding a bike-like machine behind a speedboat, but seeming to be floating above the water. A hydrofoil waterski is a monoski with two pockets to put your feet in at the front. At the rear of the ski, a shaft goes through vertically, and on the top is a seat a bit like a barstool. Underneath, the shaft continues for about 3ft (90cm), while on the bottom is a hydrofoil. You strap yourself to the seat, sit in the water and hold the tow-rope. As the boat speeds up, the hydrofoil rises to the surface and starts planing, with the rider three feet above. Balance is all-important – this isn't an easy sport to master – but other than that, it's simple. To go left you point your knees left, to go higher up you lean back, and then you're ready to learn a few tricks.

JET SKIING

AT A GLANCE

Accessibility Index: **❶❷❸❹**⑤

Fitness level: **❶**②③④⑤

Degree of Difficulty: **❶**②③④⑤

White-knuckle rating: **❶❷❸**④⑤

Equipment: hire or high cost

Season: year round

Disability friendly: ✓

Family friendly: ✓

Confident swimmer: ✓

Swim with dolphins if you like, but jet skiing is like riding the fastest creature the seas have ever seen. Fall off, and you simply swim back to where your jet ski is patiently waiting for you. The adrenalin kick and the sense of freedom is awesome. It's a motorbike that you ride across water. Unlimited by roads and speed limits, on a jet ski you can go where you please and as fast as you like (depending on where you are – there are speed limits on inland waterways, where jet skis may even be banned).

Fast, nippy and highly manoeuvrable, they're self-righting if you fall off, and can be boarded easily from a beach. Propulsion comes via an inboard engine, a propeller kept safely inside a tube and shooting a jet of water out of the back, enabling you to travel through shallow water without damaging the prop or the surface you're travelling over. Jet ski is technically the name of the Kawasaki personal watercraft (PWC), but the machine was so successful that it's now the generic term for all makes.

Despite the fun of jet skiing, they're difficult to control by novices and are a danger to their riders, and, not least, to other water users – and have been the cause of many deaths and injuries. Be sure to have full insurance before using a jet ski, follow all safety precautions and don't exceed your own abilities.

ON WATER

POPULAR LOCATIONS

Southeast: London Docklands.

Southwest: Bristol Channel, Somerset.

Central: Harwich Harbour, Suffolk.

North: Blackpool, Lancashire.

Wales: Cardigan Bay.

Scotland: The Little Minch, Skye.

WHAT EXACTLY WILL I BE DOING?

You'll be standing or sitting on a saddle with your feet on two running boards along each side. Acceleration is via a throttle on the handlebar, and steering is via a combination of handlebar and acceleration. High-powered jet skis use around 260 horsepower to reach speeds of 70mph (113kph), but even regular models for hire at your local marina are impressively nippy.

You can use a jet ski to explore rivers, gain a whale's-eye view of shipping in the harbour, travel from island or ship to shore, for fishing, even to tow waterskiers (with the use of a 'spotter' passenger). They can be used for longer trips and even go across the sea. However, jet skis are banned in many places due to the noise, the risk of oil pollution, and the danger to swimmers and other water users. You must therefore always check with the relevant authorities before using one.

HAPPY MEMORIES?

You'll probably never forget your first jet ski experience. The wonder of being able to go in any direction at top speed is breathtaking.

WHAT SHOULD I BE WORRIED ABOUT?

There are dangers both to you and other water users (see warning box). The scary thing is how much fun jet skiing is. You could lose yourself and wind up miles offshore on a machine that can easily break down, get damaged or run out of fuel. Then you're in trouble; maybe drifting towards rocks or in a shipping lane without lights, flares or radio. Up a creek, in fact, and there are no paddles on a jet ski.

WHERE DO I START?

You can experience jet skiing in many marinas and watersports centres. There has been an attempt in recent years to regulate jet ski use and stop people using them recklessly. The RYA offers a one-day training course in launching, safety, navigation, speed handling and care, for £130.

WHO CAN DO IT?

The minimum age to use a jet ski is 12, although those aged between 12 and 16 must be supervised and have the correct insurance.

WHAT SHOULD I TAKE?

A life jacket is essential.

WHAT WILL IT COST?

A new Jet ski or PWC costs at least £8,000, while rental is from £40 for half an hour.

CAMPFIRE GOSSIP

The Seabreacher (right) is an astonishing craft that looks like a dolphin and performs like a submarine and jet ski. The rider and a passenger sit inside, and the craft can submerge to a depth of 5 feet (1.5m) for up to 20 seconds (longer with a specially fitted snorkel). Yet because the Seabreacher dives only with the momentum of its own 45mph (72kph) speed, it always pops up to the surface when depowered. It costs £30,000, but must surely be the next thing in jet skis.

CONTACTS

- Cornwall Waverunner Safaris: ☎ 01208-863396, 🖳 www.cornwallwaverunnersafaris.co.uk

- Exelement: 🖳 www.exelement.co.uk/water/jet-skiing

- Jetski Safaris: ☎ 01202-706784, 🖳 www.jetskisafaris.co.uk

- Jetskier magazine: 🖳 www.jetskier.co.uk

- Maritime & Coastguard Agency: ☎ 02380-329100, 🖳 www.mcga.gov.uk

ON WATER

FLOAT TUBING/ RIVER BUGGING

CONTACTS

- British Float Tube Association:
  ☎ 07831-512008,
  🖳 www.bfta.org.uk

- Equipment: 🖳 www.wildwater.
  co.nz, www.riverbug.info,
  www.trailhead.ca/riverbug

- Organisers: ☎ 08450-178177,
  🖳 www.naelimits.co.uk,
  ☎ 01887-829706, 🖳 www.
  rafting.co.uk/bug.htm

ᗡᑎ AT A GLANCE

Accessibility Index: ❶❷❸❹⑤

Fitness level: ❶②③④⑤

Degree of Difficulty: ❶②③④⑤

White-knuckle rating: ❶❷❸④⑤

Equipment: hire or medium cost

Season: summer

Family friendly: ✓

Confident swimmer: ✓

It's floating down a river, fast or slow depending on the one you choose, bobbing along like a cork. Although people have been doing this for decades in old tractor inner tubes, the action adventure industry has now got in on the act, called 'river bugging' (invented in New Zealand) which uses a purpose-made craft called a river bug. Fly-fishermen have also realised the potential of getting closer to the fish, so you can now buy high-tech, super-strength tubes with seat attachments and multiple pockets.

Traditionally though, you choose a wide slow river and meander gently. Without the splashing of paddles and oars, fish, water voles and even otters are more likely to ignore your presence, making it a wonderful way to get close to wildlife in their own neck of the woods. It's a low impact activity that takes nothing from the river and won't even upset fishermen on the bank (except when you go blundering through their lines).

In America, where the sport grew up, people take a spare tube to hold beer, coke, sandwiches, towel, suntan lotion, iPad, Kindle... You steer by paddling with your hands, or by using flippers on your feet, but it isn't really about steering, you just go with the flow. A life jacket is always advisable, no matter how calm it is; if nothing else, it will give you more confidence.

If the river is tidal, you'll need to check tide tables to ensure that you end up going in the direction you intended. If you're doing it independently, you'll

POPULAR LOCATIONS

Southeast: River Arun, Sussex.

Southwest: River Tamar, Devon/Cornwall.

Central: River Welland, Lincolnshire.

North: River Ure, Yorkshire.

Wales: River Wye.

Scotland: River Spey.

need someone at the other end to pick you up, or face a long trudge back along the river bank.

WHERE DO I START?

You can buy tractor inner tubes on the internet or at agricultural suppliers. Organised River Bugging activities cost around £50, but for that you can buy your own 48in (122cm) inner tube. Special fly-fishing tubes cost around £300. A basic riverbug weighs 15lbs (7kg) and costs from around £600.

CAMPFIRE GOSSIP

Texas has banned the use of large iceboxes of beer being carried on its rivers and limited 'toobers' to no more than two toobs each.

ON WATER

📝 CONTACTS

- Cornwall storm-watching weekends: 🖥 www.headlandhotel.co.uk
- Met Office: 🖥 www.metoffice.gov.uk
- Maritime and Coastguard Agency: 🖥 www.mcga.gov.uk
- Weather: 🖥 www.metcheck.com

STORM WATCHING

 **AT A GLANCE**

Accessibility Index: ❶❷❸❹⑤

Fitness level: ❶②③④⑤

Degree of Difficulty: ❶②③④⑤

White-knuckle rating: ❶❷❸④⑤

Equipment: none

Season: autumn & winter

Disability friendly: ✓

Family friendly: ✓

Olympic swimming pools-sized walls of water whacking into sea defences, trees straining to stay upright, lightning turning pitch black to a flash of electric white – what's not to love? Storm watching teaches you to read the signs of British weather – the cloud formations, wind directions, red skies in the mornings – and lets you witness one of the greatest shows on earth. The artist JMW Turner once had himself lashed to the mast of a ship so he could witness the full power of a storm. Whereas quiet walks along the seashore gazing at sunsets can lead to introspection and melancholy, the power of a storm will blow away your mental cobwebs, and the calm afterwards is nice also.

Planning a storm-watching trip needn't be a total guessing game. Our weather is so well recorded that patterns, or singularities, are fairly predictable. For example, the 23rd and 24th September is a busy time for gales, late November to 12th December brings cyclonic systems, and there are many more.

Book a seaside weekend away at one of those times, or try a known stormy area – names like Cape Wrath (Scottish Highlands) are a dead giveaway – perhaps in a lighthouse or croft, or a comfy seaside hotel. A week's winter rental of a lighthouse costs from £210. The four-star Headland Hotel in Newquay costs from £75 per person per night in winter.

Storm watching is exciting for the kids and you won't even need to buy them an ice-cream or popcorn. However, a look at seaside webcams and coastguard warnings can save a disappointing trip, only to find calm seas.

WHALE WATCHING

👓 AT A GLANCE

Accessibility Index: ❶❷❸④⑤

Fitness level: ❶②③④⑤

Degree of Difficulty: ❶②③④⑤

White-knuckle rating: ❶❷❸④⑤

Equipment: none

Season: summer

Disability friendly: ✓

Family friendly: ✓

📝 CONTACTS

- Basking Shark Project:
  ☎ 01752-672020,
  🖥 www.baskingsharks.org

- Cornwall Wildlife Trust:
  ☎ 01872-273939, 🖥 www.cornwallwildlifetrust.org.uk

- Seawatch Foundation:
  ☎ 0845-202 3892, 🖥 www.seawatchfoundation.org.uk

- Whale and Dolphin Conservation Society:
  ☎ 01249-449500,
  🖥 www.wdcs.org

The largest living creatures on the planet, blue whales, were photographed off the Irish coast recently, and the second-largest, the fin whale, have been seen off Pembrokeshire. A pod of 50 killer whales have surrounded nervous Scottish fishermen, and 33 pilot whales hurled themselves onto a beach in Donegal. Maybe it's global warming, but the sea's largest creatures do appear to be coming calling more often, and you can meet them halfway.

You'll sometimes see whales, dolphins and basking sharks from the seashore – and conservationists say this is by far the best way to see them – but it's more exciting to get among them in a boat. On an organised trip, your guide will explain the 30 different kinds of whale and dolphin in British waters, so even if you don't see any, your trip won't have been wasted. Commercial whale watching trips cost from £25, or day-long excursions from £70. However, not all whale-watching trips are good for the whales, therefore it's advisable to check the operator's credentials with the Whale and Dolphin Conservation Society (see **Contacts**).

You could also do some research into their summer visiting habits and organise your own trip, maybe paddling out in a sea kayak, for example, to see the bottlenose dolphins in Cardigan Bay or the basking sharks off Cornwall (there were more than 500 sightings each month in summer 2010). Few things in nature match the thrill of a whale's tail rising languidly above your little kayak, or the dorsal fins of nosy pilot whales swimming over to sniff you out.

ON WATER

CONTACTS

- Thames Skiff Hire: ☎ 01932-232433, 🖥 www.skiffhire.com
- Oxford River Cruises: ☎ 0845-226 9396, 🖥 www.oxfordrivercruises.com

SKIFF CAMPING

A skiff is a long wooden rowing boat that's been used on the Thames for some 200 years. People love them because they're beautiful mahogany and leather crafts, which handily convert to a tent at night (or when it rains) with a detachable canvas awning and a double bed which folds out so you can make a weekend trip of it. In the 1889 novel, *Three Men in a Boat*, three witty men and a dog did just that.

Skiffs are still available to hire on the Thames for less than £400 per week, complete with awning, beds, bedding and a stove. You power the skiff by 'sculling', which is what rowing is called when you hold both oars instead of one, though there's often also a sail you can put up. You'll probably be doing what's known as the 'Thames Meander' – a relaxing trip enjoying the pubs, cafes and historical sites between Kingston and Oxford, maybe trying to catch a fish (but not too hard), and cooking and camping by the riverbank. The best part, and it will feel pretty adventurous when you're doing it, is settling down for the night in your gently rocking skiff.

7
IN
WATER

- ❖ Canyoning
- ❖ Gorge Walking/ Ghyll Scrambling
- ❖ Coasteering
- ❖ Wild Swimming
- ❖ Scuba Diving
- ❖ Snorkelling
- ❖ Freediving
- ❖ Cliff Jumping

If you live on a relatively damp island, you may as well have fun getting wet. There are numerous ways to enjoy a wet and wonderful time, with new adventures such as canyoning and coasteering, or reclaiming old pleasures with a 'wild' swim in our many beautiful coves, rivers and lakes.

Warning!

Most water sports have strict safety regulations – not imposed by Health & Safety but formulated by experts and organisers – people who are acutely aware of the dangers. With few exceptions, most of the activities in this chapter should never be attempted by novices without the supervision of a qualified and licensed organiser who knows the local area and vagaries of the weather, and who provides all the necessary safety equipment.

CANYONING

AT A GLANCE

Accessibility Index: ❶❷❸❹⑤

Fitness level: ❶❷❸④⑤

Degree of Difficulty: ❶❷③④⑤

White-knuckle rating: ❶❷❸❹⑤

Equipment: hire or low cost

Season: year round

Family friendly: ✓

Confident swimmer: ✓

Remember the scene from *Butch Cassidy and the Sundance Kid*, when they jump into the canyon to escape the law? "Why are you crazy? The jump'll probably kill you." Welcome to canyoning…

It's white-water rafting without a raft; extreme Pooh sticks and you're the stick. Canyoning is the crazier cousin of gorge walking, an adrenalin-soaked action sport where you virtually give yourself up to the elements and hope for the best. Canyoning (or canyoneering in the US), developed in America's 'slot' canyons

– deep, narrow and carved out of rock by the power of fast-flowing water. Are you beginning to see why it's so dangerous? The South Africans know it as 'kloofing', perhaps because that's the noise you make when you hit a submerged rock.

WHAT EXACTLY WILL I BE DOING?

You'll be wearing a wetsuit, helmet and life jacket, and leaping into a fast-flowing mountain stream. You bodysurf and swim down the rapids, sliding through narrow gulleys and dropping into pools. Whenever possible, canyoners like to jump from cliffs into deep pools of water. Sound easy? Wait until you do it; 30ft (9m) looks a lot higher when you're standing up there. In the water, the buoyancy of your suit and life jacket should keep you safe (unless you're sucked into a pothole), and also helps to cushion you from the buffeting by rocks as you career along. These streams are formed from melted snow so they're breathtakingly cold, but you should feel warm enough in your wetsuit. You may also need climbing or at least bouldering skills to get out of a steep-sided canyon.

WHAT SHOULD I BE WORRIED ABOUT?

Canyoning can be dangerous (18 people died in a canyoning accident in Switzerland in 1999). There are obvious inherent dangers of being in cold, deep, fast-flowing water cascading over rocks and submerged obstacles. Added to which, the source of the water may be many miles away, so if there's a sudden cloudburst far away or a naturally occurring dam collapses, a wall of water could be following you down. For these reasons, canyoning should only be done with a qualified and licensed operator who knows the area well and provides all the necessary safety equipment.

HAPPY MEMORIES?

Perhaps the single most daring thing you can do in the world is to go over Niagara Falls in a barrel. That will just get you arrested, these days, but canyoning is the next best thing. You won't have time to enjoy the view or think about the cold – you'll be busy worrying about the next waterfall or rapid – but it's an activity you won't forget in a hurry!

WHERE DO I START?

Beginners will need to sign up at an outdoor centre on one of Britain's relatively few white water rivers, as this isn't one to try at home. However, you can get in the mood by trying coasteering or gorge walking (see pages 204 and 201) and work your way up to the more extreme canyons.

IN WATER

POPULAR LOCATIONS

North: Esk, Eskdale, Lake District.

Wales: Aberdyfi, Gwynedd.

Scotland: Falls of Bruar, near Pitlochry.

CONTACTS

- British Mountaineering Council: ☎ 0161-445 6111, 🖳 www.thebmc.co.uk

- Canyoneers: 🖳 www.canyoneers.co.uk

- Organisers: 🖳 www.callofthewild.co.uk, www.canyoning.co.uk, www.naelimits.co.uk

WHO CAN DO IT?

You must be aged over 16, be fit and have the strength to pull yourself out of the water.

WHAT SHOULD I TAKE?

The activity centre will provide you with a wetsuit, helmet and life jacket.

WHAT WILL IT COST?

From £40 for a half day.

CAMPFIRE GOSSIP

Canyoning appeals to people like Aron Ralston. It was while climbing through a dry canyon in 2003 in Utah that Ralston got his hand trapped under a boulder and had to break it, then cut it off with a cheap, dull knife (aaargh!). His autobiography, *Between a Rock and a Hard Place*, was made into an acclaimed film, *127 Hours* (2010), starring James Franco and directed by Danny Boyle.

GORGE WALKING/ GHYLL SCRAMBLING

AT A GLANCE

Accessibility Index: ❶❷❸❹⑤

Fitness level: ❶❷❸④⑤

Degree of Difficulty: ❶②③④⑤

White-knuckle rating: ❶❷❸④⑤

Equipment: hire or low cost

Season: autumn to spring (and after heavy rain)

Family friendly: ✓

Confident swimmer: ✓

You're following a watercourse or stream, usually through mountainous countryside or forest. However, with gorge walking, aka ghyll scrambling (similar to Canyoning above), you walk in the stream, not on the bank. In tame, slow-moving streams you could do it yourself, just by putting on a pair of old trainers and being willing to get them wet. For faster-flowing rivers with waterfalls and rock pools, you should join an organised trip with full safety equipment such as lifejackets, helmets and wetsuits. Above all, you need to equip yourself with a try-anything-once state of mind and get off the path into the water.

WHAT EXACTLY WILL I BE DOING?

You'll be walking and climbing along the watercourse of a stream through the hills, going either upstream or down. You'll be climbing over moss-laden boulders, scrambling up and down muddy banks and wading through rock pools. There may also be some basic climbing or abseiling, but your guide will match the course to the participants' fitness and abilities, so a family with youngsters can follow a smaller, gentler stream than, for example, a stag party outing. For everyone, the highlight is getting up close and personal with the waterfalls. Some you can jump straight off, into the rock pool below, while others you can slither down – or scramble up, all with thousands of gallons of water cascading down around you, filling your ears and half blinding you. Sounds like fun…

IN WATER

POPULAR LOCATIONS

Southwest: River Erme, Devon.

Central: Peak District, Derbyshire.

North: Keswick, Lake District, Cumbria.

Wales: Bala, Snowdonia.

Scotland: Glen Feshie, Inverness-shire.

WHAT SHOULD I BE WORRIED ABOUT?

Even small streams hold hidden dangers and the risk of flash flooding, therefore novices should only do it under the guidance of experienced and qualified organisers with the correct safety equipment. Some gorge walking trips include caving: a unique combination of terrors as you follow the torrent down a pothole into a cave system.

HAPPY MEMORIES?

A walk in the hills is always nice, but with gorge walking you're up to your neck in the British countryside, and very cold it can be too. At first it will feel odd to be in the water instead of walking beside the river like any 'normal' person, but once you're thoroughly wet, and confident that your life preserver will keep you afloat, you can start to enjoy the incredible sensation of being closer to nature than you've probably ever been before.

WHERE DO I START?

You can book with an organised group or you can just follow a likely looking stream and walk in the water where safe, following it on a (waterproof) map.

WHEN'S THE BEST TIME FOR IT?

Any time. Spring is likely to have melting snow boosting the level of mountain streams, but you'll need a wetsuit.

WHO CAN DO IT?

Anyone confident in the water, though most activity centres have a minimum age of eight.

WHAT SHOULD I TAKE?

Walking boots or trainers with a good sole. The centre will provide a wetsuit and helmet.

WHAT WILL IT COST?

Around £30 for a two- to four-hour hike with a professional organiser, including safety equipment.

CAMPFIRE GOSSIP

Escaped fugitives attempting to evade capture by walking along a watercourse are usually wasting their time, slowing themselves down and also getting uncomfortably wet socks. Bloodhounds can detect as few as one or two human cells left in the air that you've walked through.

 **CONTACTS**

- British Mountaineering Council: ☎ 0161-445 6111, 🖥 www.thebmc.co.uk

- Organisers: 🖥 www.adventuremakers.co.uk, www.gorgewalkingwales.com, www.riverdeepmountainhigh.co.uk

IN WATER

COASTEERING

👓 AT A GLANCE

Accessibility Index: ❶❷❸❹⑤

Fitness level: ❶❷❸④⑤

Degree of Difficulty: ❶❷③④⑤

White-knuckle rating: ❶❷❸❹⑤

Equipment: hire or medium cost

Season: year round

Confident swimmer: ✓

Quite recently, adventurous people came to realise that if you're wearing a wetsuit, helmet and life jacket, you can pretty well jump into any body of water and, all being well, not drown. Coasteering has been described as a combination of climbing and drowning. It was developed in Wales in the late '80s and is already a major activity-centre money-spinner and a wonderful way to visit parts of the coastline that you'd never normally get to, and meet the sea life that lives there. It can certainly be dangerous, what with riptides, the freezing cold of British seawaters and large waves dashing you against sharp rocks. Which is why you should only do it with a Health and Safety Executive (HSE) certified activity centre (or a member of the International Coasteering Association)

until you're experienced and confident enough to go it alone.

WHAT EXACTLY WILL I BE DOING?

You take a bit of rugged coastline and traverse the 'intertidal zone' – the bit between low and high tides – as best you can. These being rocky coastlines with no path, you'll be scrambling over boulders, creeping along rocky ledges, and where the rocks end and sea starts you just have to jump in, possibly from quite a height. Large periods of coasteering are spent in the water – hence the wetsuit – you may even have to swim underwater to enter submerged tunnel entrances, and all while the swell and waves are pushing you against the rocks or dragging you out.

Britain has plenty of sea life, and you can easily find yourself coasteering among communities of sunbathing seals or swimming with bottlenose dolphins. But instead of just watching them from a boat you're in their backyard, close up and personal. Most sessions last around three hours, followed by a beachside barbecue, where you may even be able to eat the shellfish you collected on the way.

WHAT SHOULD I BE WORRIED ABOUT?

The jumps are what most people remember. They look so simple from the water, just a little step off the ledge and a gentle float to a splashy landing. So you clamber out of the water and climb up the cliff. You walk to the edge, a bit breathless now, and suddenly the world looks very different…

HAPPY MEMORIES?

Your first entry into the water may be a shock as the cold water slides down inside your wetsuit, but the sensation of floating in your life jacket while expending little energy, compared to swimming, feels so liberating that you may find yourself smiling. As you realise you aren't going to drown, so you start to appreciate the incredible viewpoint and your close proximity to nature.

WHERE DO I START?

Contact a coastal activity centre (see **Contacts**).

WHERE CAN IT LEAD?

If you like jumping into the sea, swap the small steps in coasteering for the giant leaps in cliff jumping (see page 217).

IN WATER

POPULAR LOCATIONS

Southeast: Seven Sisters Country Park, Sussex.

Southwest: Polzeath, Cornwall.

North: Robin Hood's Bay, North Yorkshire.

Wales: St David's Peninsula, Pembrokeshire.

Scotland: Portknockie.

CONTACTS

- British Coasteering Federation: ☎ 01637-878743, 🖳 www.british coasteeringfederation.co.uk.

- Organisers: 🖳 www.coasteering.com, www.coasteering.org

WHO CAN DO IT?

You can coasteer at any age once you're confident in the water and able to clamber over rocks. You don't even need to be a great swimmer (depending on conditions), as the life jacket will keep you afloat. However, all activity centres have a lower age limit.

WHAT SHOULD I TAKE?

All safety equipment should be provided, but take a swimsuit for under the wetsuit, and trainers.

WHAT WILL IT COST?

From £30 for a half day.

WILD SWIMMING

 **AT A GLANCE**

Accessibility Index: ❶❷❸❹❺

Fitness level: ❶②③④⑤

Degree of Difficulty: ❶②③④⑤

White-knuckle rating: ❶❷③④⑤

Equipment: none

Season: year round

Disability friendly: ✓

Family friendly: ✓

Confident swimmer: ✓

The forces of adventurous good sense are taking on the Health and Safety industry, and the battlegrounds are Britain's rivers, lakes and sea. Swimmers are freeing themselves from the shackles of lane swimming and chlorinated council baths, and diving into natural waters where people have swum for centuries. Wild swimming isn't *that* wild – you don't have to be one of those 'loonies' breaking the ice in winter, and you can wear a swimming costume, even a wetsuit. Between the wars, there were hundreds of outdoor swimming clubs, yet Britain's waterways are much cleaner now – the cleanest they've been for generations – with otters and beavers returning. Some of the clubs are also now reforming, and it's a more sociable way of swimming.

WHAT EXACTLY WILL I BE DOING?

Despite all your good intentions before you got there, standing on the riverbank or lakeside you may not want to go in. The water can suddenly look a bit cold and brown, with glimpses of furtive movements below, and you don't really fancy it. But do it anyway. Dive in, and once you've done a couple of strokes to get rid of the chill, you'll start to relax and take a look at the riverbank from an entirely new viewpoint. If you've taken a dog with you, this is where it will be looking down at you quizzically, head to one side, poring at the bank and whining, perhaps wondering whether it'll be required to rescue you.

Now you can start striking out with some proper strokes; breaststroke lets you see more. Swim round a couple of bends in the river, and you'll start to feel like you're on a proper expedition,

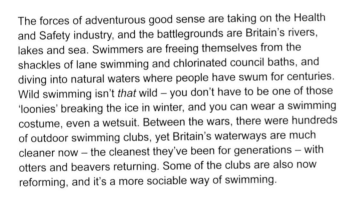

IN WATER

POPULAR LOCATIONS

Southeast: River Ouse, above Barcombe Mills, Sussex.

Southwest: Claverton Weir, near Bristol.

Central: River Cam, Grantchester, near Cambridge.

North: High Dam, Cumbria.

Wales: Cenarth Pools, River Teifi.

Scotland: Fairy Pools, Skye.

as well as getting some great exercise. Some wild swimmers opt for a wetsuit. It's far from essential (unless the water is freezing), but it aids buoyancy, keeps you warm and helps to avoid jellyfish stings at sea and nettle stings alongside rivers. The worst part is getting out – it's amazing how after just a few minutes, you start to feel quite aquatic again, and now you have to get your clothes on while standing in a field with muddy toes.

HAPPY MEMORIES?

Places where you've swum will have particular memories for you, as if by getting in the water semi-naked you've crossed a great divide and established a connection with them. Walk along a river bank and you'll barely register its presence, but get into the water and you'll know every overhanging branch intimately.

WHAT SHOULD I BE WORRIED ABOUT?

A few precautions can help avoid problems. Check the cleanliness of the water on the environment agency website. Don't enter water that smells, and in warm, dry conditions when water levels are low, cover any wounds with a plaster; don't put your head under water too much and don't swallow the water. In

cold water, hold your nose when jumping in to avoid cold water hitting your brain (yes, really). Never swim after drinking alcohol – but keep the brandy handy for a nip afterwards.

WHERE DO I START?

The book *Waterlog* by Roger Deakin inspired many wild swimmers to get in for the first time, and experience what he called 'a frog's eye view' of the world. Once suitably inspired, pick your spot, somewhere easy and accessible, and take a friend to offer moral support and hand you a towel when you get out.

WHERE CAN IT LEAD?

As your confidence in the water improves, you could start free diving (see below) to get some depth, or coasteering (see above) to add waves and even bouldering (see page 227) to really spice things up.

WHO CAN DO IT?

Anyone, including the elderly, the disabled, children, even toddlers under close supervision, should be given the chance to splash about.

WHAT SHOULD I TAKE?

What you wear – from nothing to a full 5mm wetsuit – will depend on you, but take something warming to drink afterwards, and a chunk or two of chocolate tastes especially great after a swim.

WHAT WILL IT COST?

A wetsuit jacket costs from £35, but otherwise wild swimming costs nothing.

CAMPFIRE GOSSIP

Virginia Woolf used to swim in the River Cam in Grantchester and said the water tasted of 'mint and mud', but in a good way.

CONTACTS

- The Environment Agency: www.environment-agency.gov.uk
- The Outdoor Swimming Society: www.outdoorswimmingsociety.com
- River and Lake Swimming Association: www.river-swimming.co.uk
- Swimming Holes Wales: www.swimming-holes-wales.org.uk
- Wild Swimming: www.wildswimming.co.uk

IN WATER

SCUBA DIVING

 **AT A GLANCE**

Accessibility Index: ❶❷❸④⑤

Fitness level: ❶❷③④⑤

Degree of Difficulty: ❶❷❸❹⑤

White-knuckle rating: ❶❷❸④⑤

Equipment: hire or high cost

Season: year round

Disability friendly: ✓

Confident swimmer: ✓

Space is for dreamers; for most of us, deep water is the final frontier. You aren't just floating in an alien world with incredible wildlife – you are the wildlife. Scuba is one activity that you definitely can't do untrained or alone. It stands for self-contained underwater breathing apparatus, and involves swimming with your own tank of compressed air on your back. The lower depth limit for most recreational divers is 130ft (40m), at which you can see many wrecks off the British coast, but there are several purpose-built quarry dives for beginners. It's one of the most popular adventure sports in the UK, with two million dives made by Britons annually.

WHAT EXACTLY WILL I BE DOING?

You start off in a swimming pool and with a textbook. In the pool you learn to breathe through the apparatus, clear your mask, work with a 'buddy' and get used to controlling the occasional panicky feelings you may get. Before hitting the open water, there's also some theory to learn to avoid getting 'the bends' from surfacing too fast, or nitrogen poisoning that could take you to a watery (if intensely relaxed) end. Then you're ready for water, usually somewhere like Stoney Cove, the National Diving Centre, located in an infamously chilly quarry in Leicestershire which goes down to over 130ft (40m), and has wrecks such as helicopters and boats submerged at various depths. It's weird and exciting to see everyday objects in this bluey-green alien world.

Once qualified, however, you can start going out to sea and then onto wrecks, where it gets really interesting. When a shoal of fish moves out of your way and you see the deck and railings,

a porthole or even a gun barrel appearing out of the gloom, it's an incredible experience. If you can dive in the cold and sometimes murky waters of Britain, you can dive almost anywhere.

WHAT SHOULD I BE WORRIED ABOUT?

Sometimes when you're 130ft down, it suddenly occurs to you how much water there is above you. This can be worrying, but don't panic. Decompression sickness – the bends – is where you surface too quickly and gases in your body and blood start to bubble. Combined with drowning, it kills several British divers each year, but most risks can be eradicated by following the correct procedures. It's worth remembering the oft-quoted: 'There are old divers and there are bold divers, but there are no old bold divers.'

HAPPY MEMORIES?

You're in a weightless and near-silent world, with just the sound of your breathing and the bubbling from your respirator. Strange and incredible creatures come in and out of view – close up but unafraid of you. You can move where you like in three dimensions, powered by large fins and kept warm by your wetsuit. Being at home underwater is a privilege that our ancestors might have dreamt of, but only recent generations have been able to have a weekend like this.

WHERE DO I START?

Contact the very pro-active BSAC for details of local clubs and courses.

IN WATER

POPULAR LOCATIONS

Southeast: Wraysbury, Middlesex; ☎ 01784-488007,
🖥 www.wraysbury.ws.

Southwest: Vobster Quay Diving Centre, near Frome;
🖥 www.vobster.com.

Central: National Diving Centre at Stoney Cove;
🖥 www.stoneycove.co.uk.

North: Capernwray Quarry, Lancashire; ☎ 01524-735132,
🖥 www.dive-site.co.uk.

Wales: National Diving and Activity Centre, Chepstow;
☎ 01291-630046, 🖥 www.ndac.co.uk.

Scotland: Wreck diving off the Isle of Mull;
🖥 www.ukdiving.co.uk.

CONTACTS

- British Sub-Aqua Club:
  🖥 www.bsac.com
- Gap Year Diver:
  🖥 www.gapyeardiver.com
- The National Diving & Activity
  Centre: 🖥 www.ndac.co.uk
- Professional Association of
  Diving Instructors (PADI):
  🖥 www.padi.com/scuba
- Sub-Aqua Association:
  🖥 www.saa.org.uk
- UK Divers:
  🖥 www.ukdivers.com
- UK Diving:
  🖥 www.ukdiving.co.uk

WHERE CAN IT LEAD?

Night diving is an amazing thrill, as close to a space walk as most of us will ever get. Indeed, it's better than space, because here the bright light of your torch will pick out curious fish coming to have a look at you.

WHO CAN DO IT?

Children can start from the age of eight in a pool or from ten in open water down to 40ft (12m), but many local clubs don't accept children until the age of 16.

WHAT SHOULD I TAKE?

For a first pool session, just swimming togs and a tee-shirt.

WHAT WILL IT COST?

BSAC offer a trial session for £29, and some clubs offer pool sessions from just £15. PADI (see below) also offers a variety of courses from trial sessions to full training, including e-learning. Training to be fully-qualified costs around £200 over four or five days.

CAMPFIRE GOSSIP

It's weird the things that survive in the water. Rubber boots lying next to each other by a wreck tell a horrible story; they're unlikely to have floated down and landed so close together unless someone was wearing them at the time. Many wrecks are official war graves, so check before diving to on wartime wrecks.

SNORKELLING

 **AT A GLANCE**

Accessibility Index: ❶❷❸❹⑤

Fitness level: ❶❷③④⑤

Degree of Difficulty: ❶❷③④⑤

White-knuckle rating: ❶❷❸④⑤

Equipment: low cost

Season: year round

Disability friendly: ✓

Family friendly: ✓

Confident swimmer: ✓

There's more to snorkelling than you might think. You can use weight-belts to submerge quicker, floatation devices to support you on the surface, and a few simple breathing exercises will vastly increase your time at depth. Snorkelling is a relatively natural way to be in the water, but try it on the beach with a cheap set from the beachball shop and you may get frustrated with seeing little from the surface. Learning to snorkel properly, however, takes just a few minutes and enables you to dive deeper and longer, investigate the seabed at a depth of up to 100ft (30m) and interact with the sealife you meet there. It's a perfect activity for all the family, and disabled people can snorkel as well as anybody else.

WHAT EXACTLY WILL I BE DOING?

It's important to get lessons in snorkelling if you're hoping to reach a good depth safely. After just a few deep-breathing exercises you should be able to hold your breath for 60 to 90 seconds, but using a good diving technique will also help. As well as a mask, snorkel and flippers, in UK waters you'll need a wetsuit, and because these are naturally buoyant, you'll also need a weightbelt. A snorkelling jacket is invaluable; it's a slim-line life-jacket that you just put a puff of air into in order to keep you afloat between dives. The essence of successful snorkelling, and freediving, is using very few movements. Flailing around will frighten the fish and use up energy. Therefore it's all slow, languid strokes and a dolphin-like kick with both legs.

IN WATER

POPULAR LOCATIONS

Southeast: Wraysbury Dive Centre, Middlesex.

Southwest: Wreck of the Louis Shield, Thurlestone, Devon.

Central: Stoney Cove, Leicestershire.

North: Coniston Water, Cumbria.

Wales: Llŷn Peninsula, Gwynedd.

Scotland: The Caves, Loch Long.

That may go out the window though, when you come face-to-face with your first dolphin or seal. Without all the encumbrances of scuba equipment, you'll be more nimble, able to play with them, and they also have to come up to the surface for air.

WHAT SHOULD I BE WORRIED ABOUT?

Diving is about conquering panic and fear, and knowing exactly when to surface. Divers sometimes get a build up of nitrogen, which is like being drunk – the 'rapture of the deep' –or hyperventilate and pass out, which is why it's advisable to always dive in pairs or larger groups. You should also always learn with a qualified trainer such as PADI or BSAC.

HAPPY MEMORIES?

Fish, baby seals and dolphins will be fascinated by you. You can swim to wrecks or investigate ancient submerged ruins. This isn't swimming lengths in a dreary council pool – this is snorkelling. And it's free.

WHERE DO I START?

Contact your local BSAC club. Most scuba diving centres also offer snorkelling courses or will find a course and instructor for you.

WHERE CAN IT LEAD?

Freediving (see page 216) may seem a terrifying prospect, but with a little practice, virtually anyone can hold their breath and dive deep.

WHEN'S THE BEST TIME FOR IT?

With a thick enough wetsuit you can snorkel in winter, but the most pleasant season is summer.

WHO CAN DO IT?

BSAC courses for children start at around the age of six.

WHAT SHOULD I TAKE?

You can start with just a mask and snorkel, but for the best experience you'll need flippers, weightbelt, wetsuit and a buoyancy jacket. Most dive centres will provide everything you need.

CAMPFIRE GOSSIP

The word snorkel comes from the German *schnoerkel*, meaning snout, and was first used by German U-boats in 1944. They were long air tubes that the submerged submarines could extend above the surface to get some fresh air into the sub without the risk of surfacing.

 # CONTACTS

- Bog Snorkelling:
  www.bogsnorkelling.com

- British Sub-Aqua Club:
  www.bsac.com

- PADI: www.padi.com/scuba

- Snorkeling UK:
  www.snorkeling.co.uk

IN WATER

FREEDIVING

You may not know it, but you're in possession of a 'mammalian diving reflex' which means that when your face touches cold water (below 21°C/70°F), your metabolism slows down to conserve oxygen and energy. With a little training, you can learn to hold your breath for longer than you imagine, and reach depths scuba divers can only dream of.

Freedivers do it for the freedom to dive deeper without the need for tedious decompression stops on the way back up. They're lightweight and nimble, with either super-long powerful fins, or a single giant flipper (or monofin, to be technical) that makes them look like mermaids, powering through the water with slow, powerful flicks of the hips in a graceful style that doesn't scare the fish. Spearfishing is possible, using a harpoon or even a conventional spear, and is the most ethical way to catch fish to eat.

The world depth record on a single breath is 214m (700ft) for men and 160m (524ft) for women, using a weighted trolley (sled and lift bag) to take you down fast. However, the UK record is held by Jim Lawless, who in 2010 reached a depth of 101m (331ft) on a single breath lasting 2 minutes and 7 seconds.

CLIFF JUMPING

 **AT A GLANCE**

Accessibility Index: ❶❷③④⑤

Fitness level: ❶❷③④⑤

Degree of Difficulty: ❶❷③④⑤

White-knuckle rating: ❶❷❸❹❺

Equipment: none

Season: year round

Confident swimmer: ✓

Cliff jumping is the art, science and sport of jumping off a cliff into deep water, as approached in a sober, sensible way. It isn't to be confused with tombstoning, where people get drunk and jump off a cliff, often with disastrous results (the major 'obstacles' are shallow waters and rocks). They look similar, but the people cliff jumping will be wearing safety equipment such as a wetsuit, and will have learnt cliff jumping from professionals, perhaps as part of a coasteering or canyoning session (see page 198). Once you've learnt the technique, you can find your own favourite jumping places, but you should never jump alone, however experienced you are.

For a jump of more than 30ft (9.5m), you'll need 15ft (4.5m) depth of water. Look out for currents and don't forget that you also need to be able to get out of the water – so jumping where there are sheer vertical cliffs for miles around isn't such a good idea. Above all, never jump after drinking alcohol; the endorphins and adrenalin rush you'll experience before and after a jump is addictive anyway. Start with a low jump – it won't feel low – of around five feet, learning to enter the water straight and vertical with hands by your side and your buttocks 'tight'.

Warning!

Cliff jumping can be extremely dangerous, and should only be attempted under the supervision and guidance of a licensed operator. Many reckless people die or are seriously injured doing it (i.e. tombstoning) each year. **Don't try this at home!**

IN WATER

POPULAR LOCATIONS

Southwest: Lulworth Cove, Dorset.

Wales: The Blue Lagoon, Pembrokeshire.

Scotland: Falls of Bruar, near Pitlochry, Perthshire.

 **CONTACTS**

- Go Bananas:
  🖥 www.gobananas.co.uk

- Tombstoning:
  🖥 http://tombstoning.com

- Travel Scotland:
  🖥 www.scotland.org.uk

Now you can build up height. From 10ft (3m), you'll hit the water at 17mph (27kph), but from 50ft (15m), you'll hit at almost 40mph (64kph). Over 70ft (21m) doing it wrong will break your back - and don't forget that many people use jumping off heights into water as a way of ending it all…

8

CLIMBING

- ❖ Climbing Wall
- ❖ Rock Climbing
- ❖ Bouldering
- ❖ Abseiling
- ❖ Rap Running
- ❖ Via Ferrata
- ❖ Caving & Potholing
- ❖ Cave Diving
- ❖ High-Ropes/Zip Wire
- ❖ Tree Climbing
- ❖ Aquaseiling
- ❖ Ice Climbing

"Because it's there." said a Cheshire schoolteacher, when asked why he was planning to climb Mt Everest. George Mallory learnt to love climbing in the Lake District, just one of many serious climbing areas in Britain, while for beginners there are climbing walls, boulders, trees, caves and cliffs in every corner of the land.

CLIMBING WALL

 **AT A GLANCE**

Accessibility Index: ❶❷❸❹❺

Fitness level: ❶❷❸④⑤

Degree of Difficulty: ❶❷③④⑤

White-knuckle rating: ❶❷❸④⑤

Equipment: low cost

Season: year round

Disability friendly: ✓

Family friendly: ✓

Weight restriction: ✓

There are hundreds of climbing walls in the UK, both commercially-operated sites (indoors and outdoors), and bouldering (see page 227) walls in leisure centres and children's playgrounds. They are invaluable for getting young people interested in climbing, learning holds and building strength in the right places – but they're useful for anyone who fancies a go at rock climbing, getting those muscles working again before an outdoors expedition, or just for a pleasant but testing bit of fun. What's more, they're open all year round, in all weathers and when it's dark outside.

At most commercially-run climbing walls, you need to do an introductory session first, after which you can try a few holds on a bouldering wall. When you're ready to start climbing higher, you wear a harness attached to a rope, which goes up to an anchor point at the top, then back down to someone (a belayer) holding the other end, via a 'belay device' that acts as a friction brake. You wear a harness with a waist strap and two leg loops, and tie the rope in. When you climb, the belayer holds the rope reasonably taut. You can use any route up the wall to start off with, but the holds will be coloured, and the colours refer either to routes or to grades of specific climbs, generally from grade 3 or 4 and up to grade 8. As your confidence and skill build, you'll be able to increase your grade.

The handholds have particular names, and your instructor will explain the difference between a jug, a mono, a sloper, a crimp and a pinch, and how you use them, as well as the principles of climbing. Once at the top, the belayer will release the rope gradually to let you down.

WHERE DO I START?

To start climbing, visit the BMC website (see **Contacts**) to find your nearest climbing wall. Your local leisure centre may also have one. You won't need to take anything special with you, as all necessary equipment can be hired at the centre.

CONTACTS

- Association of British Climbing Walls: 🖥 www.abcclimbingwalls.co.uk

- British Mountaineering Council (BMC): ☎ 0161-445 6111, 🖥 www.thebmc.co.uk

- Climb magazine: 🖥 www.climbmagazine.com

- Indoor Climbing: 🖥 www.indoorclimbing.com

- UK Climbing: 🖥 www.ukclimbing.com

CLIMBING

ROCK CLIMBING

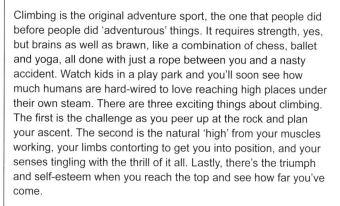

AT A GLANCE

Accessibility Index: ❶❷❸④⑤

Fitness level: ❶❷❸❹⑤

Degree of Difficulty: ❶❷❸❹⑤

White-knuckle rating: ❶❷❸❹⑤

Equipment: medium cost

Season: year round

Weight restriction: ✓

Climbing is the original adventure sport, the one that people did before people did 'adventurous' things. It requires strength, yes, but brains as well as brawn, like a combination of chess, ballet and yoga, all done with just a rope between you and a nasty accident. Watch kids in a play park and you'll soon see how much humans are hard-wired to love reaching high places under their own steam. There are three exciting things about climbing. The first is the challenge as you peer up at the rock and plan your ascent. The second is the natural 'high' from your muscles working, your limbs contorting to get you into position, and your senses tingling with the thrill of it all. Lastly, there's the triumph and self-esteem when you reach the top and see how far you've come.

WHAT EXACTLY WILL I BE DOING?

You'll be climbing or traversing a rock face using natural hand and footholds and your own strength to move you upwards. At low levels, many climbers don't use any protective equipment except perhaps a crash mat below them (see **Bouldering** on page 227). Once above 10ft (3m), you start to use ropes and anchors to support you if you fall. The safest and easiest system usually used for beginners, is 'top roping', where the rope has been fixed at the top of the climb and you're attached to it via a harness, leaving you free to focus on the climb.

'Lead roping' is where the first climber takes the rope up, and every few metres places some sort of protective anchor into the rock and puts the rope through it, so that if he falls, he'll only fall as far as the last protection. As the second climber follows, he removes the anchors below. Within this there are dozens of technical distinctions and variations, such as using pre-placed

POPULAR LOCATIONS

Southeast: Bowles Rock, near Tunbridge Wells.

Southwest: Sea cliffs, Swanage and Portland.

Central: Grinshill, Shropshire.

North: Kilnsey Crag, North Yorkshire.

Wales: Brecon Beacons National Park.

Scotland: Ben Nevis, Scottish Highlands.

protective anchors, climbing solo, sport climbing and most dangerous of all, free soloing, which is climbing at great height with no ropes or protection.

WHAT SHOULD I BE WORRIED ABOUT?

Did I connect the carabiner to that rope properly? Did I hammer that thing in enough? Do I trust the guy at the other end of this rope? You're placing your life in the hands of a rope, and it's a long way down. Beginners may find they get 'disco' leg, a wild unstoppable shaking that comes from nerves. Many of these fears are in the mind, so climbing is largely a question of mind over matter.

HAPPY MEMORIES?

You're somewhere that normal hikers never get to see, in total silence apart from the wind and the birds, perhaps enjoying a flask of tea and a sandwich on a small ledge. Great!

WHERE DO I START?

You can try indoor climbing or via ferrata (see below). The BMC (see **Contacts**) provides a list of clubs that welcome beginners, or you can take an introduction course, usually costing around £200 for a weekend, including accommodation. There are also girls-only courses in what has tended to be a male-dominated activity.

WHO CAN DO IT?

Virtually anyone of any age, by choosing the appropriate climb, and there are also special courses for the disabled.

CAMPFIRE GOSSIP

It's only in the past three or four generations that we've really begun seriously to climb mountains. Mountaineering began in

CLIMBING

CONTACTS

- ABC of Rockclimbing: www. abc-of-rockclimbing.com
- British Mountaineering Council (BMC): ☎ 0161-456111, www.thebmc.co.uk
- Climbing For All: www. thebmc.co.uk/feature. aspx?id=1914 (information for the disabled)
- The Mountaineering Council of Scotland: www.mcofs.org.uk

Europe, and specifically in the Lake District in the Victorian era, and within 100 years Britons has climbed almost everything in the world, usually after honing their skills and building their courage on our own little mountains.

BOULDERING

 **AT A GLANCE**

Accessibility Index: ❶❷❸❹❺

Fitness level: ❶❷❸❹⑤

Degree of Difficulty: ❶❷③④⑤

White-knuckle rating: ❶❷❸④⑤

Equipment: low cost

Season: year round

Family friendly: ✓

Weight restriction: ✓

If you've had enough of sitting in a playground watching your kids have all the fun on the climbing frames, bouldering could be the next step up. It's rock climbing, but a bit closer to the ground, so there's no need for the palaver of ropes and anchors. Bouldering is a test of strength, agility and mind over matter; what's more it's absolutely free and you won't even need to drive to a mountain. There are artificial bouldering walls in many kids' playgrounds, but it's worth making the effort to find the real thing.

WHAT EXACTLY WILL I BE DOING?

You'll be finding rocky outcrops, the lower reaches of larger climbs and natural or man-made boulders, and climbing them. These challenges are known as 'problems' and you start by analysing the route from the ground, looking for a sequence of hand and footholds. Once you start your attempt, bouldering becomes a test of fingertip strength, explosive energy and balance, but mental agility also. You may need to think out a new route mid-climb if Plan A goes wrong, and think your moves ahead like a chess player. The combination of mental challenge, strength and suppleness means bouldering is often compared to yoga, but instead of using a sweaty mat in a gym, you'll be in beautiful countryside with the sun and wind on your face.

The problems are short and intense, often a question of confidence and attitude. You'll build strength and suppleness, as the climb is physically demanding as you shift your bodyweight, therefore it's both an aid and a motivation to losing weight. It isn't an activity for anyone who values their dignity, however, as you'll be getting into some extraordinary contortions.

CLIMBING

POPULAR LOCATIONS

Southeast: Harrison's Rocks, Groombridge, Kent/East Sussex border; ☎ 01892-863659, 🖳 www.softrockclimbing.co.uk.

Southwest: Avon Gorge, near Bristol; 🖳 www.visitbristol.co.uk.

Central: Stanage, Derbyshire; ☎ 01629-816200, 🖳 www.peakdistrict.gov.uk.

North: Lake District; Lake District Bouldering, 🖳 www.lakesbloc.com.

Wales: Pennial Boulders, Blaenau Ffestiniog; ☎ 08708-300306, 🖳 www.visitwales.co.uk/active.

Scotland: Craigmore, near Glasgow; 🖳 www.boulderscotland.com.

Regular boulderers use a 'crash mat' for protection in case of falls, and a pair of lightweight climbing shoes. However, you can try it out first without using either, provided you don't go too high. You should also have a friend – a 'spotter' – standing underneath you in case you fall.

HAPPY MEMORIES?

Risking a manoeuvre that you're unsure you have the strength and agility to pull off, maybe grappling with a nasty overhang, and making it, is an addictive thrill.

WHAT SHOULD I BE WORRIED ABOUT?

Rock, as the name suggests, is a hard and unyielding opponent. As well as the scrapes and bruises, falling from 10-15ft (3-4.5m) can be painful and dangerous. So before you go too high, you'll need to invest in a crash mat.

WHERE DO I START?

You can just turn up at many bouldering sites on common land or parks, and start climbing. Or you can learn the basic techniques of free climbing on a course, either with a climbing company or on an indoor climbing wall (see above). If you enjoy it, local British Mountaineering Clubs (see **Contacts**) are good places to find friends to go bouldering with.

WHERE CAN IT LEAD?

As you get better at bouldering, you'll soon be looking for more technical challenges or higher rock faces. Above 15ft (4.5m), bouldering becomes highly dangerous and is known as free soloing, so by then you should be using ropes with a friend belaying (see **Rock Climbing** above). Bouldering is a great activity to combine with coasteering (see page 204).

WHO CAN DO IT?

Anyone: however, being slim and supple is a great advantage.

WHAT SHOULD I TAKE?

A crash mat, climbing shoes and chalk.

WHAT WILL IT COST?

This is a version of climbing you can tackle without any specialist equipment at all, but it's sensible to use a crash mat and climbing shoes, which each cost from around £50.

 CONTACTS

- The British Mountaineering Council: ☎ 0161-445611, 💻 www.thebmc.co.uk

- Plas y Brenin, National Mountain Centre: 💻 www.pyb.co.uk

- UK Bouldering: 💻 http://ukbouldering.com

- UK Climbing: ☎ 0114-266 2362, 💻 www.ukclimbing.com

- Routes: 💻 www.northwalesbouldering.com, www.yorkshiregrit.com

CLIMBING

ABSEILING

AT A GLANCE

Accessibility Index: ❶❷❸❹⑤

Fitness level: ❶❷❸④⑤

Degree of Difficulty: ❶❷❸④⑤

White-knuckle rating: ❶❷❸❹⑤

Equipment: hire or medium cost

Season: year round

Disability friendly: ✓

Family friendly: ✓

Abseiling is lowering yourself from a height using a rope in a controlled manner. The technique is used in climbing, caving and canyoning, and professionally by steeplejacks, tree surgeons, window cleaners, and of course, the SAS. You can also try it at many activity centres. A rope will be attached at the top of the cliff, hopefully reaching the bottom. You wear a harness with a 'descender', a device that the rope loops through, connecting you to the rope but creating tension to prevent you sliding down too fast. With the descender attached, you step out over the drop, keeping your face to the rock and your back to the drop. You sit back with your feet on the cliff, try to relax, and release a little of the tension in the rope. And you'll slide down a bit. Too fast, and you twist the rope to slow you down; too slow, and you release a bit more tension. Down you go, walking backwards at your own pace.

The joy of abseiling is being able to stand back from the cliff and look up, to the side and even down, should you wish to. It's a lovely way to examine a cliff at your own pace and without the effort of climbing it. It's also good for getting close to bird life, always being careful to avoid disturbing their nests.

Warning!

Abseiling may look easy, but it can be extremely dangerous without expert supervision and back-up systems. You must not attempt this on your own. Some of the world's greatest mountaineers have died while abseiling.

WHERE DO I START?

Contact an activity or indoor climbing centre. Children as young as seven may be accepted at an adventure centre, but they'll need someone to hold a back-up rope to ensure safety.

CAMPFIRE GOSSIP

Most climbers loathe abseiling; seeing it as a highly dangerous way to get down a cliff. In mountaineering conditions it can be difficult to find a suitable anchor at the top, and there's no back-up system. The rope could dislodge rocks above you, and any problem on the way down, such as getting your hair caught in the descender (which happens), could cause you to panic and let go of the rope. However, activity centres have plenty of back-up safety features, including an instructor holding a safety rope.

 CONTACTS

- The British Mountaineering Council: ☎ 0161-445611, 🖥 www.thebmc.co.uk

- UK Climbing: 🖥 www.ukclimbing.com

- Organisers: 🖥 www.abseiluk.com

CLIMBING

CONTACTS

- The British Mountaineering Council: ☎ 0161-445611, 🖳 www.thebmc.co.uk

- Organisers: 🖳 www.exelement.co.uk, www.naelimits.co.uk

RAP RUNNING

Warning!

Only do this with a licensed operator, never on your own.

The problem with traditional abseiling is that you go down backwards. That's fine for most people, but apparently it wasn't for Australia's Special Forces, who wanted to abseil down a building while shooting at the enemy. It now goes under many names – Australian rappelling, Geneva-style, forward-facing abseil – but whatever it's called, it's absolutely terrifying the first time you do it.

Once you're strapped in, you stand at the edge of the drop and lean forwards until you're horizontal, facing down, at 90° to the cliff or wall. Then you run down, with the rope being paid out fast through the descender. If you're doing this at an activity centre, you usually have a safety rope attached, being held by someone at the top.

VIA FERRATA

 **AT A GLANCE**

Accessibility Index: ❶❷③④⑤

Fitness level: ❶❷③④⑤

Degree of Difficulty: ❶❷③④⑤

White-knuckle rating: ❶❷❸④⑤

Equipment: hire or medium cost

Season: year round

Family friendly: ✓

Weight restriction: ✓

It means 'iron road', and was invented by the Italian Army so that they could retreat faster over the mountains. It's a combination of metal handholds, steps and cables that follow a route up, offering a taste of rock climbing, but easier. As with any climbing route, there's a thrill in seeing the ground (and your comfort zone) disappearing behind you, and the iron road may still take you over a 300ft (91m) drop or a raging torrent, so it isn't for the faint-hearted. Once at the top, you'll have a tremendous sense of achievement and possibly a few minor scrapes and bruises.

Climbing via ferrata is a popular leisure activity on the Continent, and now three routes exist in the UK. The only public via ferrata is the Elie Chain Walk in Fife, Scotland, made up of eight chains plus iron steps and footholds. It traverses half a kilometre of rugged coastline between Elie and Kincraig Point, and you'll need to time your trip to avoid high tide when it's partially submerged. Two others are part of adventure centres. At Honister, in Lancashire's Lake District, the via ferrata climbs 2,132ft (650m) to the top of Fleetwith Pike, and was originally used by slate miners. In Yorkshire, at Stean Gorge, the via ferrata is one of several ways to traverse the kilometre-long gorge (others being abseiling, caving and gorge scrambling), and takes around three hours to complete.

At privately-run centres, you'll be provided with mountaineering equipment, including climbing harness, shoes and helmet, plus a via ferrata kit of two ropes with carabiners at the end, so you're always linked by one rope. You then climb along the route keeping one line attached at all times. On the unsupervised route in Fife, climbers can bring their own equipment or just hold on.

CLIMBING

CONTACTS

- Elie Chain Walk:
  🖥 www.fifecoastalpath.co.uk

- Honister: ☎ 017687-77714,
  🖥 www.honister.com

- Stean Gorge:
  ☎ 01423-755666,
  🖥 www.howstean.co.uk

WHAT WILL IT COST?

£30 in Honister, £45 in Yorkshire and free in Scotland.

CAMPFIRE GOSSIP

You have to respect any kind of climb, even the relatively safe via ferrata. One of the world's most famous free climbers – those madmen who climb the highest rock faces without ropes – was killed in October 2010, falling from a via ferrata in Germany.

CAVING & POTHOLING

 **AT A GLANCE**

Accessibility Index: ❶❷❸❹⑤

Fitness level: ❶❷❸④⑤

Degree of Difficulty: ❶❷❸④⑤

White-knuckle rating: ❶❷❸④⑤

Equipment: hire or medium cost

Season: year round

Family friendly: ✓

Confident swimmer: ✓

Weight restriction: ✓

Working underground isn't something many people would do willingly and being trapped underground for months – as the Chilean miners were in 2010 – is most people's worst nightmare. However, cavers and potholers do it for fun. When rain, mixed with naturally occurring quantities of carbon dioxide, sinks below the topsoil and meets limestone, it dissolves the limestone a little. Over thousands of years, small streams form through the limestone, which widen into caves, then bigger caves and eventually huge chambers such as Gaping Gill (N. Yorkshire), which is large enough to contain St Paul's Cathedral. Within them, the dripping water creates incredible rock formations such as stalactites and stalagmites.

WHAT EXACTLY WILL I BE DOING?

You'll be wearing protective clothing and entering a cave system under expert guidance. Getting through the cave may involve clambering over obstacles, negotiating narrow passageways, abseiling down vertical drops, traversing subterranean cliffs, wading through flooded caverns, and even holding your breath while swimming through a flooded section. Caving can be a highly skilled and specialised activity involving ropes, diving and climbing, but equally it can be a gentle stroll through wide open canyons and astounding natural rock formations. Expert cavers delight in finding new routes to link caves: by using dyes in the streams and smoke bombs, cavers have now linked a hundred miles of tunnels between Cumbria, Lancashire and Yorkshire.

CLIMBING

POPULAR LOCATIONS

Southwest: South Devon.

Central: Forest of Dean, Gloucestershire.

North: Gaping Gill, Clapham, Yorkshire.

Wales: Brecon Beacons National Park.

Scotland: Caves of Assynt, northern Scotland.

When you enter the cave system via a vertical hole, caving is called potholing, but it's basically all the same thing. Some people refer to caving as speleology, and in America it's sometimes called spelunking (from the Greek for cave: spelunx).

HAPPY MEMORIES?

Discovering a new cave system that few, if any, human beings have ever seen before is pretty awe-inspiring, especially if you've had to negotiate obstacles such as boulder-blocked passages and flooded caverns. And there are still holes to be discovered; the UK's highest cavern (Titan Cave, 463ft/141m) was only discovered in 2000.

WHAT SHOULD I BE WORRIED ABOUT?

Caving is dangerous on many levels. You're the meat in a giant sandwich between two huge slabs of rock, and could be trapped by a rockfall (unlikely), washed down a hole by flash floods (possible), or drowned (it happens). None of these are very likely, however, and the main cause of accidents when caving is from falls, which is why you should only go caving with experienced cavers and never alone.

WHERE DO I START?

Many adventure activity companies offer caving, or you can join a British Caving Association club (see **Contacts**).

WHO CAN DO IT?

Anyone, including children under close supervision.

WHAT SHOULD I TAKE?

The activity centre will provide equipment for your first outing, but eventually you'll need a helmet, head lamp, waterproof jacket and trousers, and well-fitting wellies or walking boots.

WHAT WILL IT COST?

From £50 for a half-day experience or around £130 for a weekend course.

CAMPFIRE GOSSIP

You're not just going down a hole, you're going back in time. Limestone is made from the bodies of tiny sea creatures that lived in tropical oceans hundreds of millions of years ago – 2,500 years for each 1ft (30cm). Sometimes tucked away in the limestone you'll see a shell, or a bit of coral or maybe even part of a dinosaur. For anyone interested in what our planet is made of, caving opens the door onto a fascinating subterranean netherworld.

CONTACTS

- British Cave Research Association: ▢ bcra.org.uk

- British Caving Association: ▢ www.british-caving.org.uk and www.trycaving.co.uk

- Descent magazine: ▢ www.wildplaces.co.uk

- South Wales Caving Club: ▢ www.swcc.org.uk

CLIMBING

CONTACTS

- British Caving Association: 💻 www.british-caving.org. uk and www.trycaving.co.uk
- Cave Diving Group (CDG): 💻 www. cavedivinggroup.org.uk
- Cave Diving Website: 💻 www.cavediving.com

CAVE DIVING

👓 AT A GLANCE

Accessibility Index: ❶②③④⑤

Fitness level: ❶❷❸④⑤

Degree of Difficulty: ❶❷❸❹⑤

White-knuckle rating: ❶❷❸❹❺

Equipment: medium to high cost

Season: year round

Confident swimmer: ✓

Weight restriction: ✓

Now we're getting seriously adventurous – and dangerous. Cave diving appeals to people's desire to explore and make connections between caves. Limestone caves were created by water (see **Caving** above), and many of them are flooded. To examine them properly and find links between cave systems, you just have to get in there and start swimming. Cave divers have managed to link networks for mile after mile, deep underground. And while exploring, they get to see some of the earth's most astonishing sights, with rock formations made even more beautiful by the crystal clear water.

Safety is the number one concern, and it's all belts and braces with cave divers. They carry two independent air bottles, three lights and a guideline back to the cave entrance. Like winter climbers sometimes experiencing a white out, divers can get 'silt out', where a flipper has stirred up the silt in a narrow passage and they're blinded. They also divide air usage into three – a third out, a third back, and a third in case of emergencies. Other equipment is kept to a bare minimum, as it may have to be carried long distances through dry caves and pushed through tight gaps (always push, never pull, so that if it gets jammed you aren't trapped on the wrong side).

To be accepted onto one of the few training courses, you'll first need to be an experienced caver, and then you learn cave diving through the club structure of the Cave Diving Group (see **Contacts**).

Warning!

This is one of the most dangerous activities, which must only be attempted under expert and qualified supervision. Definitely not something for the claustrophobe.

HIGH-ROPES/ZIP WIRE

 **AT A GLANCE**

Accessibility Index: ❶❷❸❹❺

Fitness level: ❶❷❸④⑤

Degree of Difficulty: ❶❷③④⑤

White-knuckle rating: ❶❷❸❹⑤

Equipment: hire

Season: year round

Disability friendly: ✓

Family friendly: ✓

Weight restriction: ✓

A cable is slung between a high object and a lower one. You stand on a platform at the top end of the cable, and are attached to it via a harness, then pushed off the platform and go screaming along the cable, literally. The longest UK zip wire is 900ft (400m) and 60ft (18m) above the ground, which you slide down at 35mph (56kph). But it only takes a minute or two, so most activity centres now combine it into a treetop ropes course. After a safety briefing to explain all the ropes and clips, you reach the top zipwire platform by climbing a course constructed through the trees, getting higher and higher. You'll be swinging through the forest canopy on trapezes, just like Tarzan, leaping into cargo nets, climbing ladders, crossing 40ft (12m) drops on a balance beam or rope bridge no thicker than your finger, maybe over streams and waterfalls, with the beautiful countryside as a backdrop.

There'll be instructors by each danger point to check your safety ropes are securely attached, but that doesn't make it any less terrifying, especially for parents. This is a great introduction to climbing, and the perfect family day out for kids who've outgrown the climbing frame. Most activity centres accept kids as young as ten – and parents also – provided you weigh less than around 20 stones (130kg) and are fit enough to climb a rope ladder. You can do it all year and in most weather conditions – indeed, a bit of wind adds some spice – but not in snow or lightening.

CLIMBING

CONTACTS

- Organisers: Black Mountain, Wales; www.blackmountain.co.uk/ropes

- Go Ape (26 centres throughout Britain); www.goape.co.uk

- Head for Heights, Cotswolds, ☎ 01285-770007, www.head4heights.net

- Tree Surfers, Devon; ☎ 01822-833409, www.treesurfers.co.uk

WHERE DO I START?

Look for activity centres advertising ropes courses and zipwire. Many are open all week to cater for school parties and they'll be busy during the holidays, but this isn't just for kids.

CAMPFIRE GOSSIP

The origin of zip wires, according to one school of thought, goes back to the days of pirates as they would swing grappling hooks into the rigging of enemy ships and slide onto the decks at maximum speed. Which is perhaps why they're sometimes called 'deathslides'?

TREE CLIMBING

👓 AT A GLANCE

Accessibility Index: ❶❷❸❹❺

Fitness level: ❶❷❸④⑤

Degree of Difficulty: ❶❷③④⑤

White-knuckle rating: ❶❷❸④⑤

Equipment: low cost

Season: year round

Disability friendly: ✓

Family friendly: ✓

Weight restriction: ✓

The film, *Avatar*, about a peaceful, tree-climbing people trying to protect their tree-home from destruction, has revived an ancient activity that had fallen out of fashion; watching movies in 3-D. If it inspired you to climb a tree, however, you've still got them to yourself. But there's hope: people have started reclaiming the rivers with wild swimming and the countryside with wild camping; it's time for us to take to the trees also…

Trees are nature's climbing frames, complete with hand and footholds and convenient boughs to sit and rest. You can make a treehouse to watch the wildlife from – an average oak tree supports 350 species of insect for a start, as well as birds, bats and squirrels – or swing yourself to sleep in a hammock if it all gets too exciting.

There are two ways to climb trees. The old-fashioned way, up the trunk without ropes, is called 'free solo climbing'. The commercial tree-climbing organisers, however, use a double rope system suspended from a high branch. So rather than climbing the actual tree, you're climbing a rope, using a system of belays, hitches and mechanical ascenders. This may seem like cheating, but is certainly safer, and once you've learnt the technique you can always climb your own tree using the rope system as safety back-up. They also offer the opportunity to camp in a special hammock (you're strapped in), and if you have a suitable tree at home they'll come to you.

WHERE DO I START?

Try a tree with low branches for easy access, perhaps using a crash mat beneath you. When you're ready to go higher, it's safer

CLIMBING

CONTACTS

- Tree Climber International (USA): 💻 www. treeclimbing.com

- Organisers: Big Tree Climbing: ☎ 0800-055 6760, 💻 www.bigtreeclimbing.co.uk

- Good Leaf Tree Climbing Adventures, Isle of Wight; ☎ 0333-800 1188, 💻 www.goodleaf.co.uk

- Mighty Oak Tree Climbing Company, Cornwall; ☎ 07890-698651, 💻 www.mighty-oak.co.uk

- Tree Surfers, Devon; ☎ 01822-833409, 💻 www.treesurfers.co.uk

to learn the ropes at an established tree climbing centre, where they'll teach you to use a throw line and attached weight to get the rope over a high branch.

CAMPFIRE GOSSIP

Sitting in a tree gives you a special perspective on the world. You may feel a bit foolish to be discovered in a tree at first, but remember the proverb: 'don't be afraid to go out on a limb; that's where the fruit is'.

AQUASEILING

Warning!

Only do this with a licensed operator, never on your own!

CONTACTS

- Organisers: Adventure 21, Northwest England; ☎ 01257-474467, 🖳 www.adventure21.co.uk

- Activities in Lakeland, Cumbria; ☎ 01539-535999, 🖳 www.lakesactivities.co.uk

Ever fancied climbing into the washing machine when it's on a cold wash? Of course you haven't; it would be foolish (it you have, don't tell anyone). But if you have, you'll enjoy aquaseiling; which is abseiling down a waterfall. You control the speed of descent by paying the rope out through a descender, just like normal abseiling, but all the while scrabbling to get a foothold on the wet rocks, and keeping yourself out of the torrents of water that are pummelling your head. Sounds like fun!

At the bottom of the waterfall, you lower yourself into foaming water that's like a giant, ice-cold Jacuzzi. Several outdoor centres offer the experience to beginners, from around £25 for a half-day session, with full training and an instructor on hand to guide you down.

CLIMBING

ICE CLIMBING

👓 AT A GLANCE

Accessibility Index: ❶②③④⑤

Fitness level: ❶❷❸④⑤

Degree of Difficulty: ❶❷❸❹❺

White-knuckle rating: ❶❷❸❹⑤

Equipment: low or medium cost

Season: winter

Weight restriction: ✓

It's climbing frozen water: waterfalls, glaciers, gullies filled with ice, steep mountainsides covered in snow, in the most extreme conditions the British Isles can throw at you. (There are also indoor ice walls in London and Manchester). You can take ice climbing as a specialised course or as a one-day challenge, or it can be just one element on a winter mountaineering trip. It isn't usually a suitable activity for a first-time climber, and many course leaders take only clients who are experienced summer climbers. It could, however, be the first step on that campaign to climb Mount Everest before you are, let's face it, too old.

WHAT EXACTLY WILL I BE DOING?

Soon, this will be flowing water again, but for now the techniques are largely the same as for rock climbing, using

ropes and anchor points. In some ways, ice climbing is easier because you can make your own foot and handholds in the ice with crampons and ice axe. However, there's also the risk of avalanches, of 'white out' conditions where snowstorms cut visibility to zero, and of the ice coming adrift from the rockface. Ice climbs are graded in difficulty from I to VII.

The mountains in winter are such a hostile environment that all courses include survival training, and a winter mountaineering trip may even include sleeping out in the open, either in a tent or a snowhole (see page 269).

POPULAR LOCATIONS

Southeast: London Vertical Chill; 🖥 www.vertical-chill.com.

North: Lake District National Park; 🖥 www.lakedistrict.gov.uk or Manchester Vertical Chill; 🖥 www.vertical-chill.com.

Wales: Snowdonia National Park; 🖥 www.eryri-npa.gov.uk/home.

Scotland: Glenmore Lodge, Scotland's National Outdoor Training Centre, Cairngorms National Park; 🖥 www.glenmorelodge.org.uk.

WHAT SHOULD I BE WORRIED ABOUT?

Temperatures in Scotland regularly reach -20°C (-4°F), in which finding a frozen waterfall won't be a problem. But you have to add windchill to that, if you're on a mountain, and -10°C (14°F) in even a light 30mph (48kph) wind feels like -39°C (-38.2°F), cold enough to cause frostbite within minutes. Dropping your glove down the mountain in these conditions will be more than irritating. Clearly this is an activity that should only ever be attempted under expert supervision.

HAPPY MEMORIES?

Whacking you axe into the hard, blue surface and feeling it stick fast, or climbing an ice wall by kicking your crampons in, is as close as you can get to walking like a fly up a solid surface. It's a totally engrossing activity, a combination of exhilaration and immense effort, and as you conquer a tricky overhang, the cold may be far from your mind.

WHERE DO I START?

There are three indoor ice cliffs in Britain (see below). Outside, courses are available in winter walking and survival, either for total beginners or as a new skill for experienced climbers.

WHAT SHOULD I TAKE?

Don't attempt ice climbing without specialist clothing and equipment.

WHAT WILL IT COST?

Courses by their nature have to be in small groups, so you should expect to pay from £100 per day, plus accommodation. Indoor ice wall courses cost from £40.

CLIMBING

CONTACTS

CAMPFIRE GOSSIP

While struggling over the last few hundred yards of your own ice climb, you may ponder the Everest Enigma; did Mallory and Irvine die trying to reach the summit in 1924, or on their way down? Amongst the tantalising evidence; Mallory was planning to leave a picture of his wife on the summit, and when his mummified remains were found in 1999, the picture was nowhere to be found…

9

WINTER

F eel like spending all winter snuggled in a duvet? Tough luck! Human evolution decided we weren't going to be hibernators, so you may as well get out there in the snow and have fun. When we've had heavy snowfalls, here are some ideas for those with the right stuff to get the most from the white stuff.

SKIING

 **AT A GLANCE**

Accessibility Index: ❶❷❸④⑤

Fitness level: ❶❷③④⑤

Degree of Difficulty: ❶❷❸④⑤

White-knuckle rating: ❶❷③④⑤

Equipment: hire or medium cost

Season: winter/spring

Disability friendly: ✓

Family friendly: ✓

Even in bad winters, there's usually some skiing possible in Scotland and a few days on slopes in County Durham, Cumbria and Northumberland; but following three successive snowy winters, Britain's ski slopes are on a high. There are also an increasing number of real snow indoor slopes around the country, offering year-round skiing and snowboarding.

WHAT EXACTLY WILL I BE DOING?

With the growth of snowboarding, dear old skiing can seem a bit old hat, yet it's still the most popular choice of winter sports, being generally considered easier to learn than snowboarding. Traditional downhill skiing on a prepared piste (run) and with a lift to take you back to the surface, is called alpine skiing, and Scotland has over 120 runs at its five main resorts, ranging from green (easy) to black (very difficult).

Before you head onto the slopes, you'll need a lesson or two. The basic 'snowplough' allows you to stop easily (hopefully), so it's great for building confidence. Your instructor will explain how to position your legs and feet, and once you've mastered going downhill very slowly and can turn without falling over, you'll learn to bring your skis together to increase speed.

POPULAR LOCATIONS

Southeast: Hemel Hempstead; ☎ 0845-258 9000,
💻 www.thesnowcentre.com.

Central: Milton Keynes; ☎ 0871-222 5670,
💻 www.snozonemiltonkeynes.com.

North: Manchester, ☎ 0161-749 2222,
💻 www.chillfactore.com; Castleford, Yorkshire,
☎ 0871-222 5673, 💻 www.snozoneuk.com/v/castleford.

Scotland: Glasgow; ☎ 0871-222 5673,
💻 www.snozoneuk.com/v/scotland.

In addition to downhill skiing, you can also do cross country or Nordic skiing anywhere there's enough snow. It's harder work than alpine skiing and there are few prepared tracks apart from some in Scotland, but it provides a great workout.

WHAT SHOULD I BE WORRIED ABOUT?

Every piste has its risks. Even the widest and slowest has the hopeless and the hapless flying across it, and with an average speed of 15 to 20mph (24 to 32kph) down a piste, a collision can be painful; helmets are increasingly popular, especially for children. Trickier runs have bumps, jumps and moguls to keep you focused.

HAPPY MEMORIES?

People go back year after year because there's nothing in the world more thrilling than flying down a mountain on skis, and the world rarely looks better than when it's under a blanket of snow.

WHERE DO I START?

To save time on your skiing holiday, learn the basics at an indoor slope to get your muscles prepared for skiing. Booking a trip to Scotland can be problematic too far in advance, but for late-booking, the Visit Scotland website (see **Contacts**) shows the current snow conditions and even real-time webcams.

WHAT WILL IT COST?

Indoor snow centres are more expensive than artificial slopes due to the technology required, but by using them off-peak or booking a course you can get prices down to around £15 per hour, plus extra for ski hire. Scottish resorts cost around £30 for a day's lift

WINTER

📝 CONTACTS

- Lake District Ski Club:
  ☎ 015395-35456,
  🖥 www.ldscsnowski.co.uk

- Metrosnow:
  🖥 www.metrosnow.co.uk

- Resort Information:
  🖥 www.onthesnow.co.uk

- Scottish Ski Runs:
  🖥 www.nevisrange.co.uk

- The Ski Club of Great
  Britain: ☎ 0845-458 0780,
  🖥 www.skiclub.co.uk

- Ski Scotland: ☎ 0845-
  225 5121, 🖥 http://ski.
  visitscotland.com

- Skiing for the Disabled:
  🖥 www.snowsportengland.
  org.uk/disability-76.html

- Snowsport England:
  ☎ 0121-501 2314, 🖥 www.
  snowsportengland.org.uk

- Weather: Met Office,
  🖥 www.metoffice.gov.uk

pass, excluding ski hire. An all-area, all-season Scottish ski pass costs £450 for an adult and £255 for children.

CAMPFIRE GOSSIP

Who needs Verbier or Aspen? The Beckhams have given their seal of approval to indoor skiing in Britain with a family trip to the Hemel Hempstead Snow Centre over Christmas 2010. David watched Romeo and Brooklyn have lessons.

SNOWBOARDING

AT A GLANCE

Accessibility Index: ❶❷❸④⑤

Fitness level: ❶❷③④⑤

Degree of Difficulty: ❶❷❸④⑤

White-knuckle rating: ❶❷❸④⑤

Equipment: hire or medium cost

Season: winter/spring

Disability friendly: ✓

Family friendly: ✓

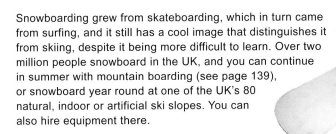

Snowboarding grew from skateboarding, which in turn came from surfing, and it still has a cool image that distinguishes it from skiing, despite it being more difficult to learn. Over two million people snowboard in the UK, and you can continue in summer with mountain boarding (see page 139), or snowboard year round at one of the UK's 80 natural, indoor or artificial ski slopes. You can also hire equipment there.

WHAT EXACTLY WILL I BE DOING?

Snowboards are around 62-73in (140-165cm) long, and 8-11in (18-25cm) wide. The boots are fixed into the boards with bindings, but the boards can travel in either direction down the slope – although it may take a rider a little longer to master this. Learning often takes longer than skiing, though lessons will help, and when you can confidently link turns and stay upright, your options for activities are wider than with skiing. Increasingly popular are snowkiting, where you're powered along by a powerkite, and snowboarder X, an Olympic sport where competitors race against each other downhill over jumps and through gates.

As well as snowboarding down pistes graded from green to black, snowboarders can go freestyle, leaping off jumps and pipes or learning tricks such as jibbing, where you slide down a metal rail or a fallen tree trunk, and aerial tricks where riders go for height, somersaults and flips. Most ski resorts have a dedicated snowboard park with objects to jump and jib from.

WINTER

POPULAR LOCATIONS

Cairngorm: ☎ 01479-861261, 🖥 www.cairngormmountain.org.

Glencoe: ☎ 01855-851226, 🖥 www.glencoemountain.co.uk.

Glenshee: ☎ 013397-41320, 🖥 www.ski-glenshee.co.uk.

Lecht: ☎ 01975-651440, 🖥 www.lecht.co.uk.

Nevis Range: ☎ 01397-705825, 🖥 www.nevisrange.co.uk.

📝 CONTACTS

- Governing body for English snowsports:
  ☎ 0121-501 2314, 🖥 www.snowsportengland.org.uk

- Ski Scotland: ☎ 0845-225 5121, 🖥 http://ski.visitscotland.com

- Snowboard Club UK:
  🖥 www.snowboardclub.co.uk

- Valuable information on the different resorts:
  🖥 www.onthesnow.co.uk

WHAT SHOULD I BE WORRIED ABOUT?

Approaching the jump, rehearsing in your mind what you'll be doing with your board and where you'll be throwing your body, and hoping you won't be coming down the mountain on a stretcher.

HAPPY MEMORIES?

It combines the pleasure of skiing with the mad excitement of acrobatics. You can do tricks just like on a skateboard, but much faster, and this is likely to be up a mountain in beautiful surroundings rather than in an underground car park.

WHERE DO I START?

Book a lesson at a dry (or artificial-snow) ski slope – there are over 50 in England alone – for training in the basics. Once confident, you can be let loose on the slopes.

WHEN'S THE BEST TIME FOR IT?

Outdoors in winter or any time on an artificial slope.

WHAT SHOULD I TAKE?

Snowboard and boots are provided by centres, but snowboard beginners spend a lot of time on their backsides, so you'll need warm, waterproof trousers or 'salopettes' (waterproof dungarees).

WHAT WILL IT COST?

For group lessons in Scotland, expect to pay £50 per day (including equipment). Lessons at indoor/artificial slopes cost from £25 an hour, plus the use of the slope (from £8 per hour).

CAMPFIRE GOSSIP

There's a whole language of snowboarding that it's probably unwise to try to learn if you're aged over 40, but you'll need to know if you're 'goofy', riding with the right foot forward, or 'regular', leading with the left. Your instructor will tell you.

DISABLED MONOSKI

There are many ways that people with disabilities can get out on the slopes, with boards and skis to suit most mobility problems. With a monoski, you sit on a moulded seat mounted (with a good suspension) on a single ski, and hold onto two skipoles/outriggers for extra balance. You ski in the usual way, and can take part in any of the usual sports events such as boarder X, freestyle, slalom or downhill.

   The monoski can be difficult to master – it requires more balance and strength – but there are easier adaptive skiing methods available if you prefer, including the skibob (see page 262). Disability needn't be a barrier to getting out on the slopes, which applies equally to an artificial ski slope in Sussex as it does to alpine skiing in the Cairngorms.

 CONTACTS

- British Ski Club for the Disabled (BSCD), www.bscd.org.uk

- Disability Snowsports UK: ☎ 01479-861272, www.disabilitysnowsports.org.uk

- Ski Scotland: ☎ 0845-225 5121, http://ski.visitscotland.com

- Snowsport England: ☎ 0121-501 2314, www.snowsportengland.org.uk

WINTER

DRY SLOPE SKIING

 **AT A GLANCE**

Accessibility Index: ❶❷❸❹❺

Fitness level: ❶❷③④⑤

Degree of Difficulty: ❶❷❸④⑤

White-knuckle rating: ❶❷③④⑤

Equipment: hire or medium cost

Season: year round

Disability friendly: ✓

Family friendly: ✓

📝 CONTACTS

- The Ski Club of Great Britain: ☎ 0845-458 0780, 🖥 www.skiclub.co.uk

- Snow365: 🖥 www.snow365.com

- UK Dry Slopes: 🖥 www.ifyouski.com/more-home/guides/dry-ski-slopes.aspx

While those unfortunate people in alpine countries can only ski in winter and spring, the high quality of artificial slopes in Britain means we can be on the piste all year. There are around 80 artificial/dry slopes in Britain, and technology is making them more snow-like each year. And it's much cheaper and easier than sloping off to the Alps.

WHAT EXACTLY WILL I BE DOING?

You'll be skiing, snowboarding or sledging down a piste created from a white plastic material that's wetted for extra slipperiness and has a feel, when skiing or snowboarding that's very much like snow. Other than the material and the fact that you can do it year round, dry skiing/snowboarding is much the same as on snow, with the same techniques, the same lifts, and 'snow parks' where snowboarders can learn tricks over jumps and pipes. Indeed, some parks even have specially created foam landing areas for you to practice your freestyle skiing techniques (see page 260). There are certain advantages to artificial slopes, including an even surface without moguls, the warmer temperatures that

POPULAR LOCATIONS

Southeast: Chatham Ski Slope; ☎ 01634-827979, 🖥 http://jnlchatham.co.uk.

Southwest: Torquay Alpine Ski Club; ☎ 01803-313350, 🖥 www.skitorquay.com.

Central: Stoke Ski Centre; ☎ 01782-204159, 🖥 www.stokeskicentre.co.uk.

North: Sheffield Ski Village; ☎ 0114-276 0044, 🖥 www.sheffieldskivillage.co.uk.

Wales: Pontypool Ski Centre; ☎ 01495-756955, 🖥 www.torfaen.gov.uk.

Scotland: Edinburgh; ☎ 0131-445 4433, 🖥 www.ski.midlothian.gov.uk.

means the slopes don't ice up like real snow slopes do, and the fact that you can ski at night under floodlights. And then again, if it does snow then you can ski on it also.

WHAT SHOULD I BE WORRIED ABOUT?

The usual accidents can happen on dry slopes, particularly as they can get even more crowded than alpine resorts. On the plus side, no-one is usually permitted on a dry slope unless they have had adequate lessons, and they're more strictly controlled than pistes on remote mountainsides.

HAPPY MEMORIES?

Most of all, dry slopes score in accessibility, as skiing and snowboarding comes within the budget and an hour or so travelling time of everyone in Britain, all year, every day.

WHERE DO I START?

You can find a local dry slope via the internet, using the links below.

WHAT WILL IT COST?

Artificial slopes start at around £10 per hour, inclusive of ski hire,

CAMPFIRE GOSSIP

If it's a while since you went on an artificial ski slope, maybe it's time to give them another spin. The upside-down-brush bristle systems of old are being superseded by a carpet-like material called Snowflex that's more like snow, softer to land on, and better for snowboard tricks such as pipes and jumps.

WINTER

OFF-PISTE SKIING & SKI TOURING

AT A GLANCE

Accessibility Index: ❶❷③④⑤

Fitness level: ❶❷❸❹⑤

Degree of Difficulty: ❶❷❸④⑤

White-knuckle rating: ❶❷❸④⑤

Equipment: hire or medium cost

Season: winter/spring

Family friendly: ✓

CONTACTS

- The Eagle Ski Club:
  💻 www.eagleskiclub.org.uk

- Equipment Guide:
  💻 www.alpin-ism.com/
  equipment/skitouring.cfm

- Huntly Nordic & Outdoor
  Centre: ☎ 01466-79442,
  💻 http://hnoc.nordicski.org.uk
  Mountain Bothies: 💻 www.
  mountainbothies.org.uk

- Ski Scotland: ☎ 0845-
  225 5121, 💻 http://ski.
  visitscotland.com

- Snowsport England:
  ☎ 0121-501 2314, 💻 www.
  snowsportengland.org.uk

- SportScotland Avalanche
  Information Service
  (SAIS): ☎ 01479-861264,
  💻 www.sais.gov.uk

- Weather: Met Office,
  💻 www.metoffice.gov.uk

The joy of off-piste skiing and ski touring is avoiding the crowds and skiing along footpaths, mountain trails, across open land and between trees, sometimes uphill, sometimes downhill, in pristine powder, out in the countryside amidst the silence and the beauty. These are fast-growing winter sports which the successive deep, crisp and even snowy winters in recent years have encouraged. There are even mountain huts in Scotland called 'bothies' that offer rudimentary shelter for those planning a longer trip, although camping and snowholing (see page 269) are also possible.

The ski technique varies. Off-piste skiing is generally done with regular downhill/alpine skis and boots, while ski touring requires special cross-country skis with free heels and grips to help with the uphill stretches, and boots that you can walk in when the snow runs out. However, this depends very much on the weather, and as novices must never attempt ski touring without a qualified guide, he'll be able to recommend the correct equipment (which can be hired).

In Scotland's ski resorts, you can join a course or do it as part of an organised activity, and once trained you can join a club or go independently, always being aware of the risk of avalanches and sudden deteriorating conditions. The weather in mountain areas can rapidly change from bright sunlight and blue skies to a 'white out', therefore you need to understand navigation and survival skills. Unlike some countries, Scotland doesn't have a mountain hut system for tourers, just some rather primitive bothies. Nevertheless, ski tourers can experience rare solitude on virgin snow in areas piste skiers can only dream about.

POPULAR LOCATIONS

Cairngorm: ☎ 01479-861261, 💻 www.cairngormmountain.org.

Glencoe: ☎ 01855-851226, 💻 www.glencoemountain.co.uk.

Glenshee: ☎ 013397-41320, 💻 www.ski-glenshee.co.uk.

Lecht: ☎ 01975-651440, 💻 www.lecht.co.uk.

Nevis Range: ☎ 01397-705825, 💻 www.nevisrange.co.uk.

WHERE DO I START?

Ski touring classes are available in Scotland, where the best snow conditions are usually in January and February. Ski touring is also a good club-based activity, with the largest in the UK being the Eagle Ski Club (see below), which meets throughout the UK.

CAMPFIRE GOSSIP

Members of the Eagle Ski Club skied the entire length of Sussex and Hampshire's South Downs Way over a snowy New Year holiday in early 2010.

WINTER

CONTACTS

- Snowsport England:
  ☎ 0121-501 2314, 🖳 www.
  snowsportengland.org.uk

- Sheffield Ski Village: 🖳 www.
  sheffieldskivillage.co.uk

FREESTYLE SKIING

For most people, just standing up on skis is challenge enough, but the freestyle skier's repertoire might include 180° spins, somersaults and backflips off a jump or half-pipe, super-fast moguls (bumps), and 'ski-across' – a four-person downhill race at astonishing speed on a course which includes jumps.

These are hard enough for snowboarders, but having two skis to control magnifies the difficulty and scares off most people, as does the need to use special skis and boots. However, some of the disciplines are now Winter Olympic sports, which is always handy for getting government/sponsorship money for training equipment and coaching. So, if you feel ready for a challenge that most of the population would run screaming from, coaches at ski centres around the country are waiting for your call this weekend.

TOBOGGANING

📝 CONTACTS

- Equipment:
  🖥 www.toboggans.co.uk

- Weather: Met Office,
  🖥 www.metoffice.gov.uk

- Organisers: 🖥 www.
  sheffieldskivillage.co.uk; www.
  xscape.co.uk/milton-keynes

👓 AT A GLANCE

Accessibility Index: ❶❷❸❹❺

Fitness level: ❶②③④⑤

Degree of Difficulty: ❶②③④⑤

White-knuckle rating: ❶❷❸④⑤

Equipment: none to low cost

Season: winter

Disability friendly: ✓

Family friendly: ✓

Tobogganing means sliding down a snowy hill while seated on… something. The latest trends are for steerable sleighs that look like go karts, inflatable sleighs, snow-tubes (inner tubes), body boards and kite-powered toboggans that will even take you back uphill again if you catch the wind right.

Tobogganing is free and fun, and one of the few things that will get children outside in cold weather to run wild. Most toboggans offer rudimentary steering and braking, at best – by putting your feet down and attempting to dig your heels in – so wearing a helmet and a little basic safety awareness is advisable. Accidents can occur when the sledge careers onto a road, wall, tree or through a wire fence, so check how and where you can stop at the bottom. If there are several people on a larger sleigh, it's generally safer to put children near the back.

Buy, or make, a sledge before the snows of winter arrive and you'll be on the slopes with the best snow first. If you already have a toboggan, get it ready for the new season by cleaning the base, applying ski wax and buffing it up.

The one drawback to sledging is the long walk back up the slope again, but taking a glass-half-full attitude, if only all aerobic outdoor exercise could combine a heavy workout with an eye-watering, thrill-ride like tobogganing does. As well as in the few days of wintry weather each year, you can also toboggan on artificial ski slopes in the UK on specially constructed toboggan runs (see above), such as at Sheffield Ski Village (see **Contacts**), which also makes a great children's party activity.

WINTER

SKIBOB/SKIBIKE/SNOWBIKE

In the competitive business of sliding down a mountain, the skibob – now usually known under the trade name skibike – has a dedicated band of devotees who wouldn't swap them for a snowboard for all the Emmental in Switzerland. They're bike-like contraptions with a long seat and a handlebar, and two skis – a fixed rear one under the seat and a front one that turns with the handlebars, just like wheels.

You ride them downhill, and they're easy to learn compared to skis or snowboard, going exceptionally fast through all types of snow. Riders sit on them, and support themselves on each side with foot-skis of around 22in (55cm) long. They have good suspension, therefore are great for tricks and jumps as well as for racing competitions.

They have become popular with disabled snowfans, including the British Limbless Ex-Servicemen's Association, but hiring is probably the best policy as some ski resorts ban their use.

SNOWSHOEING

AT A GLANCE

Accessibility Index: ❶❷❸④⑤

Fitness level: ❶❷③④⑤

Degree of Difficulty: ❶①②④⑤

White-knuckle rating: ❶❷③④⑤

Equipment: low cost

Season: winter

Family friendly: ✓

CONTACTS

- Glenmore Ski Hire:
  🖥 www.aviemoreski.co.uk

- Ski Scotland:
  ☎ 0845-225 5121,
  🖥 http://ski.visitscotland.com

The concept of snowshoes (usually written as one word in US style) is simple; they clip under your regular shoes, spreading your weight and allowing you to stroll over the deepest snow without going in up to your knees. In snowier parts of the world, they can be life savers, enabling stranded people to walk at normal pace instead of floundering up to their waist in snow, getting wet, cold and tired. Now, some ski destinations offer it as a low-impact and relaxing alternative to skiing, and many companies offer snowshoeing holidays.

They're not vast racquet-like structures, but small and lightweight, made from aluminium and nylon, easy to walk in and cheap enough that you can buy a pair for that once-a-winter emergency. Equipped with your snowshoes, you can walk anywhere, through deep snow and over ice (they have cleats to aid traction). A walking pole or stick will help you balance, but they're so easy to use you can even run in them. And when you've reached your destination, you just unclip them and are back in your normal shoes.

Walks you've done a thousand times will seem magical. Being outside on a hilltop in deep snow is an enervating experience, and you'll be able to reach places that hikers without snowshoes won't. The feeling of smugness as you go for a wintery ramble, or drag your sled to pristine virgin snowscapes will make you the envy of every snow-stranded pedestrian. Walking in snow at night is especially silent, peaceful and other-worldly.

As well as the recreational aspects, they should be standard issue for anyone who simply has to get about whatever the weather. Snowshoes cost from around £90 per pair in the UK, but much less from North American stockists (particularly if you buy them in summer).

WINTER

DOG-SLED RACING

AT A GLANCE

Accessibility Index: ❶❷③④⑤

Fitness level: ❶❷③④⑤

Degree of Difficulty: ❶❷❸❹⑤

White-knuckle rating: ❶❷❸④⑤

Equipment: high cost

Season: winter

Family friendly: ✓

Weight restriction: ✓

Who hasn't looked at their dog lolling by the fire or hogging the sofa, and wondered whether they shouldn't be doing more to pull their weight around the place? Unfortunately, your Labrador will be hopeless at this growing sport. It's unofficial name is 'mushing', and with fortnightly races attracting fields of over 100 teams, Britain's hills are alive each winter with the sound of howling hounds. At the Aviemore Sled Dog Rally in 2010 there were 230 teams and over 1,000 dogs.

To compete, you don't need dozens of dogs – a pair will do – but they do need training and a lot more exercise than your average mutt gets. There are also ways of getting into the sport without owning any dogs at all, as volunteers are needed to help look after dogs, train them and clean up after them. Many husky kennels also open for visitors to meet the dogs.

WHAT EXACTLY WILL I BE DOING?

You'll be racing around the countryside at speeds of up to 25mph (40kph), riding on the back of a sledge in snow or on a kind of tricycle if there's no snow, calling "gee" for right, "haw" for left and "whooah" for stop (or "Heeelp!" if you're heading off a mountain).

It's hard work for both man and beast, with the musher having to get off and help the team over and around tricky obstacles (and then get on again quickly or risk being left behind). Races are about 5mi (8km) long and intensely competitive, timed to the hundredth of a second.

You can get your own team or just one dog to help make up another team, with recognised sled dog breeds being the Alaskan Malamute, Canadian Eskimo Dog, Greenland Dog, Samoyed and Siberian Husky.

WHAT SHOULD I BE WORRIED ABOUT?

Let's face it, they could take you pretty much anywhere. The brakes aren't terribly effective, especially in the snow, and sled dogs are wilful and strong. Their combined power is way more than yours, so if the neighbour's cat is out for a stroll, you could both be in trouble.

HAPPY MEMORIES?

The dogs' enthusiasm is infectious, and once on the move it will take all your focus and powers of command to keep them on the straight and narrow. Racing is also about finding the right team – a football manager's job is simple compared to the demands of balancing a dog team's speed and temperament for maximum potential.

WHERE DO I START?

Visit a sled dog rally and start chatting to the rig owners. They'll be able to offer advice and maybe let you ride along to get a feel for the technique. Whatever you do, never buy dogs and kit without doing extensive research.

WHERE CAN IT LEAD?

Many UK owners take their teams to compete in alpine events in Europe.

POPULAR LOCATIONS

Races are staged throughout the UK, with the Forestry Commission being especially accommodating.

WINTER

CONTACTS

- Affiliated British Sleddog Activities (ABSA): 🖥 www.absasleddogracing.org.uk
- British Siberian Husky Racing Association: 🖥 www.huskyracing.org.uk
- Cairngorm Sleddog Centre: ☎ 07767-270526, 🖥 www.sled-dogs.co.uk
- Scottish Siberian Husky Club: 🖥 www.scottishshc.org.uk
- The Siberian Husky Club of Great Britain: 🖥 www.siberianhuskyclub.com

WHEN'S THE BEST TIME FOR IT?

With their heavy coats, winter is the season for dog-sled racing. However, exercising continues all year, and even in summer the early mornings should be cool enough for training runs.

WHO CAN DO IT?

There are junior mushing events from as young as eight years of age, although children of any age can be taken for a ride and help to care for the dogs, which aren't considered dangerous breeds.

WHAT WILL IT COST?

Two-day courses are available for around £255.

CAMPFIRE GOSSIP

Mush comes from the French 'marche', but it isn't actually a call: to start, you call "hike!"

WINTER HILL WALKING

When you hear a Severe Weather Warning for temperatures of -10ºC (14ºF), do you shudder with horror and turn the electric blanket up a notch, or get a gleam in your eye and hear the call of the wild? If it's the latter, you might see that warning more as an invitation to go winter hill walking. This isn't something to be attempted after a merry Christmas lunch. Being out in the countryside in winter anywhere requires careful thought and planning – but being out in the hills and mountains in winter requires specialist knowledge, training and equipment. The benefits of winter walking include the incredible beauty of a snowy, ever-changing landscape, yet without the summertime crowds in our National Parks.

In the wildest, highest country such as Snowdonia, Scotland and the Lake District, walking of any kind in winter is so severe

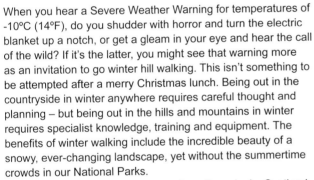

WINTER

CONTACTS

- The Mountaineering Council of Scotland: ☎ 01738-493942, 🖥 www.mcofs.org.uk/winter-hillwalking.asp

- National Parks: 🖥 www.nationalparks.gov.uk

- Organisers: High Trek, Snowdonia; 🖥 www.hightrek.co.uk/climbing/weekends/winter.htm

- Mountain Guides, Lake District & Scotland; www.mountainguides.co.uk/homepages/winter-hillwalking-skills

that it's known as winter mountaineering and usually includes elements of rock and ice climbing, using crampons and ice axes, although usually not ropes. Even a gentle slope can be lethal when it's covered in snow and ice, carrying the unwary off unless they're quick with their ice-axe, so for winter mountaineering as well as being fit and agile, you need to be alert. With conditions in the mountains so changeable, going from clear blue skies to blizzard within minutes, a winter skills course will also cover navigation and survival training.

Warning!

Winter hill walking can be highly dangerous, so take some special precautions: check the weather forecast before leaving; tell someone where you're going and when you plan to return; take a GPS unit, map and compass; keep your mobile phone fully charged, warm and dry; and if the weather turns, descend as quickly as possible or seek refuge. If in doubt, only go with an experienced local guide.

SNOWHOLING

 **AT A GLANCE**

Accessibility Index: ❶❷③④⑤

Fitness level: ❶❷❸❹⑤

Degree of Difficulty: ❶❷❸④⑤

White-knuckle rating: ❶❷❸④⑤

Equipment: hire or medium cost

Season: winter

"Darling, I've found some excellent value accommodation for our winter break. Er… shall I go ahead and book it?" It's a survival technique used for thousands of years, but largely superseded by tents. Snowholing has come back as an adventure activity, but be warned, it's hard work and requires specialist knowledge to avoid your snowhole becoming your snow tomb. Once dug, the snowhole will remain below freezing inside, but between -10-0ºC (14-32ºF) and crucially, sheltered from wind-chill.

WHAT EXACTLY WILL I BE DOING?

First you have to walk to the deepest snow. This isn't an activity for a snowy day in Surrey; it requires deep, compacted snow of at least 4-5ft (120-150cm) and guaranteed sub-zero temperatures. You need to carefully plan the position to avoid avalanche or drifting snow blocking the entrance. Assuming you aren't doing this alone, it's best to dig the hole from two sides and make it as large as possible. That usually requires two hours of hard digging with a shovel or ice-saw, and by smoothing off the ceiling you should prevent drips.

By digging the entrance lower than the chamber, you'll keep the warm, rising air inside. Once large (and deep) enough, dig shelves and alcoves into the walls for your kit, and a sleeping 'shelf' to raise your sleeping bag above the base of the cave, as the coldest air remains near the floor. Place markers and ski poles outside the entrance to warn others of your presence, otherwise you risk another climber stepping through your ceiling. Then settle down for a nice warm night.

What could be more cosy than bedding down in your home-made snowhole? The fact that it took you two hours to dig makes it extra satisfying. As you open your flask of mulled wine and curl up in your sleeping bag, you can reflect that if you were outside in the wind right now, you might never wake up.

Warning!

Being outside at night in the snow is extremely dangerous. This activity must only be attempted with a qualified and experienced guide.

WHAT SHOULD I BE WORRIED ABOUT?

You need to be aware of ventilation in the snowhole and maintain a good air supply. Only use candles or cooking equipment if you're guaranteed a good air supply, otherwise they'll burn up all your oxygen.

HAPPY MEMORIES?

Waking up on holiday in a new bed is always exciting. Although your snowhole won't have a window, so the view may not be great – not if you made it right – the sense of accomplishment when you set foot into the mountain wilderness you've just beaten, and get the bacon cooking, will taste better than any fancy five-star breakfast buffet.

WHERE DO I START?

Organise a course with an experienced operator.

WHERE CAN IT LEAD?

Taking winter navigation and survival courses could equip you for serious wild camping expeditions, both in the UK and abroad.

POPULAR LOCATIONS

You can dig a snowhole and sleep in it anywhere there's deep enough snow. For a first trip, you need to go with an expert, and most winter survival skills courses are in the Scottish mountains such as the Cairngorms.

WHEN'S THE BEST TIME FOR IT?

Winter, and the colder the better – certainly below freezing.

WHO CAN DO IT?

Inuit children have been happily sleeping in ice homes for millennia, and in America this is a popular activity for boy scouts. However, for most snowholing trips in the UK you must be aged over 18, experienced in winter hill walking, and fit enough to spend two hours hard digging.

WHAT SHOULD I TAKE?

Serious safety equipment including avalanche probes and a transceiver. You also need a shovel, gloves and spares, headtorch, sleeping bag suitable to -10ºC (14ºF) and a mat.

WHAT WILL IT COST?

Two to three-day courses cost from around £300.

CAMPFIRE GOSSIP

In an emergency, the fastest and easiest snowholes you can make are either around the base of a tree, where a natural hole forms anyway, or a snow trench. With either, you make or enlarge a hole in the snow and then construct a roof from any branches you can find, while keeping a few evergreen branches for the base of the hole.

CONTACTS

- Mountain Instruction: 🖥 www.mountaininstruction. co.uk/pages/sn_biv.htm

- Onkudu: 🖥 http://onkudu. com/other-adventures/ snow-holing-on-ben-nevis

- SportsScotland Avalanche Information Service (SAIS): ☎ 01479-861264, 🖥 www.sais.gov.uk

- Organisers: Sandy Paterson, Moray, 🖥 www. sandypaterson.co.uk/index. php?page=snow-holing

- SD Adventures, Lanarkshire; 🖥 www.sdadventures. co.uk/page12.htm

WINTER

10

COUNTRY PURSUITS

❖ Game Fishing
❖ Coarse Fishing
❖ Sea Fishing
❖ Archery
❖ Clay Pigeon Shooting
❖ Deer Stalking
❖ Falconry

"What is a weekend?" said a mystified Dowager Countess in the TV drama Downton Abbey, used to spending all week amusing herself. Well, nowadays we can all be Lords and Ladies of the Manor, with hunting, fishing and shooting – the traditional preserves of the aristocracy – now also available to the lower orders.

CONTACTS

- Anglers Net:
  www.anglersnet.co.uk

- The Angling Trust:
  ☎ 0844-770 0616,
  www.anglingtrust.net

- Fishing licenses: www.
  environment-agency.gov.uk

- Salmon and Trout Association:
  www.salmon-trout.org

- UK Fisherman:
  www.ukfisherman.com

GAME FISHING

AT A GLANCE

Accessibility Index: ❶❷❸❹⑤

Fitness level: ❶②③④⑤

Degree of Difficulty: ❶❷❸④⑤

White-knuckle rating: ❶❷③④⑤

Equipment: hire or medium cost

Season: varies with game

Disability friendly: ✓

Game fishing is about catching fish you can eat – usually trout, salmon and char – even if you decide to put it back. For most anglers, game fishing is synonymous with fly fishing, where you make something from bits of fur, feathers, hair and even tinsel that looks like a fly, then you make it behave like a fly to persuade the fish to investigate further by taking it into its mouth. There are half a million fly fishermen and women in the UK, drawn by the thrill of getting deep into the countryside and catching fish for their supper. It was once an expensive, exclusive club activity based around Scotland's salmon rivers and Hampshire's crystal clear chalk streams. Although it can still be expensive, many more lakes and ponds have now been stocked, bringing it within the budget of most people. And you can do it for nothing from the seashore.

Most game fishermen meet the fish halfway by standing in the river wearing waders, sitting in a boat or by using one of the new float-tubes (see page 190). They'll be totally absorbed in every movement of water and reed, using their knowledge of their quarry's behaviour, habits and preferences in order to catch them.

'Casting' refers to waving the rod backwards and forwards to pay out the line and deliver the fly to the target area; a fly can be 'dry' (on the surface) or wet (below the surface). As it lands the fish should strike, the rod dips and you strike to hook it. Hopefully, the

POPULAR LOCATIONS

Southeast: River Ouse, Sussex.

Southwest: River Test, Hampshire.

Central: River Coln, Cotswolds.

North: River Wharfe, Yorkshire.

Wales: River Usk, Monmouthshire.

Scotland: River Tweed, Borders.

trout comes leaping out of the water trailing spray on the end of your line.

Salmon and trout streams can be beautiful places – clear, cool and bubbling – and you're in the water with the fish, making for a more intense experience that dozing off on the riverbank with a flask of tea.

WHERE DO I START?

Book a session at a commercially run lake. Fishing licenses cost from £27 a year, or £3.75 per day. An hour's instruction and use of equipment costs around £40 per hour, while use of a commercially-run lake is £20-40 per day.

CAMPFIRE GOSSIP

The first book on angling (catching fish with a rod and line) was written by a nun in 1496. Dame Juliana Berners' *Treatyse on Fysshynge with an Angle* predated the more famous *Compleat Angler,* by Izaak Walton, by 157 years. Now the Angling Trust (see **Contacts**) is actively trying to get more women fishing.

COUNTRY PURSUITS

COARSE FISHING

 **AT A GLANCE**

Accessibility Index: ❶❷❸❹❺

Fitness level: ❶②③④⑤

Degree of Difficulty: ❶❷❸④⑤

White-knuckle rating: ❶❷③④⑤

Equipment: medium cost

Season: summer to winter

Disability friendly: ✓

Adventurous *and* relaxing? Well, yes. Fishing may have a reputation for being deeply relaxing (to put it kindly), but you're going into the countryside in the early dawn or even at night, lying in wait and using your skill and guile to snatch a wild creature out of its habitat. To get more people interested in fishing, the Angling Trust (see **Contacts**) has a proactive scheme for matching new anglers with coaches and clubs.

The target species are pike, perch, roach, bream and carp, plus at least 25 other species, known disparagingly as 'coarse' to distinguish them from the 'game' fish that the aristocracy were fishing for with their fancy 'flies'. Rod and reel, though still popular, has largely given way to fishing with a long pole of up to 40ft (12m) long. With the agreement of the landowner, you can go coarse fishing in most lakes, rivers, ponds and canals, and 850,000 people do it regularly in Britain.

The simplest form is bait fishing, where you throw ground bait onto your bit of lake or pond to get the fish interested. Then

you bait your hook with a maggot, some bread, sweetcorn, etc., and cast it into the water, with a weight to keep it in the water and a brightly-coloured float to mark it on the surface. When you see the float moving, it suggests a fish is nibbling the food, so you give it a light tug and hopefully catch the fish with the hook through its mouth. You then reel it in, which can be a tussle to avoid breaking the line until you can land it and stow it in your keep net.

Other variations include lure fishing such as spinning, where a lure or sliver of metal that looks like a smaller fish is towed through the water in order to attract a perch or pike. Ledgering is where you use a weight to take the hook to near the bottom of the water to catch bottom feeders. As you develop your techniques, you'll learn to recognise the characteristics of the many species of fish and may decide to focus on catching one species only – carp being a popular choice.

WHERE DO I START?

A trip to your local fishing tackle shop will see you kitted out with a starter pack for less than £100, and you can join a fishing club for under £50 a year and learn from local experts. Fishing on a commercial lake is regarded as a bit too easy by some purists, but it's an easy way to get started from around £20 a day, and the tackle shop can advise on the best places in your area. There are also many charities for the disabled, including 🖳 www.wheelyboats.org.

CAMPFIRE GOSSIP

Anyone can go coarse fishing, but from the age of 12 you'll need a licence from the Post Office, the cost of which depends on the kind of fish you wish to catch and your age.

 **CONTACTS**

- Angling Times magazine: 🖳 www.gofishing.co.uk/angling-times

- Angling Trust: ☎ 0844-770 0616, 🖳 www.anglingtrust.net

- Fishing licenses: 🖳 www.environment-agency.gov.uk

- Total Coarse Fishing magazine: 🖳 www.tcfmagazine.com

- Miscellaneous: 🖳 www.anglingnews.net, www.coarsefish.net, www.fisheries.co.uk, www.fishing4fun.co.uk, www.gofishing.co.uk, www.maggotdrowning.com, www.prebait.com

SEA FISHING

 **AT A GLANCE**

Accessibility Index: ❶❷❸❹❺

Fitness level: ❶②③④⑤

Degree of Difficulty: ❶❷❸④⑤

White-knuckle rating: ❶❷③④⑤

Equipment: medium cost

Season: year round

Disability friendly: ✓

If you want the biggest, wildest, tastiest fish, get out of the pond and out to sea. You can fish from the seashore, from a pier or from a boat, using rod and line which is known as angling, or just chuck a line overboard with some feathers and see if any mackerel are biting below. From the seashore and many quays, fishing is totally free, or you can take a kayak out and catch your own supper.

If you're trying to catch edible fish such as cod, plaice, sole, whiting, bass and mackerel from the shore, the most efficient method is to use a heavy rod and a beach caster to send the line out as far as 600ft (180m). From piers, sea anglers are increasingly trying lighter rods and fly-fishing techniques to catch mackerel and bass. You can also catch these off-shore, while also looking for conger eels, rays and pollock lurking around wrecks.

What could be more relaxing than watching the sunset or sunrise from the seashore while sitting in a cosy little shelter, with container ships and ferries passing on the horizon? Being there for a reason makes the spectacle even more delightful, and catching a juicy bass or cod makes a trip to the seaside extra special. Catching fish is easier when you know something about the tides, the seasons and the feeding habits of your quarry.

WHERE DO I START?

You can buy the equipment for less than £100 and have a friendly chat at your local fishing tackle shop. While there, or from the local press, you can pick up details of local boat operators offering fishing trips. Alternatively, you can join a local club via the Angling Trust (see Contacts). All organisers will be able to teach you the basics.

CAMPFIRE GOSSIP

Not so long ago, the world's most beautiful and adventurous people, including Errol Flynn, came to do their big game fishing in… Scarborough. The Yorkshire coast was teeming with giant tuna, including an 851lb (386kg) thunnus thynnus – tuna. Sadly, the hoovering of the oceans' fish by industrial commercial trawling has reduced the world's richest fishing ground – the North Sea – to a shadow of its former self.

 **CONTACTS**

- Angling Trust: ☎ 0844-770 0616, 💻 www.anglingtrust.net

- Sea Fishing UK: 💻 www.seafishingonline.com

- Miscellaneous: 💻 www. badangling.com, www. sea-fishing.org, www. fishing-blog.co.uk, www. worldseafishing.com

COUNTRY PURSUITS

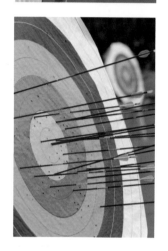

ARCHERY

 **AT A GLANCE**

Accessibility Index: ❶❷❸④⑤

Fitness level: ❶❷③④⑤

Degree of Difficulty: ❶❷③④⑤

White-knuckle rating: ❶❷③④⑤

Equipment: hire or medium cost

Season: year round

Disability friendly: ✓

Family friendly: ✓

You look along the arrow, the bright feathers by your eye and the metal tip at the end. Your focus switches to the target and you let fly. You know it isn't a real animal but it doesn't feel like that when the arrow socks into its flank with a solid thwunkkkk. The tribe will eat tonight! There's a weird excitement that comes over you as you pull that bowstring back and feel the bow bend. Is it the long-buried instincts from our ancestors, who were required by law to attend long-bow practice each Sunday?

Archery is divided into several styles. There's target archery where you shoot at a single target from a measured distance. There's clout archery where you aim to get as close as you can to a flag (the 'clout') a long distance away, and then there's field archery. This is one of Britain's fastest-growing activities, taking you out to the woods and countryside to simulate hunting wild animals (which is illegal in the UK). There are hundreds of local clubs, with field archery events staged throughout the UK each weekend. Joining in is easy and inexpensive, and you can receive full training before you need to buy a bow.

WHAT EXACTLY WILL I BE DOING?

You'll be following a course through country terrain of varying roughness, shooting arrows at life-size 3D models of wildlife. There are many different disciplines, varying according to the type of bow, from old fashioned longbows to high-tech 'compound' bows which massively increase the speed of the arrow with little effort on your part. Indeed, nowadays strength has little to do with most field archery disciplines.

Field archery competitions vary according to which governing body is organising the event, but the normal format is to shoot at 28, 36 or 40 targets over the course of a day. Distances are usually around 50yds (46m), but they can be as little as 20ft (6m) and as far as 80yds (73m). You shoot from a coloured peg, and if you miss the target you move forward to another peg, then another. Children shoot from closer than adults, which is dependent on their age. Complications may be added, such as shooting though obstacles, over undulating ground or from light to dark. And it may all be against the clock.

WHAT SHOULD I BE WORRIED ABOUT?

As you feel the power of the bow, you'll soon realise how terrifying it would have been for our ancestors to come up against a company of trained archers. But these days, if you're scared, you're probably standing in the wrong place…

HAPPY MEMORIES?

Oddly enough, you don't normally do field archery in a field – that's target archery. Field archery is mainly done in the woods and hills, where coping with the variety of terrain is half of the battle and a lot of the fun. It may mean getting wet and dirty in order to get into position for the 'kill', and if the competition is against the clock you'll be barrelling through the undergrowth loosing arrows like it was 1066.

WHERE DO I START?

Visit the National Field Archery Society or Archery GB website (see Contacts) to find a club near you. There are hundreds of clubs with exciting names such as the Black Eagle Bowmen or the Panther Bowhunters, and they usually meet at a local sports field for target practice. For obvious reasons, field archery is done mainly on private land.

WHO CAN DO IT?

Anyone – there are junior competitions, and archery for the disabled and the blind is also popular.

COUNTRY PURSUITS

CONTACTS

- Archery for the Disabled:
  www.ableize.com/
  recreation-sports/archery
- Archery GB, the governing
  body for the sport of archery in
  the UK: www.archerygb.org
- English Field Archery
  Association:
  www.efaafieldarcher.com
- National Field Archery Society:
  01206-543656 (General
  Secretary), www.nfas.net
- Scottish Archery Association:
  www.scottisharchery.org.uk

WHAT SHOULD I TAKE?

Lightweight but warm and rugged outdoor wear.

WHAT WILL IT COST?

A full, good quality, entry-level kit including bow, arrows, quiver, sight, target and all the safety equipment costs around £115. A six-week course of target archery will get you ready for field archery in six sessions for some £60, while entry to competitions costs from £15.

CAMPFIRE GOSSIP

The oldest longbow – the height of a man and usually made from yew – found in Britain was from 2665BC. At the Battle of Agincourt in 1415AD, King Henry V of England defeated a far larger French army with a force consisting mostly of (7,000) longbowmen, possibly the most famous of all battles involving archers. By medieval times, bows were so powerful that Henry VIII (1491-1547) set practice ranges at no less than 220yds (201m), and they could kill from 400yds (365m), the length of four football pitches.

CLAY PIGEON SHOOTING

 AT A GLANCE

Accessibility Index: ❶❷❸④❺

Fitness level: ❶②③④⑤

Degree of Difficulty: ❶❷③④⑤

White-knuckle rating: ❶❷③④⑤

Equipment: hire

Season: year round

Disability friendly: ✓

Family friendly: ✓

While pistol and range shooting as a sport has decreased in Britain – partly as a result of new laws brought in after the Dunblane massacre in 1996 – clay pigeon shooting has gone from strength to strength. Now a new generation of shooters are rediscovering the pleasures of a sociable activity with a high thrill factor. Shooting clays is the guilt-free option, and although it may not get you an invitation to join the Royal Family at Balmoral next Christmas, once you've hit your first flying target your hunger for clay can become addictive.

COUNTRY PURSUITS

✎ CONTACTS

- The Big Shoot:
  ☎ 0844-745 5008,
  🖳 www.thebigshoot.co.uk

- Clay Pigeon Shooting
  Association: ☎ 01483-
  485400, 🖳 www.cpsa.co.uk

- Down the Line:
  🖳 www.downtheline.co.uk

The targets, or 'pigeons', are catapulted from a trap around 50ft (15m) away from you, heading off in all directions at variable speeds. You normally do a round of 25 birds, costing from £30, with the most common discipline being 'English Sporting', where the targets vary in speed and angle just as a game bird would in the field. You'll hear the target referred to variously as a dropping duck, bolting rabbit, springing teal and many more, according to how the clay flies. Another style is called helice shooting, where a small attachment to the clay creates erratic flight and a buzzing noise. Beginners, however, normally start with Down The Line (DTL) shooting, where the targets are set 9ft (2.75m) off the ground at a distance of around 55yds (50m), more or less down a centre line.

You can usually try clay pigeon shooting from the age of 13, and no licence is required.

WHERE DO I START?

There are 450 affiliated clubs and shoots in the UK, so finding one for the weekend should be as easy as picking up the phone.

CAMPFIRE GOSSIP

The Royal Artillery Barracks at Woolwich will be the venue for the 2012 Olympics shooting events, with some 400 athletes competing for gold.

DEER STALKING

 **AT A GLANCE**

Accessibility Index: ❶❷❸④⑤

Fitness level: ❶❷③④⑤

Degree of Difficulty: ❶❷❸④⑤

White-knuckle rating: ❶❷❸④⑤

Equipment: hire or medium cost

Season: varies

Killing fellow mammals isn't everyone's idea of fun, but neither is factory farming. Deer stalking gets you closer to the brutish process of survival, and the deer will need to be culled anyway as they have no natural predators. Deer stalking is the shooting and killing of deer in the countryside after a stealthy pursuit on foot. There are more deer living wild in Britain's countryside than ever before, with indigenous red and roe deer added to by fallow deer which were introduced by the Romans, plus Muntjac, Sika and Chinese Water Deer that have escaped from private estates.

In Scotland alone, there are some 400,000 deer, and given their twin penchants for reproducing and eating crops, around 30 per cent are culled each year, throughout the UK. Unlike game birds, killed in their millions purely for fun and usually buried because there are too many to cook, deer stalking is ecologically sound and necessary. But you still need a heart of steel to do it.

Perhaps paradoxically, with the strict close seasons when hunting is banned, many deer stalkers spend most of the year shooting deer with a camera. It helps in tracking and learn the deer's habits, while still involving lying on the ground in the countryside.

WHAT EXACTLY WILL I BE DOING?

First you must be able to hit a target with a high-powered rifle. Training in stalking is done by 'ghillies', who work for the estates and (in theory) won't let you loose on a live target unless you can hit a 4in (10cm) target, three times, from 100 yards..

Most deer stalking is done at dusk or dawn. The ghillie will take you to the most likely spot to find deer and quietly, stealthily hunt them down. Shooting is strictly seasonal, with red deer stags in Scotland, for example, only stalked from July to October,

POPULAR LOCATIONS

Southeast: Kent/Sussex borders.

Southwest: Exmoor.

Central: East Anglia.

North: The Lake District.

Wales: Monmouthshire.

Scotland: The East Highlands – red and roe deer.

and the hinds from October to February. Some estates limit this even further. In order to maintain strong and stable herds, an assessment is made each year of which type of deer need to be culled. If a herd is getting too big, it's bad news for young females, while if it's too small the older males are taken. Either way, sick and very old animals are chosen first.

Some courses and holidays include butchering and preparing the carcass, which belongs to the estate, and most involve a wee dram of whisky afterwards.

WHAT SHOULD I BE WORRIED ABOUT?

Taking a weapon out to the countryside at dawn and taking aim at peaceful prey is a deep, dark, primeval pleasure that not everyone shares. Therefore, if you want to brag about the stag you bagged at the weekend, make sure that you know your audience well…

HAPPY MEMORIES?

You're in Britain's most beautiful landscapes, the glens, moors, mountains and forests, moving silently through the countryside, looking for the sight of antlers in the early morning mist, or the red hide of a deer reflecting the setting sun.

WHERE DO I START?

Contact the British Deer Society to find clubs in your area or book a stalking expedition or holiday.

WHERE CAN IT LEAD?

The British Deer Society runs courses at various levels, which include all aspects of deer identification, biology and ecology, plus shooting technique, firearms and culling law.

WHAT SHOULD I TAKE?

Standard outdoor camouflage clothing, suitable for lying down in long wet grass and for walking long distances. A deerstalker hat is optional, but midge repellent is strongly advised.

WHAT WILL IT COST?

A day's stalking costs from around £100, including the right to shoot one deer.

CAMPFIRE GOSSIP

In the 1925 novel, *John Macnab* (written by John Buchan), three bored Londoners go deer poaching in Scotland. Bagging a modern Macnab is to shoot a stag and a brace of grouse, and catch a salmon on the fly. You can take the challenge – and its many variations – with many organisers in Scotland.

 CONTACTS

- The British Deer Society:
  ☎ 01425-55434,
  🖥 www.bds.org.uk

- Deer Stalking Scotland: 🖥 www.deerstalkingscotland.co.uk

- The Home of UK Deer Stalking: 🖥 www.thestalkingdirectory.co.uk

- Stalking Directory: 🖥 www.thestalkingdirectory.co.uk

FALCONRY

AT A GLANCE

Accessibility Index: ❶❷❸❹⑤

Fitness level: ❶②③④⑤

Degree of Difficulty: ❶❷❸④⑤

White-knuckle rating: ❶❷③④⑤

Equipment: medium cost

Season: year round

Disability friendly: ✓

Family friendly: ✓

CONTACTS

- Birds of Prey and Conservation Centre, Yorks.: ☎ 01845-587522, 💻 www.falconrycentre.co.uk

- British Falconers Club: 💻 www.britishfalconersclub.co.uk

- Hawk Board: 💻 www.hawkboard-cff.org.uk

- International Centre for Birds of Prey, Glos.: ☎ 01531-820286, 💻 www.icbp.org

- Phoenix Falconry, Perthshire: ☎ 01764-682823, 💻 www.scottishfalconry.co.uk

- Sussex Falconry Centre: ☎ 01243-512472, 💻 www.sussexfalconrycentre.co.uk

In the UK, we have some of the least restrictive falconry laws in the western world, so anyone who learns to love birds of prey can own one. Falconry, strictly speaking, means using birds of prey – also known as 'raptors' – to hunt for game, usually rabbits, pheasants and smaller birds, but also foxes, ducks and hare. A peregrine falcon flies at game at 200mph (321kph), so it's an astonishing spectacle to see it dispatching an unsuspecting bunny. However, this is a bit full-on for most experience days and courses, which focus more on letting you handle the birds including hawks, eagles, kestrels, kites, owls and even vultures, and have them fly to your hand.

WHAT EXACTLY WILL I BE DOING?

First off, you'll be marvelling at the birds. Until you've seen them close up, nothing prepares you for their astonishing beauty, with the sleekest feathers and a look of disdain from beady eyes. Yet they're surprisingly light to hold and, since you can only own captive-bred birds in the UK, they're normally perfectly happy to sit on your arm and be admired.

Day experiences and courses usually involve handling a range of birds, watching them doing displays and catching lures, and even learning to swing the lure for the bird yourself. If you're hunting, you may well get to take home whatever the bird has caught. Falconry is a highly technical business involving weighing the bird to assess how far and high it will fly, and knowing when it should wear a hood, as well as being aware of its diet, knowing common illnesses, and using radio telemetry in case the bird decides to 'go native' for a while. Therefore you shouldn't get a bird before you're properly trained and understand what you're getting yourself into.

HAPPY MEMORIES?

The first time a hawk swoops down to land on your gauntleted hand, with amazing nimbleness and delicacy, you'll probably fall in love with falconry. But taking a bird into the countryside isn't like taking the dog for a walk. They appreciate calm and stillness, and will react by clenching their claw on your arm if they're upset, which can be painful. Falconers also often talk of the bond between them and their bird, which isn't like master and servant, but more like a loyal friendship based on mutual respect, admiration and understanding.

WHAT SHOULD I BE WORRIED ABOUT?

An eagle owl is a metre tall and with a wingspan to match. And they're hunters – so to develop a meaningful relationship with one, you'll need to get with the programme, put aside your squeamishness and join your bird in seeing cute woodland creatures for what they are – lunch.

WHERE DO I START?

Many country fairs have falconry displays, where you can see the birds close up and talk to their owners. If they fire your imagination, there are clubs throughout the country where you can book a day's experience and increase your knowledge and skill before considering owning your own falcon.

WHO CAN DO IT?

You need to remain still and hold the bird on your arm, therefore most courses and experience days are limited to children of 12 years and older. But children can admire the birds at any age.

WHAT SHOULD I TAKE?

Wear outdoor clothing and footwear suitable for a day in the countryside.

WHAT WILL IT COST?

A visit to the International Centre for Birds of Prey costs under £10, and half-day experiences around £65. Falconry holidays and four-day courses cost from £400.

CAMPFIRE GOSSIP

The Middle-East is the spiritual home of falconry, and there are many courses and organised holidays in places such as Kuwait. The new trend is towards parahawking, where you go hang gliding or paragliding (see page 32) with your bird of prey flying alongside you.

COUNTRY PURSUITS

11

TEAM BUILDING

- ❖ Paintballing
- ❖ Survival Skills & Bushcraft
- ❖ Assault Course
- ❖ Treasure Hunt
- ❖ School Sports Day
- ❖ Raft Building
- ❖ Duck Herding

Whether your team is your colleagues, your family or your best mates, these activities will bring you closer. You can learn how to survive in the wild, catching wild food; herding your own livestock; building shelters and rafts; tackling an assault course; competing at sports or trying to find 'treasure'; and shooting the bad guys with a paintball gun.

In addition to those described in this chapter, many other activities and sports covered in this book are also excellent team building activities and corporate events, and are offered by numerous organisers. See also the list of organisers in Appendix B.

PAINTBALLING

AT A GLANCE

Accessibility Index: ❶❷❸❹❺

Fitness level: ❶❷③④⑤

Degree of Difficulty: ❶②③④⑤

White-knuckle rating: ❶❷❸④⑤

Equipment: hire or low cost

Season: year round

Disability friendly: ✓

Family friendly: ✓

A paintball thwacking into your ear at 300 feet per second hurts, and will have you diving into the nearest ditch to avoid another. But as you climb out – muddy, bruised and 'dead' – there's only one thing on your mind: vengeance.

Paintball is genuinely thrilling, quite painful, and offers a taste of warfare (without dying). It was invented in America 30 years ago, and has developed into a sport, a training aid for the military and even a way of re-enacting famous battles. It's a great way to build rapport and camaraderie amongst workmates, and is safe. With full facemasks a legal requirement, the main risk of injury is from falling over in the excitement. It can be highly energetic but requires no special strength.

WHAT EXACTLY WILL I BE DOING?

Each player has a gun, called a 'marker', powered by gas and fitted with a hopper for the paintballs, which are small spheres containing water-soluble dye. Players are divided into teams and set against each other in a series of games, usually capturing the opposing team's flag or attacking their base. You shoot at your opponents just like in battle, and may utilise smoke bombs and 'grenades', but when you feel the bullet hit you and see the tell-tale paint-splodge on your camouflage, you leave the game.

There are paintball centres throughout the country, within easy reach of most towns and cities. You'll generally spend a day or half-day at the centre, with each game lasting around 20 minutes, though there are shorter, sharper versions. You'll experience defence and attack on a variety of terrains and scenarios, maybe including 'street fighting', but usually just in the woods.

HAPPY MEMORIES?

No-one forgets their first paintball experience. For a certain kind of person, usually a man, it's the most fun in the world; the chance to experience the thrill of combat and the bitter-sweet terror of being hunted. You'll see countryside as you've never seen it before; like an animal, for its cover and protection. The stuff you've read in books about strategy, stealth and courage: suddenly, you're living it. You're your very own action hero.

WHAT SHOULD I BE WORRIED ABOUT?

Being shot hurts. Not much, but enough to make you disinclined to make death or glory suicide runs, and that's what makes the game so good – no pain, no gain.

WHERE DO I START?

Just type paintball into Google, or even better, ask amongst friends and colleagues – you're bound to find someone with a secret hankering to try paintball, but who (not surprisingly) cannot persuade his wife to go with him.

WHEN'S THE BEST TIME FOR IT?

Winters are often better, with softer landings when you hit the deck, and cooler weather = more clothing = less pain when you're shot.

WHO CAN DO IT?

The legal minimum age is 10, with written parental consent required for those aged under 16.

WHAT SHOULD I TAKE?

Stout shoes and outdoor wear, depending on the weather. Gun, facemask and camouflage suit are provided.

TEAM BUILDING

 ## CONTACTS

- UK Paintball Sports Federation: 🖳 www.ukpsf.com
- Organisers: 🖳 http://go-ballistic.co.uk, www.paintballgames.co.uk, www.ukpaintball.co.uk

WHAT WILL IT COST?

From £10 for a half day, plus around £20 for bullets.

CAMPFIRE GOSSIP

Early in June on a riverbank in Oklahoma, the largest paintball event in the world takes place: a re-enactment of the D-Day landings, with thousands of participants divided into nationalities and even regiments.

SURVIVAL SKILLS & BUSHCRAFT

 **AT A GLANCE**

Accessibility Index: ❶❷❸④⑤

Fitness level: ❶❷③④⑤

Degree of Difficulty: ❶❷③④⑤

White-knuckle rating: ❶❷③④⑤

Equipment: none to low cost

Season: usually spring-autumn

Disability friendly: ✓

Family friendly: ✓

After completing your survival course, you'll hope western civilisation does break down. After all, with your fire lighting skills, your ability to make a cosy hat from bark, and your recipe for caterpillar soufflé, you'll probably be elected chief.

A hundred years after Baden-Powell started the Boy Scouts, bushcraft is back, inspired by the likes of Ray Mears and Bear Grylls, and a nagging suspicion that the world is going to hell in a handcart. There are now hundreds of courses teaching you how to survive in the open, help out if you happen upon an injured hiker in the mountains, or just test yourself in extreme circumstances. There are special courses for mothers and daughters, and even survival and storytelling nights for children. You can take a day course, a weekend (or longer) camping expedition, or just read a book and go it alone.

WHAT EXACTLY WILL I BE DOING?

There are four things you need in the wild: water, food, warmth and shelter. Most courses take this as a starting point and teach you how to find and store water, light a fire without matches, make a shelter and forage for food. Few of us would have the vaguest idea even how to rearrange our own clothes for maximum warmth if stranded outside, and the sad evidence is that, in extremis, people often give up too early and die of fear and misery. Yet constructing a shelter from saplings and leaves isn't so difficult when you know how, and the countryside is a well-stocked larder if you know where to look.

TEAM BUILDING

You'll learn how to nap arrowheads from flint and tie them to an arrow shaft with twine made from nettles, and catch fish and rabbits – then prepare, cook and eat them over a makeshift barbecue. Many courses are run by former soldiers, including Special Forces, who can tell you how to care for an injured companion (or how to bury them, if…), and where to find natural painkillers.

Lastly, after a while you'll probably quite like to go home, so the course will teach you how to signal to searching aircraft, work out directions from the sun and stars, and navigate your way to the nearest town.

HAPPY MEMORIES?

Learning machete skills or knowing how to track a deer will make you feel strangely good about yourself. Getting your first fire alight without the aid of matches is a terrific feeling, surpassed only by the thrill of cooking a choice morsel on it that you killed (or picked) with your bare hands. The skills you'll learn may never come in useful, but it's nice to have them anyway.

WHAT SHOULD I BE WORRIED ABOUT?

You've done the course and now you're giving it a go for real. Out in the wilderness, on your own. No tent, no mobile phone and Pizza Hut don't deliver this far. Maybe that weekend in Barcelona would have been more fun after all.

WHERE DO I START?

There are courses throughout the UK (see **Contacts**).

WHERE CAN IT LEAD?

There are also military survival courses that include an element of weapons training, camouflage and concealment, and 'games' such as hostage extraction.

WHO CAN DO IT?

Courses generally take children from year seven (ages 11 to 12), but there are family trips and courses available where you can take younger children along.

WHAT SHOULD I TAKE?

A list will be supplied by course organisers, usually including a good sheath knife

WHAT WILL IT COST?

Single days from £50 and weekend courses from £150.

CAMPFIRE GOSSIP

Stinging nettle can be converted to rope within just a few hours. Firstly, remove the leaves and side stalks. Next, gently crush the hollow stems, using a stick if not your fingers, then open them up and remove the inner pithy fibres. Dry the stems for a few hours in sunlight or by the fire. Twist the dried fibres together into a rope, and you're ready to use it for trapping animals, lashing your home together or holding your trousers up (tip from Nature's Craft, see **Contacts**).

✎ CONTACTS

- Nature's Craft:
  ☎ 07919-351640,
  🖥 www.naturescraft.co.uk

- Ray Mears Bushcraft:
  ☎ 01580-819668,
  🖥 www.raymears.com

- Wild Wise: ☎ 01803-868269,
  🖥 www.wildwise.co.uk

TEAM BUILDING

CONTACTS

- Organisers: Map Challenges,
  www.mapchallenges.
  co.uk; Exelement, www.
  exelement.co.uk; Adrenalin,
  www.adrenalinnylimited.co.uk

ASSAULT COURSE

AT A GLANCE

Accessibility Index: **❶❷❸**④⑤

Fitness level: **❶❷❸**④⑤

Degree of Difficulty: **❶**②③④⑤

White-knuckle rating: **❶❷❸❹**⑤

Equipment: hire

Season: year round

Family friendly: ✓

Weight restriction: ✓

How would you get over a 13ft (4m) wall? Try it on your own and you'll be like a spider trying to get out of a bath, yet with a couple of mates, even short ones, it's easy. Military-style assault courses are a lot of fun; popular for hen and stag parties, and for tempting teenagers away from computer games and Facebook. But they're also great for staff team-building, getting the sales team to talk to the IT department and rewarding the workforce.

There are assault course activities to suit every fitness level and for most age groups. There are also special girls-only outfits, so no-one should feel they can avoid the pain and the chance to swing, leap, crawl, climb, run and wade past obstacles.

Assault courses are often part of a whole day of outdoor team-building activities, and they're a perfect warm-up to paintballing or rafting. You'll normally be kitted out in camouflage outfit and helmet, and receive a safety briefing. Then you may face team-based challenges, such as helping each other over walls, or finding a way to cross a 'mine-field'. Or they may be a straight race over obstacles, probably with inviting names like the Torture Tunnel, Death Plunge or Stalag Escape. It isn't usually only strength that prevails; you'll need dexterity, balance, stamina and motivation.

Some assault courses are more military than others – in some you even carry a 'gun' while instructors hurl insults and bangers to recreate that Omaha Beach experience – while others focus more on co-operation and problem solving.

TREASURE HUNT

TEAM BUILDING

AT A GLANCE

Accessibility Index: ❶❷❸④⑤

Fitness level: ❶②③④⑤

Degree of Difficulty: ❶❷③④⑤

White-knuckle rating: ❶②③④⑤

Equipment: none

Season: year round

Disability friendly: ✓

Family friendly: ✓

CONTACTS

- Organisers:
  www.actiontreasurehunts.co.uk, www.huntthegoose.co.uk, www.huntfortreasure.co.uk, www.treasurehuntsuk.co.uk

If *The Apprentice* has shown us anything, it's that there's nothing more pleasing than seeing the company braggard exposed by the cold, hard truths of logic and common sense. Treasure hunts are excellent levellers and team building exercises, where everyone from the post-room to the corporate dining room gets a chance to shine, no matter how fit or popular with the bosses. They involve teams of colleagues following a course on foot, bike, quad bike, car, public transport or anything else, solving clues as they go. The various teams all meet up at the end for the results and a bit of a shindig.

Though there are companies who will organise it all for you for a fee (see **Contacts**), this is an activity that's easy to organise yourself, with formats and locations to suit you. It can be as simple as going to a series of city centre locations and having your photo taken to prove you found it, or as complicated as having to solve a fiendish set of riddles, answer general knowledge questions, find clues in tricky locations or even locate a 'spy' with your password to direct you onwards. There's also huge scope for using modern technology, with text messaging, phone cameras where you can send proof of your presence in a location instantly, and even using GPS devices.

Treasure hunts may be leisurely, or against the clock. In the country they could involve maps and compasses, just like orienteering (see page 71), but that's getting a little complicated for most company days out. A simple (though subtle) marked trail through the countryside with an element of tracking is usually challenging enough, culminating in a company picnic or barbecue, where none of you (dramatic pause) will get fired. Hopefully. Just don't make a fool of your boss…

📝 **CONTACTS**

- Organisers: 🖥 www.accolade-corporate-events.com, www.eventshouse.co.uk, www.team-motivation.co.uk

SCHOOL SPORTS DAY

👓 AT A GLANCE

Accessibility Index: ❶❷❸④⑤

Fitness level: ❶❷③④⑤

Degree of Difficulty: ❶②③④⑤

White-knuckle rating: ❶❷③④⑤

Equipment: low cost

Season: generally summer only

Family friendly: ✓

A baking hot summer's day, freshly-mown playing fields and the 100 metres course newly marked out, jugs of orange squash ready for thirsty children in short trousers, no lessons for the rest of the day... If education, as they say, is wasted on the young, that goes double for school sports day.

Sports days are too much fun to be left to the kids, so corporate entertainment providers now offer the school sports day experience as a company day out and team-building exercise for grown ups. Activities, which can take place at a local park or on private land, can be junior or senior school; the emphasis may be on silliness and fun, with egg and spoon races, a skipping contest, space hopper, wheelbarrow, sack or three-legged race, or there are more sporty versions with running races, obstacle courses, tug of war and ball games. Companies see a summer sports day as a healthy and relatively risk-free alternative to the boozy, lecherous Christmas party (though it can also be nice to see colleagues in shorts), with teams drawn from across departments, with inter-team banter encouraged and a

prize giving ceremony at the end. Even though the event should be fun, for those with ghastly memories of being picked last at games, don't think that the grown-up version will necessarily be any less humiliating. But wouldn't you just love another chance at a game of rounders on a summer's afternoon?

Around the 2012 Olympics an alternative is for a mini-Olympics, with fun versions of track and field events.

RAFT BUILDING

⌒👓 AT A GLANCE

Accessibility Index: ❶❷❸④⑤

Fitness level: ❶②③④⑤

Degree of Difficulty: ❶②③④⑤

White-knuckle rating: ❶❷③④⑤

Equipment: hire or low cost

Season: summer

Disability friendly: ✓

Family friendly: ✓

Confident swimmer: ✓

📝 CONTACTS

- Coniston, Lake District: 🖥 www.riverdeepmountainhigh.co.uk

- River Wye, South Wales: 🖥 http://blackmountain.co.uk/water/raftbuild.htm

- Snowdonia: 🖥 www.adrenalinantics.com

You and your team bring your ingenuity and skill to the task of making a raft, then climb aboard and paddle away. It's more than just a great day out, it's a metaphor. Many activity centres (see **Contacts**) offer raft building as an option, but you can also build your own at home, with plenty of instructions available on the internet, especially from America, where it's been a popular summer holiday project for kids ever since Mark Twain published *The Adventures of Huckleberry Finn*.

At an activity centre, you'll be given the tools and equipment to make your raft, usually from a collection of plastic drums and poles. The basic technique is to start by building a sturdy frame from the pipes, then laying this on the empty barrels and lashing it in place. Then you put some sort of flooring on top, load the younger members on board and push it into the water. If it floats, you then test your craft against others for speed, manoeuvrability and robustness. That could mean races, tug-of-war, even a bit of white water. Either way, you're going to get wet.

Raft building is a combination of concentration, physical activity and problem-solving. Time will slip by in a glorious haze of ropes, knots, barrels and lashing. Once it's afloat, you can lighten up for some wet and wild fun.

Warning!

Taking a home-made raft on the water can be dangerous, and should only be done under expert supervision and with the appropriate safety equipment, especially life jackets.

TEAM BUILDING

✍ CONTACTS

- Corporate entertainment/ team building: 🖥 www. derwent-pursuits.co.uk, www. corporateentertainment.net

- Longton Sheepdogs: 🖥 www.longtonsheepdogs. com

DUCK HERDING

⌐○○ AT A GLANCE

Accessibility Index: ❶❷③④⑤

Fitness level: ❶②③④⑤

Degree of Difficulty: ❶❷③④⑤

White-knuckle rating: ❶❷③④⑤

Equipment: none

Season: summer

Disability friendly: ✓

Family friendly: ✓

"Come by. Aweeee. That'll do." Ah yes, the sounds of rural Britain: a mellifluous country brogue, the pattering pads of a sheep dog, the feathery flap and quack of its quarry... Eh? Yes, it's one man and his duck, and it's all the rage in team-building.

For training sheep dogs, Indian Runner ducks are easier, cheaper and funnier than sheep and require less space. As part of a team building day out, you can learn to control the dog by both tone of voice and by what you say. The basic instructions to the dog are: 'come-by' for go left, 'away' for right, 'walk' for move in closer, 'stand' for stop and 'that'll do' for return to handler. Easy, then. Well, not really. The ducks have a mind of their own, though not an especially large one, and the dogs are easily confused by rookies who they mistakenly assume know more than they do. But getting it all wrong is part of the fun, and the ducks are inherently hilarious as they jog through tunnels, down slides, and in and out of water.

There's also the option to stay on a farm for one-to-one tuition with your own border collie and an experienced handler. Many people have collies as family pets, and all those generations of instincts are waiting to be unleashed if you have the patience to do the training.

TEAM BUILDING

12

GENTLE
ADVENTURES

- ❖ Bird Watching
- ❖ Astronomy Weekends
- ❖ Fossil Hunting
- ❖ Crop Circle Hunting
- ❖ Conservation Volunteer
- ❖ Working Farm Holidays
- ❖ Llama Trekking

We're not all adrenalin junkies who want to 'get radical' or 'pump up the action' or even 'get physical'. So if you like your adventures at a gentler or slower pace, preferably seated perhaps (and with a cup of tea and a biscuit), maybe even helping charities and your community, then these may be for you.

BIRD WATCHING

AT A GLANCE

Accessibility Index: ❶❷❸❹❺

Fitness level: ❶②③④⑤

Degree of Difficulty: ❶②③④⑤

White-knuckle rating: ❶❷③④⑤

Equipment: low cost

Season: year round

Disability friendly: ✓

Family friendly: ✓

Not so long ago, bird watchers were portrayed as weirdos in plus-fours, wandering the countryside peering into bushes. These are lesser spotted now, and being able to distinguish a warbler from a wigeon suddenly seems quite an attractive quality in a person. Birdwatching, or 'birding' as devotees prefer to call it, now claims some glamorous devotees, with Cameron Diaz, Joanna Lumley and Mick Jagger joining Bill Oddie out on the heath with the binoculars.

Birding is the identification and study of our native birds. It's a popular activity; the Royal Society for the Protection of Birds

(RSPB) has over a million members, and found in a survey that 6m people in Britain describe themselves as bird watchers. Interest has been prompted partly by the BBC's *Springwatch* and *Autumnwatch* programmes, and this is one of the few fun and worthwhile activities you can do from inside your own home. Once you've studied your local garden birds, you can visit some amazing places to see wilder birds, even sea kayaking out to remote Northumbrian islands. Dedicated twitchers will go to amazing lengths to tick off rare birds, many of which have been blown off course and have flown here by accident.

WHAT EXACTLY WILL I BE DOING?

You could start with the birds you can see in your garden or out of your window – the sparrows, starlings, blue tits, chaffinches, blackbirds, robins and greenfinches. Recognise these, and you're already ahead of 90 per cent of the population. Garden birds are easy to attract with bird food and a good feeding platform away from the reach of cats.

Next, you can start meeting birds in their own habitats, whether it's woodland to see the willow tit, wood warbler and spotted flycatcher, farmland to see the corn bunting, the yellowhammer, lapwing and kestrel, or rivers to see avocets in the mud and herons and kingfishers on the banks. Most of these can be seen by just walking around, but eventually you may want to join a club to get advice, meet like-minded people to compare notes with, and to use hides to get close up to the rarer species.

Birding isn't just about watching birds. First you have to find them, and for that you need your ears. Mobile technology has made bird identification less hit or miss; you can download birdsong onto your mobile phone or iPod to identify what you're hearing. And once you start to pick out individual bird songs, such as the beautiful, low, fluted warble of the blackbird, a walk at any time of the day suddenly starts appealing to a whole new sense.

WHAT SHOULD I BE WORRIED ABOUT?

Birdwatching isn't very worrying, but the loss of our native species certainly is. Even the humble and once ubiquitous house sparrow is disappearing.

WHERE DO I START?

Start at home, by just getting some binoculars and an internet guide to garden birds.

WHO CAN DO IT?

Anyone. The RSPB is active in recruiting and motivating younger members via its Wildlife Explorers programme.

GENTLE ADVENTURES

CONTACTS

- Bird Forum:
  www.birdforum.net

- Birds of Britain:
  www.birdsofbritain.co.uk

- British Garden Birds:
  www.gardenbirds.co.uk

- British Trust for Ornithology:
  www.bto.org

- Chatterbirds bird watching community:
  www.chatterbirds.com

- The Royal Society for the Protection of Birds (RSPB):
  www.rspb.org.uk

WHAT SHOULD I TAKE?

Binoculars – something lightweight, close-focusing 8x25 – and a book of British birds. You can buy both from the RSPB.

WHAT WILL IT COST?

Good binoculars cost from around £80 and a book less than £10, or you can buy budget and second-hand versions of each for much less.

CAMPSITE GOSSIP

Conservation efforts are ensuring that despite the loss of garden birds, which have been declining in numbers for decades, there has been a marked increase in sightings of rare birds such as the white-tailed eagle. One joined the puffins on Farne Island, Northumbria, recently.

ASTRONOMY WEEKENDS

**AT A GLANCE**

Accessibility Index: ❶❷❸❹❺

Fitness level: ❶②③④⑤

Degree of Difficulty: ❶❷③④⑤

White-knuckle rating: ❶②③④⑤

Equipment: hire or low cost

Season: year round

Disability friendly: ✓

Family friendly: ✓

It may only seem adventurous if you're reading this in a prison cell, but astronomy is a free, easy outdoor activity that takes you into the countryside at night and is a real adventure for children. As well as being interesting, scientific and thought-provoking, knowing your way round the stars might help you to navigate your way home one day.

Scotland's Galloway Forest has been named Dark Sky Park – only the fourth in the world; but any remote place away from light pollution will do, and this is the ideal activity to combine with wild camping (see page 59), as you poke your head out of the tent at 2am and calculate your place in the universe.

GENTLE ADVENTURES

CONTACTS

- Cornwall: 💻 www.roselandobservatory.com
- Devon: 💻 www.astroadventures.co.uk
- Federation of Astronomical Societies: 💻 www.fedastro.org.uk
- Holidays in Dark Skies Park: 💻 www.gallowayastro.com
- Scotland: 💻 www.forestry.gov.uk/darkskygalloway
- Space Station flights: 💻 www.spaceflight.nasa.gov

You can go it alone, with binoculars and a planisphere – a map of the stars – or join an organised astronomy weekend with proper telescopes and someone to explain what you're looking at. You'll soon recognise the Plough, Orion's Belt, Sirius and the North Star, and from these you can start linking up with other constellations and identifying planets.

Astronomy magazines (e.g. the BBC's *Sky at Night*) will keep you up to date with how the skies are changing with the seasons, as well as pointing out particular events, such as meteor showers and comets. Once you've identified Perseus, you'll know where to look for the Perseid meteor every mid-August. Joining a club will make spending long nights in the dark a lot less daunting, and you'll be able to see how various telescopes compare, before buying your own. And once you have your own and are under a nice dark sky, you'll be able to see distant galaxies such as Andromeda, whose light has taken 2.5m years to reach you.

WHERE TO START?

An easy starting point is a quick glimpse of the International Space Station, which you can often see for a few minutes just before dawn or after dusk. It's the bright light scudding across the sky from the west that you can see with the naked eye, despite it being 200mi (321km) away and travelling at 17,000mph. With even basic binoculars, you can make out its structure.

CAMPFIRE GOSSIP

Every atom in the Universe, every bit of every galaxy, star, planet, tree, person, alien, fish, flower, fly, microbe and you was once contained within an object the size of a pea – until the BIG BANG. According to Stephen Hawking, anyway – don't ask us to explain…

FOSSIL HUNTING

 **AT A GLANCE**

Accessibility Index: ❶❷❸④⑤

Fitness level: ❶②③④⑤

Degree of Difficulty: ❶❷③④⑤

White-knuckle rating: ❶②③④⑤

Equipment: none to low cost

Season: winter/spring

Disability friendly: ✓

Family friendly: ✓

Stone: it looks so solid, yet a few million years ago it was just a damp patch in the forest, into which fell a creature. Its body – maybe tiny, maybe the size of a bus – was enveloped in mud and a long chemical process took place that preserved and turned it to stone over millions of years. Layer upon layer was laid on top, tectonic plates shifted, Continents moved, forests became deserts and deserts became seabeds, seas receded, and now – oh look! Here's you, tip-tapping along the beach with your hammer…

You can go it alone with fossil hunting – and there's plenty of information online and in books – but to start, it's worthwhile signing up for a course in fossil hunting or joining a club. You're looking for where sedimentary rock is being exposed, for example in river banks, along beaches and in quarries – all of which can be dangerous. The best sites are well documented, especially along the southern coasts of England (e.g. the Jurassic Coast) and the Isle of Wight, and you can start by simply looking at the rocks along the cliff base after a storm, when wind and waves will have eroded the cliff face and, hopefully, dislodged some fossils onto the beach below.

You'll see the wildlife and learn about the big stuff from geography, geology, history and biology, not from a book in a stuffy classroom, but on site. For example, the ammonites and bivalves found in Britain's chalk cliffs were caught there when the land was on the same latitude as Gibraltar is now, and sea levels were 200m (650ft) higher than today. Which is amazing, when you stop to think about it…

WHERE DO I START?

Check out the websites below for your local fossiling highlights, and go and have a look. When you start breaking into rocks to

GENTLE ADVENTURES

✍ CONTACTS

- Discovering Fossils: 💻 www.discoveringfossils.co.uk
- The Lyme Regis Fossil Festival: 💻 www.fossilfestival.com
- Natural History Museum: 💻 www.nhm.ac.uk
- UK Fossils Network: 💻 www.ukfossils.co.uk

see inside, you'll need a specialised fossil-hunting hammer and chisel, and eye protection.

CAMPFIRE GOSSIP

Mary Anning, an ordinary girl from Lyme Regis, became one of the world's greatest fossil hunters in the early 19th century, after she discovered an ichthyosaur when she was just 12 years old. But fossil hunting can be dangerous: she lost her dog and very nearly her own life in a rock fall.

CROP CIRCLE HUNTING

AT A GLANCE

Accessibility Index: ❶❷❸④⑤

Fitness level: ❶❷③④⑤

Degree of Difficulty: ❶②③④⑤

White-knuckle rating: ❶②③④⑤

Equipment: none

Season: spring and summer

Disability friendly: ✓

Family friendly: ✓

Crop circles are images and geometric patterns – some simple, some incredibly complex – that have been forming in fields of corn and other crops since the mid-'70s. Numbers vary from year to year, but generally between 100 and 200 turn up each year – 2009 was a bumper crop, including a 600ft (183m) jellyfish pattern. The majority are found in Wiltshire, a county already known for spirituality and ancient mysteries at Stonehenge and for the stone circle at Avebury, Merlin, King Arthur, etc.

Despite people coming forward to admit to making them, many devotees still believe that most circles have natural or supernatural origins to do with natural energies, wind, water, gravitational fields, or maybe even a message from Gaia (the earth's spirit) warning us about pollution and global warming. There have been many scientific studies and no-one has yet found proof either way, although it seems unlikely that a jellyfish image was formed entirely naturally. Some circles are amazingly complex and detailed, and many CAD experts would be pushed to reproduce them on a computer.

You can view most crop circles from public footpaths, and there's usually an honesty box for you to leave £1 for the farmer whose crop has been damaged. You may want to examine what caused the stems of the crop to lie flat, but if you go inside the circles, be careful to use the 'tramlines' left by the tractor wheels and not spoil any more of the crop. There are also helicopter tours, though Gaia might be unimpressed if you take this approach.

GENTLE ADVENTURES

 CONTACTS

- 🖥 www.cropcircleconnector.com
- 🖥 www.cropcircleresearch.com
- 🖥 www.silentcircle.co.uk
- 🖥 www.ukcropcircles.co.uk
- 🖥 www.visitwiltshire.co.uk

Either way, it's summer, it's the West Country and you're out in the countryside – what could be lovelier?

WHERE DO I START?

You cannot predict when a crop circle will appear, therefore the safest option is to head to Wiltshire when the crops are out and hope for the best. There's plenty to do between sightings. New circles are publicised on crop circle websites (see **Contacts**) and in the many local cafés and pubs where devotees gather to swap photos and theories.

CAMPFIRE GOSSIP

Artists love a landscape, so it's no surprise that local artists are prime suspects in artificial crop circle making. Thus you have the chance to see some of England's most beautiful landscapes gilded by its up-and-coming artists, or not…

CONSERVATION VOLUNTEER

👓 AT A GLANCE

Accessibility Index: ❶❷❸④⑤

Fitness level: ❶❷③④⑤

Degree of Difficulty: ❶②③④⑤

White-knuckle rating: ❶②③④⑤

Equipment: none

Season: year round

Being a tourist is nice, but sometimes just relaxing on holiday and looking at things can leave you feeling a little unconnected, and you just want to do *something* – especially if you're on your own.

Which explains why volunteering holidays have become so popular. The National Trust runs 450 volunteer holidays each year, both for weekends and whole weeks. Accommodation in a farmhouse, cottage or apartment and food is included in the minimal price, and there's plenty of time to relax with the other volunteers, who are grouped according to age, from 16 up. You can opt to volunteer in something you have no experience of – you'll be given full training and be well supervised – and of course it all helps on a CV for younger people. Typical work includes gardening, construction, conservation and helping to organise events.

The National Trust isn't alone. You can help clear vegetation from the tracks of heritage railways, dig through decades of mud to clear a clogged canal for waterway charities or help with animals at a rescue centre. Several government agencies can help you find the volunteering option that most suits you, which include opportunities for the whole family to get involved. It's the perfect way to make likeminded new friends, and physical activity has been shown to be highly beneficial to a person's sense of wellbeing.

CONTACTS

- Countryside Restoration Trust: 🖳 www.livingcountryside.org.uk

- Muck In 4 Life (families): 🖳 http://muckin4life.direct.gov.uk

- National Trust: 🖳 www.nationaltrust.org.uk
Volunteering England: 🖳 www.volunteering.org.uk

- Volunteering Made Easy: 🖳 www.do-it.org

- Waterscape: 🖳 www.waterscape.com

- Woodland Trust: 🖳 www.woodlandtrust.org.uk

GENTLE ADVENTURES

CONTACTS

- Enjoy England:
  www.enjoyengland.com
- Devon Farms:
  www.devonfarms.co.uk
- Farm Stay UK:
  www.farmstay.co.uk

WORKING FARM HOLIDAYS

AT A GLANCE

Accessibility Index: ❶❷❸④⑤

Fitness level: ❶②③④⑤

Degree of Difficulty: ❶②③④⑤

White-knuckle rating: ❶②③④⑤

Equipment: none

Season: spring to autumn

Disability friendly: ✓

Family friendly: ✓

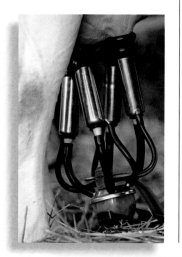

Farm stays make a wonderful weekend away. The recent recession perked up Britain's rural tourism industry, bringing us glamping (glamorous camping) and staycations on a farm. Suddenly, farmers are welcoming city folk onto their land – bits of it anyway – creating imaginative water features where once was just a rusty tractor, and putting bijou tents, yurts and teepees in their pastures.

Coming face to face with farm animals is exciting at any age. It won't only be city kids who have never seen a bull close up, been gently butted by a pygmy goat or been transfixed by the calming sight of horses munching hay from a haynet. Farms are wonderful places to explore, climb haybales and trees, and jump bareback onto the pony for a trot around the meadow. Of course, there are also dangers. Farms have huge lumps of machinery moving around and highly unpredictable animals, therefore farmers won't leave kids completely free to wander where they like. All the same, these are holidays that the kids are likely to remember for a long time, and it will teach them where their food comes from (without them even realising it) and the value of animal-friendly farming.

What you get varies. Some farms are geared up to welcome families with children, letting the children collect eggs and feed pigs. Some are more upmarket, providing reflexology treatments in your tent or a day's fly fishing or clay pigeon shooting. Accommodation may be a self-catering apartment, bed and breakfast in the farmhouse – even Prince Charles has gone for this option in the past – or maybe a tent so sumptuous it would impress a Bedouin potentate.

LLAMA TREKKING

You can't ride a llama, but you can walk along beside it while it carries your picnic, or even your camping equipment, in saddle bags. Llama trekking is a simple and accessible way to make a family walk more exciting. Llamas are friendly and inquisitive creatures, lovely to be around and used to looking after children and their owners. They are available to hire just for a walk, or for a weekend camping trip that the kids will definitely remember.

On holiday with a llama or donkey, you'll be securely rooted in the countryside. There's no nipping off to a theme park, leaving your new friend tethered outside. It's also a slow holiday – moving at around two miles an hour and no more than 7-10mi (10-16km) per day, leaving plenty of opportunity to enjoy the meadows, forests and hamlets that you pass through.

 **CONTACTS**

- Organisers: 🖳 www. llamapark.co.uk, www. llamatrekking.co.uk, www. nationalforestllamatreks.co.uk

GENTLE ADVENTURES

13

ODDBALL

To do many of the adventures in this book, you'll need some level of fitness, skill, training or common sense. Not here, though. With these, you just turn up and do something stupid but fun, memorable and a little bit brave – probably while falling off a high platform, screaming. Enjoy!

BUNGEE JUMPING

 **AT A GLANCE**

Accessibility Index: ❶❷❸❹⑤
Fitness level: ❶②③④⑤
Degree of Difficulty: ❶②③④⑤
White-knuckle rating: ❶❷❸❹❺
Equipment: none
Season: year round
Disability friendly: ✓
Weight restriction: ✓

You wear a harness around your ankles, from which is attached a long, stretchy cord. You leap from a platform and experience freefall, before bouncing around spectacularly and then being lowered gently to the ground. Most bungee operators work from a crane or bridge, often at fairgrounds, festivals or special events, but also from permanent sites. Either way, it's terrifying!

The highest bungee jump in the UK is 400ft (122m), equivalent to around 40 storeys. For many people, it's about conquering a fear of heights and experiencing the rush of adrenalin that is the natural physical response to fear. Regular jumpers do it for the thrill of freefall, the wind rushing past, and in wet weather falling faster than the rain. For others, it's all about style: a swallow dive, arms outstretched, head up and out, followed by a graceful bounce up with arms still outstretched…

Judging by the number of last minute refusals, indoor bungee jumps are most terrifying and jumps over water the 'easiest'. But there's no easy way to leap from a high platform and plummet to earth head first. Our minds just aren't geared up for it.

WHERE DO I START?

There will definitely be a bungee operator somewhere near you this weekend, if you have the courage to find it. If you're nervous, you could try the Reverse Bungee, where you're catapulted upwards.

CAMPFIRE GOSSIP

Bungee diving originated in a fertility rite on the remote Pacific island of Bunlap, where village men would climb the tallest tree, tie a liana vine around their ankles and leap off, hoping it would break their fall. Members of the Oxford University Dangerous Sports Club saw a documentary about this in 1979, and tried their own version off Bristol's Clifton Suspension Bridge, while dressed in top hat and tails and attached by a home-made rubber/nylon rope…

 **CONTACTS**

- Bungee Extreme: ☎ 01538-300528, 🖳 www.bungee.co.uk
- UK Bungee Club: ☎ 07000-286433, 🖳 www.ukbungee.co.uk

ODDBALL

ZORBING/SPHERING

 **AT A GLANCE**

Accessibility Index: ❶❷❸❹⑤

Fitness level: ❶②③④⑤

Degree of Difficulty: ❶②③④⑤

White-knuckle rating: ❶❷❸④⑤

Equipment: hire

Season: mainly summer

Disability friendly: ✓

Family friendly: ✓

Weight restriction: ✓

It goes under many different names – zorb, orb, OGO, sphere/sphereing, ballule – but the principle's the same. You're inside a large ball made of clear, soft plastic, which is itself suspended inside a 12ft (3.5m) diameter ball to provide total cushioning. And you're rolling around. You can go all sorts of places in it; rolling down a hill, over water, you can even walk along in it like a hamster ball. It's gained popularity as an 'extreme' sport in New Zealand (where they probably roll down mountains), and it's a hilarious experience, either rolling helplessly down a hill or attempting to power yourself along the street.

There are three options. Harness hill rolling, where two people are strapped into the insides of the ball opposite one another and roll down a hill at speeds of up to 30mph (48kph),

spinning round and round, over and over. Not weird enough? Aqua or Hydro hill rolling is where up to three people share the inside of the ball with a bucketful of warm water. You aren't strapped in so just tumble, surf and splash along like you're inside a washing machine. Don't do this with your boss on a team-building day out or you'll never be able to look him/her in the eye again – it's best experienced with **really good** friends. Lastly, you're inside a blacked out orb, tumbling around in total darkness like an astronaut lost in outer space. Very weird…

You probably won't stop laughing from the moment you go into the orb until at least an hour after you finish. There's just something about the experience that causes wild hilarity.

WHERE DO I START?

Check online or see the links below – there are zorbing sites throughout the country.

CAMPFIRE GOSSIP

The orb or *ballule* was invented by a young French architect and inventor named Gilles Ebersolt in the mid-'70s. And he has the photos to prove it. The world speed record is 55mph (89kph). Sounds beatable doesn't it? No problem…

CONTACTS

- Orb 360 (South Downs): ☎ 08456-434360, 🖥 www.orb360.co.uk

- Sphere Mania: ☎ 0844-800 3045, 🖥 www.spheremania.com

- Sphereing UK: 🖥 www.sphereing.co.uk

- Zorbing UK: ☎ 0845-430 3322, 🖥 www.zorbing.co.uk

ODDBALL

CONTACTS

- Organisers: ▣ www.
exelement.co.uk/experience/
the-powerfan-plummet-1413.
php, www.powerfan.co.uk,
www.ukbungee.co.uk

POWERFAN

It's like bungee without the bounce, the gentlest way to scare yourself silly. You throw yourself off a platform, and experience 87 per cent of freefall velocity before slowing down and being softly lowered to earth. The powerfan is a 'fan descender', originally developed by the military to train parachute jumpers. You wear a harness, from which is attached a rope that's fixed to the device. You throw yourself from something high, and as you plummet to earth, the rope flies through the machine and turns a fan, which slows the rope, allowing you to come to a gentle stop roughly equivalent to stepping off a small kerbstone (say the manufacturers).

The highest parachute simulators are 101ft (31m) – the equivalent of a ten-storey building, and the fan kicks in around halfway down, giving you five floors to wonder whether the machine really works…

For 'at a glance' ratings, see **Bungee Jumping** above.

SCAD DIVING

It stands for Suspended Catch Air Device, but SCAD is a pretty good description of how you'll feel at the top of the platform. Like many white-knuckle rides, SCAD takes you 164ft (50m) up in a crane and you fall off, but its unique scarifying proposition is that you have no rope or bungee cord attached – you just freefall at 65mph (105kph) into a giant net. Even worse, you fall backwards, so cannot be entirely sure that the net is there for the three **looong** seconds that it takes between starting to fall and the net catching you.

To ensure you land the right way, you wear a harness that makes you look a bit like a Ninja turtle, and the net – actually, there are two nets – is kept in place by several 1,100lb (500kg) weights, so an unfortunate gust of wind won't blow it out of the way at the last minute. The joy of SCAD is that the supersoft net provides a lovely gentle landing with very low G forces.

CONTACTS

- British Elastic Rope Sports Association (BERSA): 💻 www.bungeezone. com/orgs/bersa.shtml
- Scad Freefall: 💻 www.scadfreefall.co.uk

BRIDGE SWINGING

Bridge swinging involves wearing a harness, tying a rope to the parapet of a high bridge, then tying the other end to your own harness, and jumping off. To get a proper swing, you can't jump from exactly where you've tied it on, or it becomes a rather harsh bungee jump without the bounce, so usually the rope is tied on the parapet of one side of the bridge, then passed under the bridge and the jumper leaps off the other parapet.

If two bridges are close together, the rope can be tied onto one bridge and the jumper goes off the other bridge, though the rope must be shorter than the drop (for obvious reasons). You then need someone to lower you down the rest of the way, which will often be to a stream or a river, making this an excellent starting point for a canyoning trip (see page 198). Although popular in New Zealand (where many suicidal activities were invented), bridge swinging is only just starting to catch on in the UK, but is being introduced by some activity centres, usually as part of a canyoning or gorge walking expedition.

CONTACTS

- Splash: ☎ 01887-829706, 💻 www.rafting.co.uk/bridge.htm
- Vertical Descents: ☎ 01855-821593, 💻 www.verticaldescents.com

Warning!

Bridge swinging is an extremely dangerous and foolhardy activity unless it's done at a certified activity centre. Many people who have tried doing it DIY have died, usually from falling out of the harness or from miscalculating the angle of swing. Do not try this at home!

🖉 CONTACTS

- Maldon Mud Race, Essex:
  🖥 www.maldonmudrace.
  com

- Bog Snorkelling, Powys:
  🖥 http://tinyurl.com/bogsnorkel

BOG SNORKELLING

AT A GLANCE

Accessibility Index: ❶②③④⑤

Fitness level: ❶❷❸④⑤

Degree of Difficulty: ❶❷③④⑤

White-knuckle rating: ❶❷③④⑤

Equipment: low cost

Season: varies

It's the kind of thing that could get a nation branded as eccentric. Bog snorkelling, inevitably, started out as a conversation in a British pub and is rapidly becoming a worldwide phenomenon – okay, very slowly. There's even a World Bog Snorkelling Championship (but it isn't yet an Olympic event).

The original version started in Llanwrtyd Wells in the middle of Wales, and involves wearing flippers, mask and snorkel and swimming two 60yd (55m) lengths of a channel cut out of a peat bog. The tricky part – oh those devilish Welsh – is that you cannot use any recognised swimming strokes, only the power of your flippers, and so you flap along through thick mud trying to keep the top of your snorkel from filling with gunk. The record is around 90 seconds, but make no mistake – this is a tough event that many competitors don't finish (especially those who do it in fancy dress or carrying handbags – yes, really!).

Another version in the same location is the Mountain Biking Bog Snorkelling Championship, where you ride a modified and weighted mountain bike into a deeper bog, and cycle a short course keeping your eyes and snorkel, hopefully, out of the water. The shortest time wins.

Meanwhile, over in Maldon, Essex, another pub and yet another challenge, this one being to cross the Blackwater River at low tide in January. The name says it all – black water – otherwise known as mud, which at low tide is 55yd (50m) wide, freezing cold and deep enough to drown a pony. This one is a straight race with all 250 or so competitors starting together and running, crawling, rolling, whatever, for two crossings of the river and a stretch along the bank. The trick is to get out ahead before the mud gets too churned up, because while the winners do it in under four minutes, the back markers often have to be pulled out with ropes after half an hour. And the showers are cold.

ODDBALL

APPENDICES

❖ Further Reading
❖ Useful Websites
❖ Maps

APPENDIX A: FURTHER READING

This appendix contains a selection of magazines and books for adventurers, sports people, and anyone else wishing to spice up their weekends and holidays. The lists aren't meant to be inclusive.

Magazines

General

Adrenamag: http://adrenamag.co.uk

Adventure World: www.adventureworldmagazine.com

Outdoor Adventure Guide: http://outdooradventureguide.co.uk

Scouting: www.scouts.org.uk/magazine

Trail: www.livefortheoutdoors.com

Country & County Magazines

Adventure Cornwall: www.adventure-cornwall.co.uk

Anglia Afloat: www.angliaafloat.co.uk – covers Cambs, Essex, Norfolk & Suffolk

Bird Watching: http://birdwatchingmag.blogspot.com

Birdwatch: www.birdwatch.co.uk

BBC Countryfile: http://info.bbccountryfilemagazine.com

Britain: www.britain-magazine.com

Bushcraft & Survival Skills: www.bushcraftmagazine.com

Camping magazine: www.outandaboutlive.co.uk/magazines/default.asp?magazine=6

Camping & Caravanning: www.campingandcaravanningclub.co.uk – magazine of the Camping & Caravanning Club

Country Life: www.countrylife.co.uk

Country Walking: www.livefortheoutdoors.com

The Countryman: www.countrymanmagazine.co.uk

Cumbria Life: www.cumbrialife.co.uk

Dartmoor: www.dartmoormagazine.co.uk

Exmoor: 🖳 www.theexmoormagazine.com

The Field: 🖳 www.thefield.co.uk

Irish Countrysports & Country Life: 🖳 www.countrysportsandcountrylife.com

Lakeland Walker: 🖳 www.outandaboutlive.co.uk

Scotland: 🖳 www.scotlandmag.com

The Scots Magazine: 🖳 www.scotsmagazine.com

Scottish Field: 🖳 www.scottishfield.co.uk

This England: 🖳 www.thisengland.co.uk

Trail: 🖳 www.livefortheoutdoors.com

Welsh Country: 🖳 www.welshcountry.co.uk

BBC Wildlife: 🖳 www.discoverwildlife.com

Yorkshire Life: 🖳 http://yorkshire.greatbritishlife.co.uk

Boating & Sailing

Boat International: 🖳 www.boatinternational.com

Boatmart: 🖳 www.boatmart.co.uk

Boating Cornwall: 🖳 www.boatingcornwall.co.uk

Canal Boat & Inland Waterways: 🖳 www.canalboat.co.uk

Dinghy Sailing: 🖳 www.dinghysailingmagazine.co.uk

Motor Boat & Yachting: 🖳 www.mby.com

Motor Boats Monthly: 🖳 www.motorboatsmonthly.co.uk

Practical Boat Owner: 🖳 www.pbo.co.uk

Sailing Today: 🖳 www.sailingtoday.co.uk

Yachting Monthly: 🖳 www.yachtingmonthly.com

Yachting World: 🖳 www.yachtingworld.com

Yachts & Yachting: 🖳 www.yachtsandyachting.com

Country Pursuits

Anglers Mail: 🖳 www.anglersmail.co.uk

Angling Times: 🖳 www.gofishing.co.uk/angling-times

Boat Fishing Monthly: 🖳 www.boat-fishing-monthly.co.uk

British Horse Society: 🖳 www.bhs.org.uk

Equestrian Life: 🖳 www.equestrianlifemagazine.com

Eventing: 🖳 www.eventing.com

APPENDICES

Horse: 💻 www.horsemagazine.co.uk

Horse & Hound: 💻 www.horseandhound.co.uk

Horse & Pony: 💻 www.yourhorse.co.uk

Horse & Rider: 💻 www.horseandridermagazine.co.uk

Pony: 💻 www.ponymag.com

Shooting Gazette: 💻 www.shootinggazette.co.uk

Shooting Times: 💻 www.shootingtimes.co.uk

Sporting Gun: 💻 www.sportinggun.co.uk

Sporting Shooter: 💻 www.sportingshooter.co.uk

Cycling

Bicycling: 💻 www.bicycling.com

Bike: 💻 www.bikemag.com

Cycle Sport: 💻 www.cyclesport.co.uk

Cycling News: 💻 www.cyclingnews.com

Cycling Plus: 💻 www.cycling.magazine.co.uk

Cycling Weekly: 💻 www.cyclingweekly.co.uk

Cycling World: 💻 www.cyclingworldmagazine.co.uk

DIG BMX: 💻 http://digbmx.mpora.com

Dirt: 💻 http://dirt.mpora.com

Dirt Bike Rider: 💻 www.dirtbikerider.co.uk

Mountain Bike Rider: 💻 www.mbr.co.uk

Mountain Biking UK: 💻 http://magazine.bikeradar.comcategory/mountain-biking-uk

Procycling: 💻 http://magazine.bikeradar.com/category/procycling

Ride UK BMX: 💻 http://rideukbmx.mpora.com

Singletrack: 💻 www.singletrackworld.com – monthly mountain bike magazine

What Mountain Bike: 💻 http://magazine.bikeradar.com/category/what-mountain-bike/

Miscellaneous Sports

200 Triathlon: 💻 http://info.220triathlon.com

Autosport: 💻 www.autosport.com (F1 mortorsport)

Boards: 💻 http://boards.mpora.com (windsurfing)

Canoeist: 💻 www.canoeist.co.uk

Climb: 💻 www.climbmagazine.com

Daily Mail Ski & Snowboard: 💻 www.metrosnow.co.uk

Dive: 💻 www.divemagazine.co.uk

Diver: 💻 www.divernet.com

Document Snowboard: 💻 www.fall-line-media

Fall-Line Skiing: 💻 www.fall-line.co.uk

Flyer: 💻 www.flyer.co.uk

Good Ski Guide: 💻 www.goodskiguide.com

IKitemag: 💻 www.ikitemag.com

Karting: 💻 www.kartingmagazine.com

Motor Sport: 💻 www.motorsportmagazine.co.uk

Onboard: 💻 http://onboard.mpora.com

Pilot: 💻 www.pilotweb.aero

Powerkite: 💻 www.powerkite-magazine.co.uk

Quad: 💻 www.quad.tv

Runner's World: 💻 www.runnersworld.co.uk

Running Free: 💻 www.runningfreemag.co.uk

Skier & Snowboarder: 💻 www.skierandsnowboarder.co.uk

BBC Sky at Night magazine: 💻 www.skyatnightmagazine.com, For amateur astronomers.

Singletrack: 💻 www.singletrackworld.com – monthly mountain bike magazine

Surf Europe: 💻 http://surfeurope.mpora.com

Surfer's Path: 💻 http://surferspath.mpora.com

Trek & Mountain: 💻 www.trekandmountain.com

Books

Listed below is a selection of books (by subject) for adventurers, sportsmen/women and others who enjoy the outdoor life (the title is followed by the name of the author and the publisher's name in brackets). Some of the books listed may be out of print, but you may still be able to find a copy in a library or bookshop.

General

Adventure Britain, Demi Taylor (Footprint)

Britain & Ireland's Best Wild Places: 500 Ways to Discover the Wild, Christopher Somerville (Allen Lane)

APPENDICES

Britain's National Parks: A Visitor's Guide, Roland Smith (New Orchard Editions)

Chris Packham's Nature Handbook, Chris Packham (Dorling Kindersley)

Britain's Wildlife, Plants and Flowers (Readers Digest)

Coast: A Celebration of Britain's Coastal Heritage, Christopher Somerville (BBC Books)

Coast: Our Island Story: A Journey of Discovery Around Britain's Coastline, Nicholas Crane (BBC Books)

Countryside Detective: How to Discover, Observe and Enjoy Britain's Wildlife, David Bellamy (Readers Digest)

Great British Journeys, Nicholas Crane (Phoenix)

The Highways and Byways of Britain, David Milner (Macmillan)

John Craven's Countryfile Handbook, John Craven (BBC Books)

The Most Amazing Places on Britain's Coast (Readers Digest)

The Most Amazing Places to Visit in Britain's Countryside (Reader's Digest)

The Most Amazing Places to Walk Britain (Readers Digest)

National Parks of Britain, Roly Smith (AA)

Nature Tales: Encounters with Britain's Wildlife, Michael Allen & Sonya Patel Ellis (Elliott & Thompson)

Over The Hills And Far Away, Candida Lycett Green (Black Swan)

The Peak District, Fran Halsall (Frances Lincoln)

Places to Hide: In England, Scotland and Wales, Dixe Wills (Icon Books)

RSPB Complete Birds of Britain and Europe, Rob Hume (Dorling Kindersley)

RSPB Pocket Nature Wildlife of Britain (Dorling Kindersley)

RSPB Wildlife of Britain, Allen Et Al Coombes (Dorling Kindersley)

Somerville's Travels, Christopher Somerville (AA Publishing)

Springwatch & Autumnwatch, Bill Oddie, Kate Humble & Simon King (BBC Books)

Steve Backshall's Wildlife Adventurer's Guide: A Guide to Exploring Wildlife in Britain, Steve Backshall (New Holland)

Unwrecked England, Candida Lycett Green (Oldie Publications)

Where to Watch Birds in Britain, Simon Harrap & Nigel Redman (Christopher Helm)

The Wildlife Trusts Handbook of Garden Wildlife, Nicholas Hammond (New Holland)

Climbing

Learning to Climb Indoors, Eric J Horst (Falcon Press)

Mountain Skills Training Handbook, Pete Hill & Stuart Johnson (David and Charles)

Mountaincraft and Leadership, Eric Langmuir (Sportscotland)

Rock Climbing: Essential Skills & Techniques, Libby Peter (Cordee)

Rock and Wall Climbing: The Essential Guide to Equipment & Techniques, Steve Long (A & C Black)

Scotland's Mountain Ridges: Scrambling, Mountaineering and Climbing, Dan Bailey (Cicerone Press)

Winter Skills: Essential Walking and Climbing Techniques, Andy Cunningham (UKMTB)

Country Pursuits

The BASC Handbook of Shooting: An Introduction to the Sporting Shotgun (Quiller Publishing)

Breaking Clays: Target Tactics, Tips and Techniques, Chris Batha (Swan Hill Press)

Clay Shooting for Beginners and Enthusiasts, John King (John King Coaching)

Coarse Fishing Basics: A Beginner's Guide, Steve Partner (Bounty Books)

The Coarse Fishing Handbook: A Guide to Freshwater Angling, Tony Miles (Apple Press)

Complete Horse Riding Manual, William Micklem (Dorling Kindersley)

The Deer Stalking Handbook, Graham Downing (Quiller Publishing)

Foraging: Discover Free Food from Fields, Streets, Gardens and the Coast, Paul Chambers (Remember When)

Getting the Most from Riding Lessons, Michael W. Smith (Storey Books)

Hedgerow (River Cottage Handbook), John Wright (Bloomsbury)

The Horse Riding and Care Handbook, Bernadette Faurie (New Holland)

John Wilson's 1001 Top Angling Tips, John Wilson (Green Umbrella)

Mushrooms: River Cottage Handbook No.1, John Wright (Bloomsbury)

APPENDICES

Sea Fishing (River Cottage Handbook), Nick Fisher (Bloomsbury)

Sea Fishing Properly Explained, Ian Ball (Right Way)

Starting Fishing, Lesley Sims & H. Edon (Usborne)

Where to Sea Fish in Britain and Ireland, John Bailey (New Holland)

Cycling

100 Greatest Cycling Climbs: A Road Cyclist's Guide to Britain's Hills, Simon Warren (Particular Books)

Cycling Anatomy: Your Illustrated Guide for Cycling Strength, Speed, and

Cycling Britain, Etain O'Carroll (Lonely Planet)

The Cyclist's Training Bible, Joe Friel (Velopress)

Cyclopedia: It's All About the Bike, William Fotheringham (Yellow Jersey)

Endurance, Shannon Sovndal (Human Kinetics Europe)

The London Cycling Guide, Tom Bogdanowicz (Batsford)

Mountain Biking, John Olsen (Stackpole Books)

Mountain Biking: The Essential Guide to Equipment & Techniques, Herman Mills (New Holland)

Mountain Biking in the Lake District, Ian Boydon (Cicerone)

The Time-crunched Cyclist: Fit, Fast and Powerful in 6 Hours a Week, Chris Carmichael (VeloPress)

Extreme Sports

50 50 Secrets I Learned Running 50 Marathons in 50 Days, Dean Karnazes (Grand Central Publishing)

500 Adrenaline Adventures, Lois Friedland et al (Frommer's)

Adventure Sports: 52 Brilliant Ideas for Taking Yourself to the Limit, Steve Shipside (Infinite Ideas)

Beyond Adventure An Inner Journey, Colin Mortlock (Cicerone Press)

Born to Run, Christopher McDougall (Profile Books)

Build the Perfect Survival Kit: Custom Kits for Adventure, Sport, Travel, John D. McCann (KP Books)

Extreme Running, Kym McConnell (Pavilion)

Extreme Sports: a Guide to the Most Extreme Sports in the World, Nicotext (Van Horne Industries Ltd)

Feet in the Clouds: A Story of Fell Running and Obsession, Richard Askwith (Aurum Press)

Guide to Adventure Sports, Emma Drew & Irvine Conner (A & C Black)

Life on the Run: Coast to Coast, Matt Beardshall (Arima publishing)

Personal Growth Through Adventure, David Hopkins & Roger Putnam (David Fulton)

Philosophy, Risk and Adventure Sports, Mike J. McNamee (Routledge)

The Psychology of Risk: Glynis M. Breakwell (CUP)

The RHP Companion to Outdoor Education (Russell House Publishing)

Running for My Life, Ray Zahab (Insomniac Press)

Running Through the Wall: Personal Encounters with the Ultramarathon, Neal Jamison (Breakaway Books)

Safety, Risk and Adventure in Outdoor Activities, Bob Barton (Sage Publications)

Survival Of The Fittest: The Anatomy of Peak Physical Performance, Mike Stround (Yellow Jersey)

Ultramarathon Man, Dean Karnazes (Jeremy P. Tarcher)

Sailing

Dinghy Sailing: The Essential Guide to Equipment and Techniques, Sarah Ell (New Holland)

Dinghy Sailing: Start to Finish, Barry Pickthall (John Wiley)

Learn to Sail in a Weekend, John Driscoll (Dorling Kindersley)

The New Complete Sailing Manual, Steve Sleight (Dorling Kindersley)

The Sailing Handbook: A Complete Guide for Beginners, Halsey C. Herreshoff (Adlard Coles Nautical)

Start Sailing: Beginner's Handbook (Royal Yachting Association)

Walking

100 Greatest Walks in Britain (David & Charles)

101 Best Hill Walks in the Scottish Highlands and Islands, Graeme Cornwallis (Fort Publishing)

1001 Walks in Britain (Automobile Association)

365 Pub Walks & Cycle Rides (Automobile Association)

APPENDICES

Britain's Great Views: 50 Walking Routes to Britain's Most Spectacular Views, Ramblers' Association (Frances Lincoln)

Footpaths of Britain: North West (Parragon Books)

Great British Walks: 'Countryfile' – 100 Unique Walks Through Our Most Stunning Countryside, Cavan Scott (BBC Books)

Hill Walking: The Official Handbook of the Mountain Leader & Walking Group Leader Schemes, Steve Long (UKMTB)

Mountain Weather: A Practical Guide for Hillwalkers and Climbers in the British Isles, David E. Pedgley (Cicerone Press)

Somerville's 100 Best Walks, Christopher Somerville (The Armchair Traveller)

Time Out Book of Country Walks: 52 Walks Within Easy Reach of London (Time Out)

Walk Scotland: A Guidebook For All Seasons, Bruce Sandison (Mainstream Publishing)

Walker's Britain in a Box: Britain's Best Walking Guide, David Hancock & Nick Channer (Duncan Petersen)

Walking in Britain, Sandra Bardwell et al (Lonely Planet)

Walking in Scotland, Sandra Bardwell (Lonely Planet)

Walking and Orienteering, Peter G. Drake (Southwater)

Winter Sports

All-Mountain Skier: The Way to Expert Skiing, R. Mark Elling (McGraw-Hill Contemporary)

Go Ski, Warren Smith (Dorling Kindersley)

Go Snowboard, Neil McNab (Dorling Kindersley)

Illustrated Guide to Snowboarding, Kevin Ryan (McGraw-Hill Contemporary)

Ski School, David Anderson (New Holland)

Snowboarding, Greg Goldman (New Holland)

Snowboarding Skills: The Back to Basics Essentials for All Levels, Cindy Kleh (Firefly Books)

Sports Resorts in the World, Chris Gill (NortonWood Publishing)

Ultimate Skiing: Master the Techniques of Great Skiing, Ron LeMaster (Human Kinetics)

Where to Ski and Snowboard 2011: The Definitive Guide to the 1,000 Best Winter

White Weekends: Where to Ski, Where to Stay, Where to Eat, Where to Party, Tom Robbins (Bantam Press)

Miscellaneous

Adventure Sport Scuba Diving, Jack Jackson (New Holland)

Be Expert with Map Comp: The Complete 'Orienteering' Handbook, Kjellstrom (Hungry Minds)

Beginning Gliding, Derek Piggott (A & C Black)

Canoe and Kayak Handbook: British Canoe Union, Franco Ferrero (Pesda Press)

The Complete Caving Manual, Andy Sparrow (The Crowood Press)

The Glider Pilot's Manual, Ken Stewart (Air Pilot Publisher)

Gliding: The Theory of Flight, British Gliding Association (A & C Black)

Hang Gliding and Parasailing, John E. Schindler (Gareth Stevens)

Kayaking and Canoeing for Beginners, Bill Mattos (Southwater)

Orienteering: Skills - Techniques – Training, Carol McNeill (The Crowood Press)

Parachuting: The Skydiver's Handbook, Dan Poynter (Para Publishing)

River Running, David & Cheryl Young (Cheryl Young)

RYA Start Windsurfing (Royal Yachting Association)

Touching Cloudbase: A Complete Guide to Paragliding, Ian Currer (Air Supplies)

Understanding Flying Weather, Derek Piggott (A & C Black)

Water Sports (Extreme Sports), Jim Gigliotti (Raintree)

Waterlog: A Swimmer's Journey Through Britain, Roger Deakin (Vintage)

White Water Safety and Rescue, Franco Ferrero (Pesda Press)

Wild Swim, Kate Rew (Guardian Books)

Wild Swimming: 150 Hidden Dips in the Rivers, Lakes and Waterfalls of Britain, Daniel Start (Punk Publishing)

Wild Swimming Coast: Explore the Secret Coves and Wild Beaches of Britain, Daniel Start (Punk Publishing)

Windsurfing: The Complete Guide, Ian Currer (Air Supplies)

Windsurfing: The Essential Guide to Equipment and Techniques, Simon Bornhoft (New Holland)

APPENDICES

APPENDIX B: USEFUL WEBSITES

This appendix contains a selection of useful websites (by subject) for readers wishing to find out more about a particular organisation, activity or region – or maybe just find some inspiration. Website addresses are also listed throughout the book, particularly those relating to individual sports and activities.

National Organisations

Adventure & Environment Awareness Group (💻 www.aea-uk.org). Environmental awareness group for the Lake District National Park.

Areas of Outstanding Natural Beauty (💻 www.aonb.org.uk). See page 18.

British Ecological Society (💻 www.britishecologicalsociety.org). Dedicated to advancing ecology and making it count.

British Trust for Conservation Volunteers (💻 www2.btcv.org.uk). Charity for environmental volunteers in the UK and around the world.

British Waterways (💻 www.britishwaterways.co.uk/home). See page 19.

Byways & Bridleways Trust (💻 www.bbtrust.org.uk). Charity which protects the public rights over the many ancient lanes that form part of the British landscape.

Campaign for National Parks (💻 www.cnp.org.uk). The CNP's aim is to protect, stand up for and expand the National Parks family.

Camping & Caravanning (💻 www.campingandcaravanningclub.co.uk). The premier organisation for campers and caravanners in Britain.

Car Free Walks (💻 www.carfreewalks.org). Website for people who love walking but want to reduce their impact on the environment.

Conservation Foundation (💻 www.conservationfoundation.co.uk). Established as a means for all people to work together for environmental causes.

Countryside Alliance (💻 www.countryside-alliance.org.uk). Website for everyone who enjoys the rural way of life.

Countryside Recreation Network (💻 www.countrysiderecreation.org.uk). CRN provides easy access to information and people concerned with countryside and recreation related matters in Britain and Ireland.

Department for Environment, Food and Rural Affairs (⌨ www2.defra.gov.uk). The Government department concerned with everything from general environment issues to British wildlife and animal welfare.

Duke of Edinburgh's Award (⌨ www.dofe.org). The leading youth charity that gives young people the chance to fulfil their potential through adventure activities.

Environment Agency (⌨ www.environment-agency.gov.uk). Government agency charged with protecting and improving the environment.

Forestry Commission (⌨ www.forestry.gov.uk). See page 19.

Girl Guides (⌨ www.girlguiding.org.uk). The equivalent of the scouts (see below) for girls.

Good Beach Guide (⌨ www.goodbeachguide.co.uk). The website of the Marine Conservation Society, the charity caring for Britain's seas.

Green Tourism Business Scheme (⌨ www.green-business. co.uk). Government scheme for promoting green and sustainable tourism.

Joint Nature Conservation Committee (⌨ www.jncc.gov. uk). Statutory adviser to the UK Government and devolved administrations regarding nature conservation.

The Land is Ours (⌨ www.tlio.org.uk). Land rights campaign for Britain.

The Long Distance Walkers Association (⌨ www.ldwa.org.uk). Meet other like-minded walkers and learn about long distance walking events and routes throughout the UK.

Marine Conservation Society (⌨ www.mcsuk.org). Charity that cares for Britain's seas.

The Met Office (⌨ www.metoffice.gov.uk). The UK's national weather service.

Mountain Weather Information Service (⌨ www.mwis.org. uk). Daily weather forecasts for the English, Scottish and Welsh mountains.

National Parks (⌨ www.nationalparks.gov.uk). See page 17.

National Trails (⌨ www.nationaltrail.co.uk). See page 18.

National Trust (⌨ www.nationaltrust.org.uk). Leading charity that conserves and protects Britain's heritage, including historic buildings, forests, beaches, gardens, ancient monuments and nature reserves. See also National Trust Scotland below under **Scotland**.

Nature on the Map (⌨ www.natureonthemap.org.uk). Natural England's interactive mapping website.

APPENDICES

Open Spaces Society (💻 www.oss.org.uk). The country's oldest national conservation body, the OPS protects open spaces, common land, village greens and public paths in England & Wales.

Ordnance Survey (💻 www.ordnancesurvey.co.uk). Britain's national mapping agency.

Ramblers (💻 www.ramblers.org.uk). Britain's walking charity, working to safeguard the country's footpaths and countryside.

River Access Campaign (💻 www.riversaccess.org). A campaign funded by Canoe England to raise awareness of the access issues on inland waterways in England and Wales.

Royal National Lifeboat Institution (💻 www.rnli.org.uk). Charity that saves lives at sea, on beaches (through its lifeguards) and during floods.

Royal Society for the Protection of Birds (💻 www.rspb.org.uk). Europe's largest conservation charity working for the conservation of wild birds, other wildlife and the places in which they live.

Scouts (💻 www.scouts.org.uk). Leading outdoor adventure organisation for boys.

Sites of Special Scientific Interest (💻 www.sssi.naturalengland.org.uk). See page 18.

UK Campsite (💻 http://ukcampsite.co.uk). Online resource for campers and caravanners.

Waterscape (💻 www.waterscape.com). Britain's official guide to canals, rivers and lakes in the UK.

Wild About Britain (💻 www.wildaboutbritain.co.uk). Charity and home to hundreds of thousands of pages about British wildlife, the environment and the great outdoors.

Wildlife Trusts (💻 www.wildlifetrusts.org). A voluntary organisation dedicated to conserving the UK's habitats and species.

Wildfowl & Wetlands Trust (💻 www.wwt.org.uk). Leading conservation organisation saving wetlands for wildlife and people in the UK and across the world.

Woodland Trust (💻 www.woodlandtrust.org.uk). The UK's leading woodland conservation society, dedicated to maintaining a countryside rich in native woods and trees.

Youth Hostel Association (💻 www.yha.org.uk). The YHA maintains a network of youth hostels thoughout England and Wales.

England

Broads Authority National Park (💻 www.broads-authority.gov.uk). Information about Britain's largest wetland.

Campaign to Protect Rural England (💻 www.cpre.org.uk). CPRE works to protect the British countryside in all localities.

Cycling England (💻 www.dft.gov.uk/cyclingengland). Promotes the benefits of cycling and contains useful information on safety and transportation issues.

Dartmoor National Park (💻 www.dartmoor-npa.gov.uk). Seasonal guided walks programme and fact files about Dartmoor life.

English Heritage (💻 www.english-heritage.org.uk) Protects and promotes England's spectacular historic environment.

Enjoy England (💻 www.enjoyengland.com). The official website for tourism in England.

Exmoor National Park (💻 www.exmoor-nationalpark.gov.uk). The official Park authority site, including a site search facility.

Lake District National Park (💻 www.lakedistrict.gov.uk). Information on local conservation areas, community planning and things to do.

Natural England (💻 www.naturalengland.org.uk). Information on conserving and enhancing the natural environment of England.

New Forest National Park (💻 www.newforestnpa.gov.uk). Information for local residents, students and visitors.

North York Moors National Park (💻 www.northyorkmoors.org.uk). All you need to know about this special part of England, where the national park was founded in 1952.

Northumberland National Park (💻 www.northumberlandnationalpark.org.uk). Borderland culture, Hadrian's Wall and much more.

Peak District National Park (💻 www.peakdistrict.gov.uk). Comprehensive information about living in, learning about, visiting and looking after the Peak District, Britain's first national park.

South Downs National Park (💻 www.southdowns.gov.uk). Conservation issues and development within Britain's newest national park (2010).

Yorkshire Dales National Park (💻 www.yorkshiredales.org.uk). Information about this spectacular National Park, which takes in both Cumbria and part of North Yorkshire.

APPENDICES

Scotland

Active Scotland (🖵 http://active.visitscotland.com). An official branch of Scotland's national tourism organisation.

Cairngorms National Park (🖵 www.cairngorms.co.uk). Works to ensure that the unique aspects of the Park are cared for, sustained and enhanced by the many partnership projects undertaken locally.

Glenmore Lodge (🖵 www.glenmorelodge.org.uk). Scotland's National Outdoor Training Centre.

Historic Scotland (🖵 www.historic-scotland.gov.uk). Dedicated to safeguarding Scotland's heritage and historic environment.

Loch Lomond & The Trossachs National Park (🖵 www.lochlomond-trossachs.org). Comprehensive information for locals, students, visitors and volunteers.

National Trust Scotland (🖵 www.nts.org.uk). The Scottish equivalent of the National Trust (see **National Organisations** above).

Outdoor Access Guide Scotland (🖵 www.outdooraccess-scotland.com). Explains how to enjoy Scotland's great outdoors responsibly.

Scottish Countryside Alliance (🖵 www.*countryside-alliance.org.uk)*. Represents the vital interests of rural communities and businesses across Scotland.

Scotland Natural Heritage (🖵 www.snh.org.uk). The Government funded body that looks after all of Scotland's nature and landscapes.

Scottish Natural Heritage (🖵 www.snh.gov.uk). Responsible for Scotland's 40 National Scenic Areas (NSA).

Scottish Youth Hostel Association (🖵 www.syha.org.uk). The SYHA maintains a network of youth hostels thoughout Scotland.

Visit Scotland (🖵 www.visitscotland.com). Scotland's national tourism organisation.

Wilderness Scotland (🖵 www.wildernessscotland.com). Adventure travel and ecotourism in Scotland's wild places.

Wales

Brecon Beacons National Park (🖵 www.breconbeacons.org). Things to do, local archaeology and education programmes, plus job opportunities.

Cadw (🖵 www.cadw.wales.gov.uk). Cadw (meaning 'to keep' in Welsh) is the Welsh Assembly Government's division dedicated to protecting the historic environment of Wales.

Countryside Council for Wales (🖵 www.ccw.gov.uk) Interactive maps and data, and information on open access and protected sites.

Pembrokeshire Coast National Park (🖥 www.
pembrokeshirecoast.org.uk). Descriptions of coasts, beaches and
islands, plus links to other sites.

Snowdonia (🖥 www.visitsnowdonia.info). General visitors'
website.

Snowdonia National Park (🖥 www.snowdonia-npa.gov.uk).
Information on the 823mi² of diverse landscapes that comprise
Snowdonia National Park – home to Britain's highest mountain
and over 26,000 people.

Visit Wales (🖥 www.visitwales.co.uk). Welsh national tourist
organisation.

Wales (🖥 www.wales.com). The official gateway to Wales.

Safety & Training

Adventure Activities Licensing Authority (🖥 www.hse.gov.uk/
aala). Part of the Health and Safety Executive (HSE).

Adventure for All (🖥 www.adventureforall.org.uk). Outdoor
activity centres for people with special needs.

Adventuremark (🖥 www.adventuremark.co.uk). Comprehensive
adventurous activities scheme.

Adventure Activities Industry Advisory Committee (🖥 www.
skillsactive.com). Umbrella organisation working to ensure that
the sports and active leisure sector has the professionally trained
and qualified staff it needs.

Dart Training Group (🖥 www.darttraininggroup.co.uk). Instructor
training courses for those wishing to work within the 'outdoors'
industry.

Mountain Leader Training (🖥 www.mltuk.org). Mountain leader
training schemes with course dates information.

Mountain Rescue (🖥 www.mountain.rescue.org.uk). Covering
England and Wales.

Mountain Training School (🖥 www.
mountaineeringtrainingschool.com). Climbing school whose
classroom is the mountains and glaciers of Patagonia.

Outdoor Instructor Academy (🖥 www.
outdoorinstructoracademy.com). Independent outdoor education
centre for training for careers in the outdoor pursuits industry.

Outdoor Instructor Training (🖥 www.outdoor-instructor-training.
co.uk). Fast-track outdoor instructor training.

Royal Society for the Prevention of Accidents (🖥 www.rospa.
com). The main efforts of RoSPA's Leisure Safety department are
focused on reducing the several hundred drowning deaths that
occur each year in the UK.

Safesport (🖥 www.safesport.co.uk). Provides comprehensive
safety advice and information.

APPENDICES

Scottish Mountain Rescue (🖳 www.mrcofs.org). Website of the Mountain Rescue Committee of Scotland.

Surf Life Saving Great Britain (🖳 www.slsgb.org.uk). Beach life-saving and life-saving sports site.

Training Expertise (🖳 www.training-expertise.co.uk). Integrated training programmes for those operating in outdoor and wilderness environments.

Trinity House (🖳 www.trinityhouse.co.uk). Looks after the safety of shipping and the wellbeing of seafarers.

Wilderness Expertise (🖳 www.wilderness-expertise.co.uk). Runs overseas expeditions in developing countries focusing on personal development for young adults aged 14-24.

Help for the Disabled

The Accessible Guide (🖳 www.accessibleguide.co.uk). *Accessible Britain* book for the handicapped, published by Rough Guides.

Archery for the Disabled (🖳 www.ableize.com › Recreation & Sports). Archery sports clubs and facilities for the disabled and wheelchair users in the UK.

Bendrigg Trust (🖳 www.bendrigg.org.uk). Established in 1978 to specialise in courses and activities for disabled and disadvantaged young people.

BLESMA (🖳 www.blesma.org). The British Limbless Ex Service Men's Association is the national charity for limbless serving and ex service men and women,

British Disabled Flying Association (🖳 www.aerobility.com). Enables disabled and profoundly ill adults and children to share the magic of flying light aircraft.

Calvert Trust (🖳 www.calvert-trust.org.uk). Challenging disability through outdoor adventure.

Climbing For All (🖳 www.thebmc.co.uk/feature.aspx?id=1914). Climbing for the disabled.

Disability Now (🖳 www.disabilitynow.org.uk). UK newspaper with adverts, articles, links and an archive.

Dukes Barn (🖳 www.dukesbarn.org). Provides outdoor adventure activities for young people, irrespective of their ability, special need or disadvantage.

Equal Adventure (🖳 www.equaladventure.org). Provide opportunities for people with diverse needs to pursue adventure sports and active lifestyles.

Fieldfare Trust (🖳 www.fieldfare.org.uk). Fieldfare works with people with disabilities and countryside managers to improve access to the countryside for everyone.

Flyability (💻 www.flyability.org.uk). The disability initiative of the British Hang Gliding and Paragliding Association.

Jubilee Sailing Trust (💻 www.jst.org.uk/default.aspx). The JST owns and operates *Lord Nelson* and *Tenacious*, the only two tall ships in the world designed and built to enable people of all physical abilities to sail side-by-side as equals

Kepplewray Project (💻 www.kepplewray.org.uk). Operates an inclusive education and outdoor activity centre in the Lake District for disabled and non-disabled people.

Lifesavers (💻 www.lifesavers.org.uk). The website of the Royal Life Saving Society.

Low Mill Outdoor Centre (💻 www.lowmill.com). Outdoor education centre adapted to accommodate those with special needs and disabilities.

Motability Information Service (💻 www.mis.org.uk). The UK's foremost resource for physically disabled people who drive or want to drive.

QE2 Activity Centre (💻 www.qe2activitycentre.co.uk). Caters for people of all ages with learning disabilities, autism, physical disabilities and other specific needs.

Red Ridge Centre (💻 www.redridgecentre.co.uk). Outdoor centre dedicated to enabling persons of all abilities to participate in outdoor pursuits.

Riding for the Disabled Associations (💻 www.riding-for-disabled.org.uk). Horse riding for people with disabilities.

RYA Sailability (💻 www.ryasailability.org.uk). Sailing programmes for the disabled.

Skiing for the Disabled (💻 www.snowsportengland.org.uk/disability-76.html). Skiing and snowboarding for the disabled.

Speyside Trust (💻 www.badaguish.org). A Charitable Trust providing a special service to those with disabilities, where they can explore and develop new skills in safety in the Cairngorms National Park.

Walking on Air (💻 www.walkingonair.org.uk). A Scottish charity enabling people with disabilities to soar like birds.

The Wheelyboat Trust (💻 www.wheelyboats.org). Boating for the disabled.

Charities & Volunteering

Action (💻 www.action.org.uk). 100-mile cycle rides for Action medical research charity for children.

Charity Challenge (💻 www.charitychallenge.com). The world's leading fundraising charity challenge operator.

Do-it (💻 www.do-it.org). Volunteering made easy.

APPENDICES

Fix the Fells (💻 www.fixthefells.co.uk). The Fix the Fells teams work to repair and maintain upland paths with funding from donations, partners and the Heritage Lottery Fund.

Game & Wildlife Conservation Trust (💻 www.gwct.org.uk). The leading UK charity conducting scientific research to enhance the British countryside for public benefit.

Greenspace (💻 www.green-space.org.uk). A registered charity that works to improve parks and green spaces by raising awareness, involving communities and training skilled professionals.

John Muir Trust (💻 www.jmt.org). The leading wild land conservation charity in the UK.

NSPCC Challenge (💻 www.nspcc.org.uk/get-involved/join-an-event/get-active/get-active-hub_wdh72070.html). Fundraising for the NSPCC.

Snowdon 500 (💻 www.snowdon500.co.uk). Challenge walk for the Prostate Cancer Research centre.

Vinspired (💻 www.vinspired.com). Connects 16-25 year-olds with volunteering opportunities in England.

Extreme & Adventure Sports

Active Edge (💻 www.activeedge.co.uk). Kites, gliding, hang-gliding and para-gliding.

Adrenalin Antics (💻 www.adrenalinantics.com). Premier adventure & activity holiday organisers based in Snowdonia.

Adventure Activities Portals (💻 www.reviewing.co.uk/outdoors/links.htm). A guide to portal sites for outdoor adventures/activities news.

Adventure Sport (💻 www.adventuresport.co.uk). A wide range of activities for team-building and individuals.

Aerial (💻 www.aerial.org). Aerial sports 'club' that organises sports involving falling or flying.

Anglesey Adventures (💻 http://angleseyadventures.com). Adventure activity company that provides adventure days and breaks on Anglesey and throughout North Wales.

Bike Radar (💻 www.bikeradar.comblogs/cyclingplus). Cycling magazine with useful addresses and contact details.

Blue Dome (💻 www.bluedome.co.uk). Outdoor activities, from adventure racing to mountain rescue.

British Information (💻 www.britishinformation.com/extreme-sport). Directory of extreme sports organisers.

Ebo Adventure (💻 www.eboadventure.co.uk). Specialists in extreme sports and instruction in outdoor pursuits.

Exelement (💻 www.exelement.co.uk). Extreme sports activity days.

Free Spirits (💻 www.freespirits-online.co.uk). Adventure activities in Scotland.

Gasp Action Sports (💻 www.gaspactionsports.com). Dedicated to 'alternative action' (extreme) sports.

London Airsports Centre (💻 www.londonairsports.com). All kinds of flying experiences and training, from power kiting to small aircraft.

Mpora (💻 http://mpora.com). Action Sports Community.

Nae Limits (💻 www.naelimits.co.uk). Adventure sports organiser specialising in water-based activities in Scotland.

North Wales Active (💻 www.northwalesactive.co.uk). Outdoor specialist offering a wide range of activities.

Outdoor Magic (💻 www.outdoorsmagic.com). Outdoor gear and equipment reviews, friendly forums and walking routes.

The Outdoors Show (💻 www.theoutdoorsshow.co.uk). The largest UK show for outdoor sports enthusiasts.

Outlook Expeditions (💻 www.outlookexpeditions.com). The leading independent expedition and adventure holiday provider for schools.

Planet Fear (💻 www.planetfear.net). Adventure and travel sports.

Plas y Brenin, National Mountain Centre (💻 www.pyb.co.uk). Welsh centre offering a wide range of adventure sport courses, holidays and expeditions.

Pro Adventure (💻 www.proadventure.co.uk). Offers a huge range of activity breaks, courses and holidays in North Wales.

TOAD (💻 www.toad.uk.com). Excellent online activity directory. sports video, photos and news from across the globe.

Scottish Quads (💻 www.scottishquads.co.uk). Quad biking treks in Scotland.

Snowdonia Adventures (💻 www.snowdonia-adventures.co.uk). Adventurous activity courses and holidays in Snowdonia.

Spice UK (💻 www.spiceuk.com). Adventure sports, leisure events and holidays.

Sport & Adventure (💻 www.sportandadventure.co.uk). Tandem sky-diving and other extreme sports.

Surf Lines (💻 www.surf-lines.co.uk/adventure/index.asp). Adventure courses for schools and colleges.

Thrill Seekers Unlimited (💻 www.thrillseekersunlimited.com). Extreme sports holiday packages.

Tree Surfers (💻 www.treesurfers.co.uk). Exciting woodland activities in the Tamar Valley.

UK Active Outdoors (💻 www.ukactiveoutdoors.co.uk). Information about outdoor sports and activities in the UK.

APPENDICES

UK Extreme Sports (🖥 www.ukextremesports.co.uk). Extreme sports directory.

Ultra Sport EU (🖥 www.ultrasporteu.com). Extreme sports equipment distributors with interesting blogs.

Yumping (🖥 www.yumping.co.uk). Guide to leisure and adventure sports.

Xtreme Gap Year (🖥 www.xtremegapyear.co.uk): specialists in extreme sports and adrenalin activities.

Team Building & Corporate Events' Organisers

Accolade Corporate Events (🖥 www.accolade-corporate-events.com). Team building events throughout the UK.

Action Days (🖥 www.actiondays.co.uk). Organisers of customised company days and team building events.

Action Treasure Hunts (🖥 www.actiontreasurehunts.co.uk). Corporate team building events.

ATP Events (🖥 www.atpevents.co.uk). Bespoke activity days for team building and staff motivation.

Bouncy Bounce (🖥 www.bouncybounce.co.uk). Leisure corporate and organised themed-events organiser (fun events rather than extreme sports).

Chilli Sauce (🖥 www.chillisauce.co.uk). Unique activities for corporate events and team building days.

Costello Events (🖥 www.costelloevents.co.uk). Corporate entertainment and events.

Events House (🖥 www.eventshouse.co.uk). Team building events and corporate fun days.

Go Ballistic (🖥 http://go-ballistic.co.uk). The UK's largest paintball organiser with over 100 sites.

Group Games (🖥 www.group-games.com). Database for team building activities.

Hunt the Goose (🖥 www.huntthegoose.co.uk). Specialist treasure hunt organiser for corporate and team building or just for fun.

Hunt for Treasure (🖥 www.huntfortreasure.co.uk). Corporate entertainment events.

Kaleidoscope (🖥 www.kaleidoscope-events.co.uk). Teamwork ideas and activities.

Paint Ball Games (🖥 www.paintballgames.co.uk). Paintball equipment, locations, prices and programmes.

Phoenix Leisure (🖥 www.phoenixleisure.co.uk). Team building involving a wide range of indoor games and outdoor events and sports.

Sandstone (🖥 www.sandstone.co.uk/team-building). Working to build winning teams.

Team Build Events (💻 www.teambuildevents.co.uk). Team building events throughout the UK and Europe.

Team Building (💻 www.teambuilding.co.uk). Fun corporate team building activities.

Team Motivation (💻 www.team-motivation.co.uk). Organiser of over 50 indoor and outdoor fun events (as opposed to extreme sports).

Treasure Hunts (💻 www.treasurehuntsuk.co.uk). Treasure hunt activities in the UK for team building.

UK Paintball (💻 www.ukpaintball.co.uk). One of the UK's largest paintball organisers with over 45 venues.

Wildersom (💻 http://wilderdom.comgames/initiativegames.html). Initiative games and group problem-solving exercises.

Will 4 Adventure (💻 www.will4adventure.com). Active adventure holidays and team building courses and events.

Adventure Travel Organisers

Action Challenge (💻 www.actionchallenge.com). Specialist organiser of challenge events in the UK and across the globe.

Adventure Company (💻 www.adventurecompany.co.uk). Over 230 worldwide adventure holidays.

Adventure Sports Holidays (💻 www.adventuresportsholidays. com). Adventure holidays & outdoor activities worldwide.

Direct Adventures (💻 www.directadventures.co.uk). Active adventure trip organiser.

Dragoman (💻 www.dragoman.com). Adventure travel worldwide.

Explore (💻 www.explore.co.uk). Adventure holidays and other activities in over 130 countries worldwide.

Intrepid Travel (💻 www.intrepidtravel.com). For travellers with a yearning to get off the beaten track.

Neilson (💻 www.neilson.co.uk). Outdoor activity holidays abroad.

Outdoor Travel (💻 www.outdoorstravel.co.uk). Active holidays in the UK and abroad.

Rock and Sun (💻 www.rockandsun.com). Climbing holidays and rock-climbing courses.

Travel the Unknown (💻 www.traveltheunknown.com). For those who want to really get off the beaten track.

Windows on the Wild (💻 www.windowsonthewild.com). Wildlife, activities and experiences worldwide.

APPENDICES

Inspiration

Adventure Travel Live (🖥 www. adventuretravellive.com). The UK's biggest adventure travel event.

The Adventurists (🖥 www.theadventurists.com). Join the Adventurists in their battle against an increasingly boring, sanitised world.

Because It's There (🖥 www.becauseitisthere.co.uk). Kevin Shannon's zero emissions odyssey, circumnavigating the globe.

Ben Fogle (🖥 www.benfogle.com). The website of the well-known presenter, writer and adventurer.

Coast Alive (🖥 www.coast-alive.eu). EU-funded project that aims to get more people to use local paths and outdoor facilities for recreation and for fitness.

Design Juices (🖥 www.designjuices.co.uk/2010/05/hdr-extreme-sports-photography). Extreme sports photography.

Dive (🖥 www.bvents.com). The International Sub-Aqua and Watersports Show held at the NEC in the autumn.

Dive Show (🖥 www.diveshows.co.uk). London International Dive Show at ExCel, London (March) for scuba diving enthusiasts.

Extreme (🖥 www.extreme.com). Source of high quality extreme sports videos.

Extreme Dreams (🖥 www.extremedreams.co.uk). Information, photographs and videos on a wealth of extreme sports.

Globetrotters Club (🖥 http://globetrotters.co.uk). Travel club for independent travellers & travel enthusiasts of all ages, established for over 60 years.

James Cracknell (🖥 www.jamescracknell.com). Inspiring athlete and extreme sports adventurer.

London Bike Show (🖥 www.thelondonbikeshow.co.uk). Held at ExCel, London (January).

London Boat Show (🖥 www.londonboatshow.com). The UK's premier boat show staged at ExCel in January.

Nat Geo Adventure (🖥 www.natgeoadventure.tv/uk). Website from *National Geographic* (magazine, TV, etc.) that inspires people to get the most out of exploring the planet.

Outdoors Show (🖥 www.theoutdoorsshow.co.uk). The UK's largest adventure and extreme sports show, held at ExCel, London (January).

Ranulph Fiennes (🖥 www.ranulph-fiennes.com). The website of Britain's most famous explorer.

Royal Geographic Society (🖥 www.rgs.org). Founded in 1830, the RGS is a world centre for geography; supporting research, education, expeditions and fieldwork; and promoting public engagement and informed enjoyment of our world.

Secret Compass (💻 www.secretcompass.com). Inspiration for adventurers from an independent expeditionary service

Travel Photographer of the Year (💻 www.tpoty.com). Inspiring photographs to get you out and about.

Wanderlust Magazine (💻 www.wanderlust.co.uk). Inspiration for adventure travellers.

Wildlife Whisperer (💻 www.wildlifewhisperer.tv). Inspiring wildlife community on the web.

APPENDICES

APPENDIX C: MAPS

The maps in this appendix show the most popular areas in England, Scotland and Wales for many of the activities featured in this book.

ENGLAND

SCOTLAND

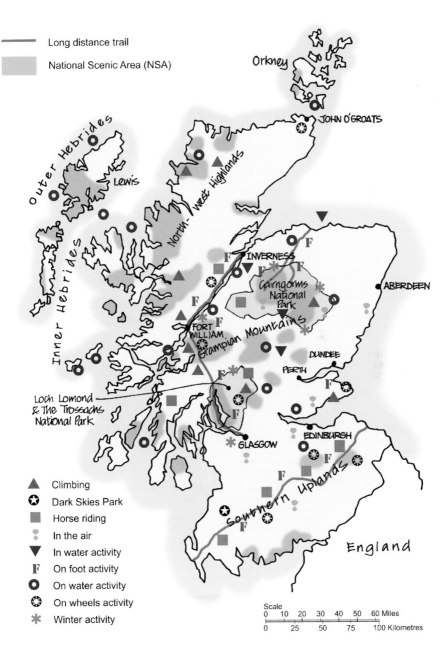

Long distance trail

National Scenic Area (NSA)

Orkney

JOHN O'GROATS

Outer Hebrides

Lewis

North-West Highlands

Inner Hebrides

INVERNESS

Cairngorms National Park

ABERDEEN

FORT WILLIAM

Grampian Mountains

DUNDEE

PERTH

Loch Lomond & The Trossachs National Park

GLASGOW

EDINBURGH

Southern Uplands

England

▲ Climbing
✪ Dark Skies Park
■ Horse riding
⋮ In the air
▼ In water activity
F On foot activity
◎ On water activity
✪ On wheels activity
✳ Winter activity

Scale
0   10   20   30   40   50   60 Miles
0   25   50   75   100 Kilometres

APPENDICES

WALES

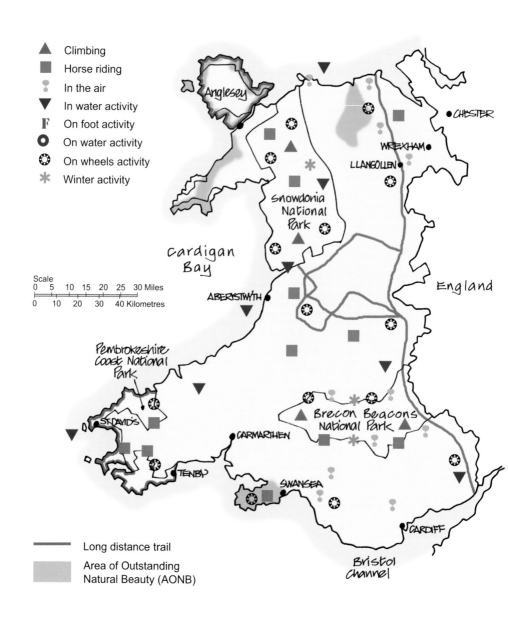

Legend:
- ▲ Climbing
- ■ Horse riding
- In the air
- ▼ In water activity
- F On foot activity
- ◉ On water activity
- ✽ On wheels activity
- ✳ Winter activity

Anglesey

Snowdonia National Park

Cardigan Bay

CHESTER

WREXHAM

LLANGOLLEN

England

ABERYSTWYTH

Pembrokeshire Coast National Park

St DAVID'S

Brecon Beacons National Park

CARMARTHEN

TENBY

SWANSEA

CARDIFF

Bristol Channel

Scale
0 5 10 15 20 25 30 Miles
0 10 20 30 40 Kilometres

─── Long distance trail

▨ Area of Outstanding Natural Beauty (AONB)

INDEX

A

B

C

D

E

Survival Books was established in 1987 and by the mid-'90s was the leading publisher of books for people planning to live, work, buy property or retire abroad.

From the outset, our philosophy has been to provide the most comprehensive and up-to-date information available. Our titles routinely contain up to twice as much information as other books and are updated frequently. All our books contain colour photographs and many are printed in two colours or full colour throughout. They also contain original cartoons, illustrations and maps.

Survival Books are written by people with first-hand experience of the countries and the people they describe, and therefore provide invaluable insights that cannot be obtained from official publications or websites, and information that is more reliable and objective than that provided by the majority of unofficial sites.

Our Books are designed to be easy – and interesting – to read. They contain a comprehensive list of contents and index and extensive appendices, including useful addresses, further reading, useful websites and glossaries to help you obtain additional information as well as metric conversion tables and other useful reference material.

Our primary goal is to provide you with the essential information necessary for a trouble-free life or property purchase and to save you time, trouble and money.

We believe our books are the best – they are certainly the best-selling. But don't take our word for it – read what reviewers and readers have said about Survival Books at the front of this book.

Order your copies today from
🖳 www.survivalbooks.net

Culture Wise Series

Our **Culture Wise** series of guides is essential reading for anyone who wants to understand how a country really 'works'. Whether you're planning to stay for a few days or a lifetime, these guides will help you quickly find your feet and settle into your new surroundings.
Culture Wise guides:

- Reduce the anxiety factor in adapting to a foreign culture
- Explain how to behave in everyday situations in order to avoid cultural and social gaffes
- Help you get along with your neighbours
- Make friends and establish lasting business relationships
- Enhance your understanding of a country and its people.

People often underestimate the extent of cultural isolation they can face abroad, particularly in a country with a different language. At first glance, many countries seem an 'easy' option, often with millions of visitors from all corners of the globe and well-established expatriate communities. But, sooner or later, newcomers find that most countries are indeed 'foreign' and many come unstuck as a result. **Culture Wise** guides will enable you to quickly adapt to the local way of life and feel at home, and – just as importantly – avoid the worst effects of culture shock.

Culture Wise – The Wise Way to Travel

The essential guides to Culture, Customs & Business Etiquette

Buying a Home Series

B uying a home abroad is not only a major financial transaction but also a potentially life-changing experience; it's therefore essential to get it right. Our Buying a Home guides are required reading for anyone planning to purchase property abroad and are packed with vital information to guide you through the property jungle and help you avoid disasters that can turn a dream home into a nightmare.

The purpose of our Buying a Home guides is to enable you to choose the most favourable location and the most appropriate property for your requirements, and to reduce your risk of making an expensive mistake by making informed decisions and calculated judgements rather than uneducated and hopeful guesses. Most importantly, they will help you save money and will repay your investment many times over.

Buying a Home guides are the most comprehensive and up-to-date source of information available about buying property abroad – whether you're seeking a detached house or an apartment, a holiday or a permanent home (or an investment property), these books will prove invaluable.

**For a full list of our current titles, visit our website at
www.survivalbooks.net**

Living and Working Series

Our Living and Working guides are essential reading for anyone planning to spend a period abroad – whether it's an extended holiday or permanent migration – and are packed with priceless information designed to help you avoid costly mistakes and save both time and money.

Living and Working guides are the most comprehensive and up-to-date source of practical information available about everyday life abroad. They aren't, however, simply a catalogue of dry facts and figures, but are written in a highly readable style – entertaining, practical and occasionally humorous.

Our aim is to provide you with the comprehensive practical information necessary for a trouble-free life. You may have visited a country as a tourist, but living and working there is a different matter altogether; adjusting to a
new environment and culture and making a home in any foreign country can be a traumatic and stressful experience. You need to adapt to new customs and traditions, discover the local way of doing things (such as finding a home, paying bills and obtaining insurance) and learn all over again how to overcome the everyday obstacles of life.

All these subjects and many, many more are covered in depth in our Living and Working guides – don't leave home without them.

The Expats' Best Friend!

Other Survival Books

The Best Places to Buy a Home in France/Spain: Unique guides to where to buy property in Spain and France, containing detailed regional profiles and market reports.

Life in the UK - Test & Study Guide: essential reading for anyone planning to take the 'Life in the UK' test in order to become a permanent resident (settled) in the UK.

Renovating & Maintaining Your French Home: The ultimate guide to renovating and maintaining your dream home in France.

Retiring in France/Spain: Everything a prospective retiree needs to know about the two most popular international retirement destinations.

Running Gîtes and B&Bs in France: An essential book for anyone planning to invest in a gîte or bed & breakfast business.

Rural Living in France: An invaluable book for anyone seekingthe 'good life', containing a wealth of practical information about all aspects of French country life.

Shooting Caterpillars in Spain: The hilarious and compelling story of two innocents abroad in the depths of Andalusia in the late '80s.

For a full list of our current titles, visit our website at
www.survivalbooks.net

PHOTO CREDITS

PHOTO

CREDITS

Travelling the World
A Guide to Planning the Trip of a Lifetime

by Samantha Wilson

ISBN: 1-978-907339-39-7 £13.95

A comprehensive guide for independent travellers planning a 'once in a lifetime' round the world trip. Covers everything from choosing where and when to go; getting the best deals on travel and accommodation; safety and security; and most importantly, helping readers avoid disasters that can turn their dream trip into a nightmare.

Buy your copy at www.survivalbooks.net